LEADERSHIP IN
INTERNATIONAL RELATIONS

Leadership in International Relations

The Balance of Power and the Origins of World War II

Ariel Ilan Roth

palgrave
macmillan

LEADERSHIP IN INTERNATIONAL RELATIONS
Copyright © Ariel Ilan Roth, 2010.

First published in 2010 by PALGRAVE MACMILLAN® in the United States—a division of St. Martin's Press LLC, 175 Fifth Avenue, New York, NY 10010.

Where this book is distributed in the UK, Europe and the rest of the world, this is by Palgrave Macmillan, a division of Macmillan Publishers Limited, registered in England, company number 785998, of Houndmills, Basingstoke, Hampshire RG21 6XS.

Palgrave Macmillan is the global academic imprint of the above companies and has companies and representatives throughout the world.

Palgrave® and Macmillan® are registered trademarks in the United States, the United Kingdom, Europe and other countries.

ISBN: 978-0-230-10690-1

Library of Congress Cataloging-in-Publication Data is available from the Library of Congress.

Roth, Ariel Ilan.
    Leadership in international relations: the balance of power and the origins of World War II / Ariel Ilan Roth.
        p. cm.
    Includes bibliographical references.
    ISBN 978-0-230-10690-1 (alk. paper)
    1. Balance of power—Case studies. 2. Political leadership—Case studies. 3. Political leadership—Great Britain. 4. Great Britain—Foreign relations—1910-1936. 5. Great Britain—Foreign relations—1936-1945. 6. World War, 1939-1945—Diplomatic history. I. Title.

JZ1313.R68 2010
940.53'22—dc22   2010011562

A catalogue record of the book is available from the British Library.

Design by Scribe Inc.

First edition: October 2010

10 9 8 7 6 5 4 3 2 1

Printed in the United States of America.

To Steven R. David and Benjamin Ginsberg
and
To the memory of Nicole Süveges (1970–2008)

CONTENTS

ACKNOWLEDGMENTS

No book is written as a solo endeavor and thanks for the present volume are owed to many. Jeannette Pierce, now at Loyola University, was the political science librarian at Johns Hopkins who made exertions to obtain material and provide resources without which this project would have been far poorer. The Department of Political Science at Johns Hopkins provided financial support, which facilitated the archival research reflected herein, as did the Office of the Provost at Goucher College.

The idea for this book was born during the summer of 2004 when I participated in the Columbia University Summer Workshop on Military Analysis and Strategy (SWAMOS). Thanks especially to Richard Betts, Eliot Cohen, Stephen Biddle, Tami Davis Biddle, Eric Ouellet, Zachary Mears, Mark Smith, Reuben Brigety Jr., Christine Grafton, and Joshua Baron, who helped primordial idea take relevant shape. Robert C. Self, perhaps the world's greatest living expert on Neville Chamberlain, is also thanked for being so willing to talk to a cheeky American who rang him out of the blue.

I am indebted to Mark Blyth who steered me right all along. Daniel Deudney has likewise played a key role in helping me sort many theoretical issues out. I am also fortunate to have the support of the best group of colleagues that anybody could ask for. Kathy Wagner, Dorothea Israel Wolfson, Alexander Rosenthal, Mark Stout, and Rameez Abbas from the Governmental Studies Program at Johns Hopkins all inspire me and make work a happy home away from home.

My wife Nanci has been the pillar that supports me in this and in all things. Although he will not know this for years, I owe thanks to my son Savi, whose imminent arrival was the Damoclean sword that motivated me to spend endless hours working on this project from before dawn until well into the night, all the while mumbling my mantra: "It's the baby, stupid!"

This book is dedicated to Steven David and Ben Ginsberg. Steven has been my teacher and my friend for ten years now, and it is impossible to imagine my career without his influence. Although he is not a scholar of international relations (for which he is forgiven), Ben Ginsberg has been instrumental in helping me navigate these early years. It is no exaggeration to say that without Steven there never would have been a book and without Ben it would never have been published!

Finally, this book is also dedicated to the late Nicole Süveges. Nicole was my closest friend in graduate school and would have been a tremendous asset to our profession. Nicole died on June 24, 2008, in Baghdad, Iraq, while working in the most literal way to bring the wisdom and insight of political science to make people's lives better and safer. She is deeply missed.

Blame for the many errors left uncaught is mine.

Acronyms and *Dramatis Personae*

CAS	Chief of Air Service
CID	Committee on Imperial Defence
CIGS	Chief of the Imperial General Staff
DC(M)	Ministerial Committee on Disarmament
DPR	Defence Policy Requirements Committee
DRC	Defence Requirements Committee
TA	Territorial Army

Baldwin, Stanley	Lord President of the Council, August 1931–May 1935; Prime Minister, May 1935–May 1937.
Chamberlain, Neville	Chancellor of the Exchequer, August 1931–May 1937; Prime Minister, May 1937–May 1940.
Chatfield, Sir Ernle	Admiral of the Fleet
Duff Cooper, Alfred	Secretary of State for War, November1935–May 1937
Ellington, Air Marshal Sir Edward	Chief of the Air Staff
Eden, Anthony	Minister for League of Nations Affairs and Foreign Secretary
Eyres-Monsell, Sir Bolton	First Lord of the Admiralty
Fisher, Sir Warren	Secretary to the Treasury
Hailsham, Lord	Secretary of State for War, November 1931–June 1935

Hankey, Colonel Sir Maurice — Secretary to the cabinet and Committee on Imperial Defence

Londonderry, Lord — Secretary of State for Air, November 1931–June 1935

MacDonald, John Ramsay — Prime Minister, August 1931–June 1935; Lord President of the Council, May 1935–May 1937.

Montgomery-Massingberd, Field Marshal Sir Archibald A. — Chief of the Imperial General Staff

Simon, Sir John — Secretary of State for Foreign Affairs

Swinton, Lord — Secretary of State for Air, June 1935–May 1938

Vansitart Sir Robert — Permanent Head of the Foreign Office

Weir, Lord — Industrial Advisor to the Defence Policy Requirements Committee

INTRODUCTION

While the case study in this book is Britain, this book is really about leadership and the role that leaders play in the formation of effective balances of power. This book was written with the expectation that the balance of power as a mechanism for preserving systemic stability and geopolitical independence has returned to prominence in recent years. Absent world government and in the anarchic order in which international politics plays out, the ability of great powers to forcibly deny the territorial and geopolitical ambitions of other great powers historically has been crucial in preventing any one state from exercising complete hegemony over the international system and controlling global resources for its exclusive use. In more recent times, arguments have been advanced that posit that the sharp edges of international politics can be blunted by channeling interactions through the agency of international institutions but, even according to theorists oriented to this approach, the ultimate guarantor of independence in the international system lies in the ability to deny the ambitions of others by force.[1]

The balance of power has a bad reputation. Overt appeals to its restoration as a motivating factor in World War I led to a disavowal of the concept in the interwar years and the architects of the post–World War II international system stridently denied that their new system, embodied as it was in the Charter of the United Nations, was cementing a new balance. In the Cold War, the balance of power became a balance of terror as the Americans and the Soviets held each other's spheres of influence in check through a robust network of civilization-ending nuclear arms. The end of the Cold War and with it the (prematurely declared) "end of history" made the balance of power seem like an antiquated relic of an age in which international politics was marked by clashes of will instead of the harmonious pursuit of wealth under benign American leadership.[2]

The first decade of the twenty-first century, however, has seen the rekindling of international politics and the unheralded return of the balance of power. Fueled by the profits of high commodity prices, Russia, while still a shadow of its former self, is rising again and pushing back against the encroachment of the North Atlantic Treaty Organization (NATO) in areas formerly under its control. China, whose ascendancy has been foretold for more than a half century, is making a bid for greatness that is expressing itself not only in remarkable economic dynamism but also in the development of a complex security industry that includes an impressive blue-water navy and a program of manned space exploration. North Korea shows no signs of disarming itself from its recent nuclear acquisitions, and so doubts about the credibility of the U.S. security guarantees to South Korea and Japan have raised the prospect again of whether those countries will pursue their own nuclear futures.

The return of competition to international politics is perhaps lamentable (at least from the perspective of the Americans, whose decade or so of unquestioned preponderance is now over), but it is not surprising. With world government a no more realistic prospect today than in the past, the most likely order for a still anarchic world is the relative stability of the balance of power in which the ambitions of each of the major players in the international system are kept in check by the capabilities of others and the mutual independence of each thereby vouchsafed.

The return of the balance of power makes it all the more important to understand how balances form and are maintained, and that is where this book comes in. The structural variant of realism, a paradigm of international relations theory, posits that balances of power are the near automatic result of the competition between great powers. This book argues that this not true. An *effective* balance of power, which is a balance of power wherein a would-be aggressor is either deterred from acting on aggressive intent or denied success in such an effort, is a deliberate act of policy. At the heart of that policy are leaders.

Leaders carry many burdens and multiple responsibilities, but in the realm of international relations and foreign policy there are three main tasks that determine their success as providers of national security. First, leaders diagnose the severity, urgency, and direction from which threats to national security emerge. Second, leaders prescribe policies to counter those threats. Third, leaders mobilize support for those prescriptions from the relevant constituencies involved.

Leadership is a peculiar variable for international relations theory. On the one hand, the idea that leadership matters is intuitively obvious. Although some conflicts have root causes that do not hearken back to any specific leaders, the way that conflicts play out very often is dependent on the leadership of the time. World War II, for example, had many causes, ranging from the questions of power and hegemony left unresolved in the wake of World War I to the indignities and excesses of the Versailles settlement. However, World War II as we know it, with death camps and the promotion of a racist Aryan agenda, can be tied to Adolf Hitler specifically. That the war that occurred was the racially idiosyncratic Hitler's war is of great significance for later international politics including, but not limited to, its role as a partial justification for the creation of the State of Israel.

For scholars of international relations, on the other hand, leadership is rarely considered a variable in its own right. A significant part of the reason why leadership does not get its due consideration in international relations theorizing is because it is deemed incompatible with scientific rigor, yet theories that are consistent with aspirations to scientific rigor frequently fail the litmus test of being able to explain important past events in international politics accurately, let alone predict events yet to come.

Structural realism is one such approach. Structural realism, which posited that many predictions about behavior in international politics can be generated on the basis of knowing only the organizing principle of the international system and the distribution of capabilities within that system, took the world of international relations theory by storm in the late 1970s and still exercises considerable influence today. In attempting to generate elegant and parsimonious theory, however, structural realism has become a leading example of an elegant theory that fails to explain important past events accurately. The result of this pattern of inaccurate explanation is not merely egg on the face of its adherents but the rather more serious problem of poor guidance for the policy decision makers who often turn to scholars for advice.

This book's arguments about the role of leaders in establishing effective balances of power are based on an examination of British behavior in the decade before World War II. For more than a half century, both scholars and laymen, including one former president, have mined the British experience in the 1930s for key lessons. The popular lesson most often associated with the period is that of the danger of appeasing dictators.

For international relations theory, however, and especially for structural theory, this epochal time is actually a great puzzle. Structural realist theory expects that the competition between Great Powers in their quest for security will result in the formation of a balance of power between them. By most accounts, the interwar years in Europe defy that expectation. Specifically, Britain is believed to have not balanced against Germany during the 1930s. Given the seismic impact of World War II, the glaring noncompliance of the era to what seems to be an otherwise robust generalized prediction threatens the credibility of structuralism as a whole. After all, what good is a theory if it cannot explain the most central event under its purview?

Structural thinkers have developed two competing theories that attempt to account for the variance that Britain's unexpected behavior during these years represents while maintaining the primacy of material-structural variables in explaining international outcomes. Both arguments are mentioned briefly here and will be discussed at length in Chapter 1.

The first such theory is buck-passing. Buck-passing, or externalizing the costs of defense on to a second, similarly threatened nation, is a mechanism that undermines the tendency of states to form balances of power in multipolar international systems. Thus, the multipolar international system created an incentive for Britain to attempt to externalize the costs of confronting Germany to France or Russia, which resulted in a meager British effort and the resultant imbalance.

The second argument, advanced by Randall Schweller, is tripolarity. In this argument, the claim is that the behavior of Great Britain is consistent with the expected behavior patterns of states in a system in which aggregate power is divided between three major poles. Scholars of this school argue that Great Britain sought to offer up France and her eastern allies to Germany in the hope that Germany's appetite for conquest might be sated by these offerings and Britain herself spared.

There are significant problems in both of these explanations, all of which will be addressed in each of the coming chapters. In general, however, despite what the scholars who advocate both buck-passing and tripolar theories assert, Britain did not attempt to either externalize the costs or responsibilities for defense to France or to offer France up to Germany in her stead.

The great problem with the structural theories that purport to explain British behavior in the 1930s is that they mistake an ineffective balance for a nonexistent one. British behavior is identified as being evidence of nonbalancing because Britain is perceived to have not tried to arm itself effectively against Germany. That perception is false. Britain did attempt to arm against Germany and expected that its efforts would result in the formation of a balance of power between them.

British armament in the 1930s was relegated largely to aerial power. That focus reflected the belief of Britain's civilian leadership that the creation of offensive air power could and would serve as both an effective deterrent to war or as a striking tool if deterrence failed. The idea of using air power in such a way reflects a great misunderstanding of how particular kinds of weapons can be effective against one kind of threat yet completely ineffective against another. Specifically, it reflects a flawed understanding of what British air power could do to Germany and, more, what little British air power could do to stop a German attack on Britain.

The challenge, then, is not to explain why Britain did not balance but, rather, why Britain did not balance *effectively*. The explanation for why Britain failed to effectively balance against Germany and thereby either deter war or acquit herself better in the early days of combat lies in the relative inadequacy of her political leadership during the years leading up to the war. It was leaders who ordered the armament plan with its nearly exclusive aerial focus, and leaders who made it happen. It was the choice to focus on air power to the exclusion of other forms of military might, particularly land forces, which resulted in an ineffective balance to German might.

Given this, this book aims to accomplish two things. The first is to solve a puzzle for international relations theory: namely, why Britain did not balance effectively when its structural circumstances suggested that it should. The second task is to show the key role of leaders in the creation of effective balances of power. The role of leaders in the process of creating power is the lesson of greater value that is drawn from this work and one that is relevant for today.

OUTLINE OF THE BOOK

The remainder of this introduction provides a historical review of the events that will be discussed in subsequent chapters before turning to questions of methodology and a discussion of the role of counterfactual modeling in qualitative international relations theory. A comprehensive treatment of the origins of structural neorealism, its general predictions for behavior in the international system, and its predictions for the specific behavior of Britain in the 1930s are examined in Chapter 1. Challenges and problems with the structural approach, both generally and as it relates to this specific case, will be explored there as well. Chapter 2 provides a qualitative model for leadership and generates certain null hypotheses on effective decisions in relation to the formation of a balance of power in the 1930s against which the leaders of Britain at the time can be tested. In Chapters 3, 4, 5, and 6, the leadership of Stanley Baldwin and Neville Chamberlain, Britain's leaders during the years in question will be evaluated. Finally, the conclusion hosts a discussion of what the lessons of this book, that an effective balance of power is a deliberate act of policy and that leaders are central to ensuring the same, suggest for our own times and for the future. An epilogue explores the challenges of balancing power in the twenty-first century.

Before turning to that, however, it is important to provide a brief review of the events, the deep-rooted causes of which are explained herein.

HISTORICAL REVIEW

On September 1, 1939, the Nazi army invaded Poland. Two days later, His Majesty's government, along with the government of France, declared war on Nazi Germany. The tentative peace that had endured through the 1920s and the peace that had been more fiction than fact since the Abyssinian crisis of 1935 was over. Fighting between the two sides—the British and the French on the one and Nazi Germany on the other—did not commence immediately. After a rush to occupy positions along both sides of the fortified frontier, the French behind their famed Maginot line and the Germans holding fast behind the Siegfried line, the "war" in the west was nonexistent. It was not until nearly nine months later that the "phony war" between Germany and the Allies lost its phoniness in an instant.

On May 10, 1940, Germany invaded France. The French had expected a repeat of the Schlieffen plan, which had come so close to giving Germany success in August 1914. That plan, named for the long-time German army chief who authored it, had envisioned an attack in which a large right wing would sweep through Holland and Belgium and wheel around Paris pushing the French armies before it and crushing them against the anvil-like left wing, which had held fast during the opening salvos. In 1940, the French, in fact, sought to guarantee that the Germans would funnel their attack through Belgium just as they had in 1914. As the French saw things, the problem during the Great War had been the loss of great swathes of their industrial heartland to the Germans, which, along with the reality of having nearly a third of its territory under enemy occupation, had seriously hobbled their war effort.

The purpose of the Maginot line was not, as popular myth would later have it, to make France invulnerable. It was rather, meant to discourage the Germans from launching an attack across the Loire Valley and violating French territory proper. The Maginot line was meant to funnel a German attack into Belgium by creating fortifications comprehensive enough so as to make the appeal of flanking them far outweigh the appeal of attacking them head on. The French plan envisioned that upon the commencement of hostilities French forces would rush north into Belgium where both custom and the realities of Maginot would have compelled the Germans to launch their attack.[3] Once there, two possibilities could occur: either there would be a decisive battle in which France might win, or, more likely, a front would develop and stabilize much as it had in the fall of 1914. This time around, however, the French were determined that the front should stabilize in Belgium and not, as it had in the Great War, in France.

The Germans did not accommodate French plans. The "Plan Yellow" of 1940, crafted by Erich von Manstein and executed by Heinz Guderian, called for a push by an independent armored force through the unfortified Ardennes forest in what was called a "sickle cut" (*sichelschnitt*), which, taking a curving trace across northern France, would push to the channel ports, thereby cutting off British aid. This cutting off of the channel ports was a crucial aim of the German army, as their perception of the Great War had been that it was Britain's participation that had kept them from achieving victory well before the arrival of the Americans in 1918 made that outcome impossible.

As it turned out, the German plan was executed almost flawlessly. Gerd von Rundstedt's army group pushed through the Ardennes cutting underneath the French army, which had, as planned, rushed headlong into Belgium. The German army formed a barrier between the French armies in Belgium and any reinforcements that might be brought up from France. Within weeks, the Germans had mopped up the French armies north of the Ardennes. The token British expeditionary force, which had been sent to France in 1939 along with nearly one hundred thousand French soldiers, escaped elimination only by executing a near-miraculous evacuation under fire from the channel port at Dunkirk during the week between May 27 and June 4, 1940.

With the defeat of the French forces north of the Ardennes and the cutting off of any hope of British aid, the Germans turned their attentions to France proper. On June 13 the Germans took Paris and on June 23 France surrendered.

For Britain, a nightmare had come. From the summer of 1940 until the German operation against Russia began in June 1941, they stood alone against the Nazis—and, indeed, did so in the compromised position of having the German army, and more importantly, the German *Luftwaffe* based just across the channel in France and the Low Countries instead of at a greater distance behind the Rhine. It had been precisely this outcome that the British chiefs of staff had warned of as early as 1934 when they responded to a query by government ministers on defense priorities by stressing "the vital importance of denying the Low Countries to Germany as an advanced air base for an attack on Britain. They [the chiefs of staff] estimated than an air attack from the Low Countries would be initially 80 percent stronger than if launched from bases in Germany."[4] As will be discussed at greater length later in this book, the chiefs of staff took the task of denying German access to aerodromes in France and the Low Countries as well as denying the German navy submarine bases on the Atlantic coast to be the *sine qua non* of British security. To that end, the chiefs, including the air and navy commanders, advocated for increasing the strength of the British army, which had to that point been so starved of funds such that it was but a shadow of what it was at the end of the Great War and without a hint of what it could and later would, be. Their call was acknowledged by Stanley Baldwin, who nonetheless did little to answer it either as lord president of the council until 1935 or as prime minister thereafter until 1937.

Neville Chamberlain, the chancellor of the exchequer for the entire period until 1937 and prime minister thereafter until the fall of France, rejected the call of the chiefs entirely, using his control over the purse strings to deny the funds needed to build the army.

Even with events turning out as they did, Britain did not lose the war. Thanks to innovations developed during the 1930s including, but not limited to, radar and the forceful advocacy of certain politicians in developing fighters even in opposition to the preferences of the air staff for building bombers, Britain was able to withstand the punishing bombardments that came during 1940 and later.[5] The German plan for an invasion of the British Isles, Operation Sealion, collapsed even before Germany decided to launch its war against Russia.

That said, although Britain would not have been conquered by Germany, there is fair reason to speculate that were it not for the subsequent follies of Hitler in both attacking Russia and, equally foolishly, declaring war on the United States, Britain would have had to negotiate a separate peace, likely as not with a near vassal status for at least the foreseeable future. Britain may have wished to starve out Hitler as she had Napoleon, but Napoleonic France did not have submarines as Germany did, and the British mastery of the seas was far less in 1940 than it had been in the days of Nelson.

Thus, the full measure of Britain's independence was secured only by the less than wise decisions on Hitler's part to attack Russia and declare war on the United States. The victory for Great Britain turned out to be the very definition of Pyrrhic. The year 1947, just two years after the war's end told the scope of the cost of victory. India, the crown jewel of the empire was freed, mandatory authority over Palestine, held since General Allenby had marched into Jerusalem was surrendered to the United Nations and, finally, Britain was compelled to abdicate its role in the defense of Greece and Turkey—and with it, its place as world leader, to the United States, pleading the inability to continue.

HOW THE FALL OF FRANCE
MIGHT HAVE BEEN AVOIDED

The fall of France was avoidable and, with it, the subsequent exhaustion of the British Empire as it clung to life during the remainder of the war. Among the possible paths that may have spared Europe, two bear mentioning. The first is if France had had a better understanding of the various doctrines, which might govern the use of armor in a future war. At the time of the invasion, French armor exceeded in quantity the German armor, which was the key to the German victory. Where the French fell short was in operational doctrine. Had France heeded the calls of Charles de Gaulle during the interwar years for the creation of independent armored forces, instead of armored units integrated within infantry units, the outcome of events in May 1940 might have been different if only because the French would have been more likely to identify the Ardennes as a point of vulnerability.

Nonetheless, as Chapter 1 will make clear, international relations theory and practice are informed by the notion that in the international system there is no greater power than the states that compose the system. From this condition of anarchy, a number of general principles are derived. First among them is that the international system demands of its constituent states that they help themselves in the procurement of security. States are responsible for their own safety. As such, even though France could have, in theory, defended itself and—by way of positive externality—Britain, that in no way excuses Britain from making appropriate exertions on her own part for the attainment of security.

This leads to the second path by which the fate of Europe and Britain could have been different. The fault for the fall of France and the subsequent exhaustion of the British Empire can be found in the relative inadequacies of the leaders of Britain during the period between the rise of Hitler and the invasion of France in 1940.

As will be more fully discussed in Chapter 2, leadership can be broken down into three core tasks:

1. Leaders diagnose a situation, including identifying potential rivals and strategic realities.
2. Leaders prescribe corrective policies in light of their diagnoses.
3. Leaders mobilize support for that prescription

The leaders of Great Britain during the years in question proved weak in at least one of these core tasks and, more often, more than one. The coming chapters explore precisely what Stanley Baldwin and Neville Chamberlain, the undisputed leaders of the United Kingdom did during the years in question with an eye to evaluating how each of them performed the tasks of leadership as it relates to the issue of the possibility of a war with Germany and preparation for it.

The fall of France could have been prevented if the political leadership in Great Britain had behaved differently in the face of the rise of

Nazism. If the United Kingdom had developed a competent, rapidly deployable, mechanized army it is likely that Germany would have either refrained from attacking Western Europe or in the event that she did attack, would have been held at positions significantly further back from the English Channel than she found herself in June 1940 and so eased the burden on Britain in the years to come.

One avenue of approach that could have, and should have, been pursued in relation to the equipping of an efficient army but that was thwarted by the political leadership, was the development of British armor. In the late 1920s, "everyone agree[d] that . . . Britain led the world in terms of both the technical development of armoured forces and their tactical handling."[6] Additionally, "until 1931, despite the small size of the British specialist armament industry, Britain led the world not only in the theory of armoured warfare and in the training and tactical handling of armoured forces but also (with the Sixteen Tonner) in the technical development of tanks."[7] In the early 1930s, however, all development of medium tanks was abandoned and was not restarted until April 1937. The consequence of the dropping of development of medium tanks was that the one thing that "would have given the British a chance to perform really well in armoured warfare in the early stages of the Second World War" was snapped.[8] By the time the war came, "Britain went to war without a single effective armoured division or a coherent doctrine of armoured warfare."[9] At the time that France was invaded, Britain only had two battalions of the Royal Tank Regiment in Europe and found herself with an "almost total incapacity to conduct armoured operations."[10] This is compared with the fact that by the time the war against Poland started, the Germans already had six full Panzer divisions and added another four divisions in the time between the Polish war and the invasion of France in May 1940.

The cost that this abandonment and lack of preparedness would garner was presciently decried in a memorandum by Major General Percy Hobart from October 1937:

> The Western theatre will be decisive for us. Elsewhere, we have to accept risks. . . . Not much more than static defence can be expected from Infantry formations against a first class enemy. Our allies already dispose of considerable defensive strength. The greatest threat from our point of view is a German drive to secure advanced air bases. German armoured formations, leading such a drive, can be countered by defence where it is ready, but only by armoured counteroffensive otherwise. . . . In relation to the forces of our allies the greatest value

we can provide is offensive armoured formations to assist to counter the German drive.

We are expending an uneconomical proportion of our resources, in the provision of lighter forces, to the detriment of the provision that we might make for a more effective offensive contribution.[11]

Hobart is himself a living example of the teaching that "a prophet hath no honor in his own country." Hobart's evangelism on the merits of an independent armor division was treated with a certain degree of scorn in Britain even as generals in the new German army, for example, Heinz Guderian, were consuming his ideas voraciously. As Basil Liddel Hart commented on Hobart, "His ideas of how an armoured force should be handled, and what it could achieve when operating in strategical independence of orthodox forces, had been contrary to the views of more conservative superiors. His 'heresy,' coupled with an uncompromising attitude, had led to his removal from command in the autumn of 1939—six months before the German panzer forces, applying the same ideas, proved their practicability."[12]

When the war came, Hobart volunteered in the Home Guard and was given the rank of corporal. It was from this duty that he was summoned by Churchill based on a newspaper article by Liddel Hart on "wasted brains": talents who could have been serving the nation and were not. Hobart was quickly restored to command and played a significant role in subsequent armored fighting, earning for himself a knighthood in the United Kingdom and being awarded the Legion of Merit in the United States.[13]

In the next two chapters I will situate the discussion of the role of leadership within the broader context of international relations theory and develop a qualitative model for leadership performance. The remainder of this book explores how it was that Britain failed to take the necessary steps in order to vouchsafe its own security. It explores the roles played by Stanley Baldwin and Neville Chamberlain in the armament process that resulted in the focus on air power that yielded such disastrous results in the early years of the war. It also examines how both leaders diagnosed the rise of Germany and her rearmament. It will explore how they perceived that threat and what, if anything, they thought should have been done about it. Finally, it will examine how well both leaders mobilized support for corrective measures.

This book uses a simple counterfactual null hypothesis against which Baldwin and Chamberlain will be compared. It argues that British leaders should have perceived Hitler's Germany as a military threat that needed to be countered and balanced against. They should have advised that the way to meet that threat was through an aggressive rearmament campaign that would further the goal articulated above by the chiefs of staff of keeping Germany from acquiring air and sea bases in France and the Low Countries. Finally, they should have convinced the government, Parliament, and ultimately, the people that such rearmament was the necessary course of action and mobilized their willingness, both financial and moral, for the task of preparing for the coming war.

The terms of the null hypothesis are what we would expect to see given the material realities facing Britain in the 1930s. Structural neorealism predicts that states that are faced with a threat coupled with a credible means to execute it will enhance their own capabilities in response through a combination of alliances and the intensification of their own military efforts. To the extent that the expected outcomes of the neorealist-based null hypothesis are not met, whatever deviations exist between the null hypothesis and events as they occurred must be explained theoretically.

It is important to note at this point that while this book is about leadership, it is not a psychobiography of the leaders. Although it does identify recurring behaviors among the leaders with whom it is concerned, it does not seek to identify the cause of those behaviors in any but the most cursory ways. As a rule, Stanley Baldwin preferred compromise to confrontation. This is a fact that can be established by examination of his policies in regards to the General Strike of 1926, India, Italy, and even Germany. A psychobiographer may have some insights into the conciliatory nature of Baldwin's personality as stemming from his being raised in a business environment or being from a more relaxed rural environment. Similarly, perhaps explanations for Chamberlain's actions and motivations can be found in his living in the shadows both of his brother Austen and their revered father Joseph. Rather than concerning itself with why each leader was as he was, this work simply takes their personalities as a given.

Next, there is the question of method. There are, of course, serious problems with generalizing from this single case of inadequate balancing to a more general theory of leadership. Within the scholarly community, much has been made of the relative merits of various research methodologies. For the purposes of generalizing, it is usually conceded that, a large sample size is to be preferred. The larger the sample size the greater the likelihood that a single case cannot misrepresent reality for the whole sample group. In our own situation, it would be preferable if we had a very large number of cases of ineffective balancing against which we could test. Ineffective balancing among great powers is, however, a rather rare occurrence. As such, the generally accepted wisdom of correcting for a small sample size by seeking to increase the number of cases as much as possible is difficult in this case.[14] To the extent that the sample can be increased from a single observation, of say, Baldwin, it has been to include Chamberlain. Even so, the doubling of the number of observations does not, in this case, increase the sample size by a significant enough factor so as to allow for detailed statistical analysis.

What we are left with is the question of whether or not the case study is an appropriate means and method for producing theory in international relations. Even those authors such as Lijphart who espouse a clear preference for large sample size studies acknowledge that case studies have both their place and their merits. Thus, "the great advantage of the case study is that by focusing on a single case, that case can be intensively examined even when the research resources at the investigator's disposal are relatively limited."[15]

Many scholars in addition to Lijphart recognize that meaningful theory can be built from case studies. Alexander George has observed that "most theories are in need of shaper formulation and a fuller statement of the network of parameters, independent and intervening variables that influence the variation in outcomes of the dependent variable. It is precisely one of the advantages of controlled comparison and single case studies . . . that they can facilitate this task."[16] The means by which they facilitate this greater understanding of the impact on the dependent variable is because of the depth to which they penetrate the topic as opposed to the more superficial treatment that any particular case receives in a large sample study.

Another methodological issue that bears explicit treatment is whether counterfactual reasoning should be considered legitimate in the development of political science theory. In the case at hand, the suggestion that different leadership would have resulted in different outcomes is the entire theoretical *raison d'être* of the project.

James Fearon has written a strong statement on the role of counterfactuals that begins with the assertion that "scholars in comparative politics and international relations routinely evaluate causal hypotheses by discussing or simply referring to *counterfactual cases* [italics in original] in which a hypothesized causal factor is supposed to have been absent."[17] That is, the use of counterfactuals is an established fact. What is generally lacking, Fearon claims, is that "researchers who use counterfactual argument to support causal hypotheses should be methodologically aware of what they are doing and should make their counterfactual arguments as explicit and defensible as they can."[18]

Every counterfactual argument is flawed, if only because there is no such thing as *ceteris paribus*. Robert Jervis has long ago disabused political science of the notion that one variable can be swapped for another without impacting on anything else.[19] That said, the null hypothesis of this book is that different leaders deciding differently, or in fact, the same leaders, had they adopted different decisions, may have attained different ends. Thus, for example, Hitler is known to have remarked that had he met the least resistance to his remilitarization of the Rhineland in 1936 he would have desisted immediately. From this we can surmise that had Baldwin taken more decisive action at that time, events may have turned out appreciably different than they did.

Because a goal of this book is to go beyond merely explaining ineffective balancing to argue that throwing out explanatory variables because of their predictive *problematique* may make the discipline more scientifically rigorous, but less relevant, to the world, acknowledging the role that leaders play in determining outcomes will assist us in understanding reality better. In so doing, it will also make the efforts of international relations theory more useful to those in a position to influence international affairs.

To the extent that this argument is inconsistent with some of the preferred strictures of scientific method, I urge a recollection of the origins of this discipline. Alexander George has written, "In an earlier era, the education of political scientists included training in history; but in the modern era the two disciplines, which once shared a common epistemological and methodological approach, drifted steadily apart as political science responded to the challenge of the scientific 'behavioral' movement in the social sciences."[20] At the time of his writing he foresaw that the pendulum would swing back the other way, bringing the study of history and political science closer together. That has not fully been borne out. This book straddles the middle ground; it is historically grounded while at the same situating its argument within the debate of international relations theory.

History provides the data set from which the theories of international relations are drawn; using historical methods to get at the root of a theoretical problem in the international relations literature is a good way to help reconcile the discipline to its origins.

Finally, there are two conventional narratives of this era that need to be addressed. The first is the commonly held idea that British air power saved Britain in 1940. The second is the claim that the problem was that Winston Churchill was not the prime minister nor, in fact, in any position of power at all from the time of his resignation from Baldwin's shadow cabinet in 1931 and until Neville Chamberlain brought him in to the war cabinet as first lord of the admiralty once the war had already begun.

The question with regards to air power depends on what is meant when we say that air power saved Britain. Certainly, the existence of interceptor aircraft and the superhuman exertions and sacrifices of the men who flew and serviced them minimized the suffering of Britons during the bombing raids of 1940–41. But did air power save Britain from invasion? Probably not. Although it is true that Hitler had drawn up plans for an amphibious invasion of Britain, that plan was shelved, albeit not as a consequence of British air power. In the end, Hitler, like Napoleon before him, reached the conclusion that given the nearly insuperable challenge of a cross-channel amphibious invasion of the British Isles, the better course to take against Britain was simply to make her stand alone. For Napoleon, that had meant the creation of the "Continental System," which excluded Britain from trade with Europe. For Hitler, it meant the same and more. It meant occupying Europe and making trade and communication between Europe and Britain near impossible. It also meant using his newly acquired position on the Atlantic coast to compound British misery with submarines in a way that Napoleon could not by making British trade and communication with other parts of the globe difficult as well. Hitler, of course, also could marshal air forces to make the pains of war real for Britons in an immediate and personal sense. Bonaparte did not have similar tools.

The chief threat to British security and the highest aim of her foreign policy always has been understood to be denying the attainment of hegemony in Europe by a continental power. It was to prevent that outcome that the Duke of Marlborough made war against the Hapsburgs. It was to prevent that outcome as well that Wellington had been sent to Europe during the Napoleonic wars. The attainment of German hegemony in Europe was an outcome not averted by British air power during the Second World War. Germany's rule, like that of Napoleon, extended from the Atlantic to Moscow, and it was turned back by the arduous labor of the hard-suffering Russians and, only much later, of the United States and Britain.

The second common narrative of this era concerns Winston Churchill. The claim, articulated by Churchill himself in his *Memoirs of the Second World War*, is that he saw what he called the "gathering storm" of an ascendant and revisionist Germany on the horizon, well before even the rise of Hitler. Furthermore, he would not have allowed the condition of the British armed services to reach the sorry state that they did. Additionally, had he inherited the leadership at any point during the 1930s, he would not have been so slow in rearming.

There is much to validate this point of view. Certainly, Churchill was not reticent in sharing his concerns about Germany during the interwar period. The pages of the Hansard are filled with speech after speech in which the member for Epping implored the government to accelerate the pace of their rearmament. As much as can be offered to validate the suggestion that the fate of the empire would have been different if Churchill had not been in the political exile he was, there is equally much to suggest that even had he been in the active leadership the outcome may not have been substantially different.

Although it is true that Churchill advocated a swift rearmament, he, like Baldwin and Chamberlain, fixated on air power as being the cureall to the German menace. The necessary prescription was not for air power as such, but for a strengthened army, with independent armor divisions and a firm continental commitment that could have, as General Hobart suggested, counter the highly effective German independent armor formations. A small example to demonstrate the degree to which Churchill was not on this track will suffice for the present. On March 8, 1934, during a House of Commons debate on the air estimates (budget) for that year, Churchill rose and, in a speech to which we will return in a later chapter, begged the government to do more, to do faster, to call for rearmament in a loud and clarion voice. A week later, during the debate on army estimates for the same year, a debate that dealt in large measure with the state of lavatories for married personnel, Churchill is not even recorded as being in attendance. His invective was indeed aimed against Germany and in favor of rearmament, although not necessarily of the kind that would have mattered.

In the end, however, the claims that Churchill made about what may have been different if he had been in the leadership will not be explored because the simple fact remains that he was not. These years find Churchill in the political wilderness. He was not involved in the process of making decisions on defense and not privy to the secrets that other leaders were. The research in this book is based on the historical record, archival data, speeches, and minutes of meetings of both the cabinet and its special subcommittees. Churchill was not involved in any of these.

The leadership of Churchill belongs to a different era, that of the Second World War, and his historical legacy determined by his actions therein. To judge him kindly, as Stanley Baldwin in fact did, the nation would need Churchill when the war came but not before.[21]

CHAPTER 1

STRUCTURAL NEOREALISM
AND THE BRITISH CASE

The ascendancy of structural neorealist theory in international relations that coincided with the 1979 publication of Kenneth Waltz's *Theory of International Politics*[1] gave rise to expectations across the discipline. It was believed that by discovering recurrent trends that seemed to be at a divorce from specific national attributes such as language, history, and culture, Waltz had found a way to generate elegant, parsimonious, and predictive theory on the basis of a scant number of variables. If true, it was felt that this development would allow the discipline of international relations to shift toward economics with its more robust predictive abilities and putative scientific neutrality and away from its mangled legacy as a mongrelized version of political science, philosophy, and diplomatic history.

Among the recurrences that Waltz had discovered, two bear particular mention. The first is that systemic-structural factors intervene between the intentions of actors in international politics and the outcomes of their interactions. Waltz argued that states very often want peace yet get war, not because of some factor inherent in human nature or even in the regime type of the interacting states, but rather because of the international system with its underlying anarchy. Anarchy, for the purposes of international relations theory, refers to the absence of a sovereign authority above the level of the state. That systemic anarchy, in which all states must be the guarantors of their own security, drives states toward security competition, which can result in war.

The second recurrent pattern that Waltz observed was that the competition spawned by the structure of the international system conditioned states to emulate the successful practices of others in their pursuit of security. In so doing, there was a certain convergence of capabilities that resulted in the formation of a balance of power. Waltz argues that the formation of balances of power need not be the result of a deliberate policy of "balancing" as some earlier scholars suggested.[2] Balancing is, rather, an unintentional response to the pressures that drive states to converge in their capabilities.

The balance of power is perhaps the central concept in international relations theory. For the most part, scholars writing on the balance of power frame balancing as a form of alignment that "occurs when a state brings its policies into close cooperation with another state in order to achieve mutual security goals."[3] This definition refers to "external" balancing, in which the efforts at attaining security are characterized by the pursuit of alliances. Another variant of balancing, called "internal" balancing, also exists. Internal balancing occurs when a threatened state seeks to enhance its security by bolstering its own power by such means as increasing military strength and the like.

Waltz's theory does not attempt to explain when specific balances will form and when they will not. Waltz argues that while he expects balances to form all the time, other factors that "lie outside of the theory's purview" can explain why they occasionally do not.[4] Other scholars, discussed later, have found the lack of predictive specificity in Waltz to be disheartening. While having knowledge of recurring systemic tendencies is interesting, it is far more exciting to be able to generate prediction on how any given state in any given situation will react. That information is relevant and useful both to scholars and the policy makers they inform. Randall Schweller, Jack Snyder, Thomas Christensen, and Stephen Walt have all developed theoretical approaches that provide a greater specificity in terms of predicting outcomes while remaining within the structural Waltzian framework.

GOALS AND ARGUMENTS

The goal of this book is to discuss leaders as a determinative variable in both explaining and predicting outcomes in international politics. That goal is advanced through three main arguments and three distinct targets. The first argument is against Waltz's claim that it is systemic-structural factors that intervene to explain why intentions and outcomes so rarely match up in international politics. Waltz is right that there is a variable that intervenes; however, it is not systemic structure but leadership.

The second argument is against neorealism's underspecified conception of the balance of power. Waltz himself and the many scholars who have followed his structural approach have all failed to unpack the concept of power and in so doing, failed to recognize the often-subtle distinction between nonbalancing and ineffective balancing.

That criticism feeds into the third and final argument that is not against Waltz but against the other neorealist scholars writing about the British case who have attempted to modify Waltz's work from within the structural framework in their efforts to generate specific predictions of when and under what circumstances balancing will occur.

The variable that intervenes between intentions and outcomes is the relative skills of leaders in identifying potential rivals and creating policies that meet the threat posed by those rivals that most explains why outcomes in international politics diverge from what the actors in the system wish for. British leaders in the 1930s intended to arm themselves against Germany and to form an effective balance against her rising might. That outcome failed to occur because of the relative inaptitude of Britain's leaders for appreciating what the situation they faced demanded in terms of the armament decisions they make. It was the leaders' own skills and limitations that intervened between their intention to balance and the ineffective balance that resulted.

The case of British armament behavior helps us understand two general phenomena: The first is how leaders intervene between intention and outcome in international politics. The second is what an effective balance of power is and how it is formed. Looking at the British case accomplishes this second task by showing how neorealist theory is underspecified in relation to the balance of power. The key error of neorealist theory is that it treats the concept of "power" vaguely. Not all types of power are the same. Many scholars writing about the influence of the United States in world politics, for example, focus on "soft power" elements, such as economic, social, and cultural influences through which they claim much of American influence is exerted.[5] But even within the more traditional dimensions of so-called hard power, that is, military power, not all power is of a single block. Some modalities of power work well against one type of rival and one kind of threat while doing little against a different rival who presents a different sort of threat.

Because not all modes of power are appropriate for every situation, the first task in the creation of an effective balance of power requires national leaders to determine who the rival to be balanced is. Once that is accomplished, leaders must analyze their own national vulnerabilities as well as those of their would-be rivals. Leaders must then prescribe policies that minimize their own vulnerabilities and, at the same time, find the appropriate policies to exploit the vulnerabilities of their rivals. Finally, leaders must mobilize support for those policies among the governing institutions, the people, or both, depending on the type of regime.

The formation of an effective balance of power is the result of the careful matching of the capabilities of state A to the vulnerabilities of state B. Other than by happenstance, that is the result of a deliberate process of identification, prescription, and mobilization that leaders undertake. If leaders perform all three tasks well, then one of two possibilities is likely. The first is that a balance of power will develop. That balance need not deter all wars from breaking out, but it will deter the cataclysmic wars that threaten to destroy the polar order of the international system. Order destroying wars are those in which at the end of the war the international system that was configured in one way, say with multiple great powers at its core, finds itself in a new and potentially less stable order. A balance of power which restrains cataclysmic war is the likely outcome when the target of balancing recognizes their own vulnerability and how the capabilities of the balancing state put it in a position to exploit them. The development of secure second-strike nuclear delivery vehicles during the Cold War, for example, was appreciated by both the Soviet Union and the United States, who recognized the existence of such weapons made it impossible to land a "war-winning" first strike. That recognition certainly contributed to the maintenance of nonbelligerence between the superpowers.[6]

The second outcome may be a war, one in which the first state will acquit itself well on the field of battle because it has looked after its own weak points while developing the appropriate means to exploit the weaknesses of their rival. This outcome is possible, although not necessarily likely, if the target state either does not assess its vulnerability correctly or misperceives how the capabilities of the balancing state take advantage of their weakness. Saddam Hussein's misperception of the willingness of the United States to fight Iraq both in 1991 and in 2003 illustrates how misperceptions on the part of leaders can lead to war.

Finally, when several scholars, such as those mentioned earlier, find the root of specific balancing behavior to lie in a combination of the malevolent intentions of actors combined with a specific distribution of powers within the system, they, too, like Waltz, underspecify power by not unpacking the concept to accommodate theoretically how different kinds of hard power are task and case appropriate.

The failure of an effective balance to form between Britain and Nazi Germany in the 1930s is the example to which this study looks both for the rejection of neorealism and for the substantiation of its own arguments. The case of Britain and Germany in the interwar years highlights some of the specific problems inherent in Waltz. To put it bluntly, World War II was, arguably, the most epochal and world-shaping event of the twentieth century. Yet an effective balance failed to form between Britain and Germany. Waltz's theory excuses itself from having to answer for that outcome by limiting its scope to predicting general trends but not specific outcomes. With humility, one must ask what utility and benefit comes from a "theory of international relations" that cannot account for the most important events in international politics, like the origins of the Second World War, and does not even try to.

Waltz's silence on this topic has discomfited Christensen and Snyder, Schweller, and Walt, who have all insisted that structural neorealism must have a mechanism to explain both the specific case of World War II as well as when states will balance and when they will not more generally if international relations theory is to be relevant. Where Walt makes a broad-spectrum argument about when balancing will occur and when it will not, Christensen and Snyder, as well as Schweller, build systemic-structural arguments that they contend explain the specific case of the inadequacy of Britain's response to the rise of Germany.

The documentary record of Britain in the 1930s confounds the arguments of the structuralist scholars such as Christensen, Snyder, and Schweller by showing that the logic that underpins their theories on why Britain did not balance effectively were not in operation at the time. Rather than having their behavior motivated by the factors related to either buck-passing or distancing (discussed later), the record shows that British leaders fully intended to balance against Germany. The reason that effort failed was because British leaders proved inaccurate and inadequate in their diagnoses, myopic and misguided in their prescriptions, and timid in their efforts at national mobilization. The record shows that the recognition of the nonfungiblity of power modes was known at the time but that specific leaders intervened to have their personal policy preferences for power generation implemented at a high ultimate cost to British security.

The remainder of this chapter will be occupied with situating leadership within the evolving realm of international relations theory.

INTERNATIONAL RELATIONS THEORY I: CLASSICAL REALISM

As this project is a reaction to Waltzian structuralism as advocated by both Waltz himself and other structuralist thinkers, Waltz and the subsidiary structural theories that purport to explain British behavior in the 1930s are a reaction to the scholars who preceded them. The effort embodied in this book represents a synthesis between the scholars to whom Waltz was reacting and Waltz himself. It accepts from Waltz the important observation that the variance between intention and outcome can be explained by the operation of an independent variable. It learns from those Waltz was reacting to the importance of including nonmaterial, ideational variables such as leadership, in order to accurately explain the origins of real-world international political phenomena.

International relations theory, as an academic discipline, has its modern origins in the work of E. H. Carr and Hans Morgenthau from the years immediately before and during the Second World War. It is important to understand what Waltzian structuralism was reacting to in order to appreciate the synthetic approach to international relations theory embedded in this study.

As Waltz represents a reaction to Carr and Morgenthau, the latter were responding to the heady optimism of the years after the First World War. Revulsion from the horrors of the Great War engendered a series of international agreements, some of them famous, others less so, that proposed the legal banishment of all war as a means of resolving conflict. The most posthumously notorious of these was the 1928 Pact of Paris, better known as the Kellogg-Briand Pact. This treaty, signed by all, save one, of the combatants of the First World War,[7] committed the signatory nations to "condemn recourse to war for the solution of international controversies, and renounce it, as an instrument of national policy in their relations with one another."[8] In so declaring, Kellogg-Briand was echoing the Treaty of Locarno from three years earlier in which the major combatants of the First World War, again, save Russia, vowed "that they will in no case attack or invade each other or resort to war against each other."[9] History would of course tell the lie to both of these agreements in fairly short order.

Both Carr and Morgenthau demurred from the trends that Locarno and Kellogg-Briand reflect. For Carr, the flaw of the internationalist school, of which President Wilson was a member and that spawned both Locarno and Kellogg-Briand, was that it was based on a false assumption of a "harmony of interests." This concept, extrapolated from the domestic discourse of economics as taught by Adam Smith, postulates that all sectors of society, whether producers or consumers, capital providers, or workers, have a harmony of interests between them such that conflict is only possible as the result of misunderstood realities not objective truth. Political thinkers of the late nineteenth and early twentieth centuries held that what was true for individuals was true for nations as well.[10] However, as Carr notes, the principle of the harmony of interests had been debunked as it related to individuals as soon as a century after it had first been promulgated. It turned out that the harmony of interests in economics existed only as long as there were no machines and no specialized labor skills. Once, however, machines and labor specificity came, workers could not just shift from one employment to the next, so capital grew at the expense of labor because owners had the advantage of being able to force lower wages on workers who could not easily shift to a more profitable sector because that would require a skill set or training that they did not possess. This early phase of industrialization resulted in the Dickensian description of big cities that we are familiar with from the mid-nineteenth century. It also inspired Marx to believe that workers would not allow this relative degradation to continue in perpetuity and that they would eventually rebel against the system. In recognition of the dangerous tendencies that result from unfettered capitalism, states, first Germany and later others, took steps to correct some of the most egregious of the disparities in their economic societies.[11]

Carr pointed out the irony of the harmony of interest being adopted as an international political truth at just the time that its domestic validity was being denied. Nonetheless, Carr went on to point out the extreme fallacy of the harmony of interests for international relations. There is in every age, Carr wrote, some powers that are satisfied with the current alignment of power and others who are dissatisfied by it. As long as those who hold power at the conclusion of the last test phase of power, that is, the last major war, continue to hold their place relative to the defeated powers, the system will appear to be universally interested in the maintenance of the status quo.[12] Once, however, the power capacity of the defeated state begins to rise, it expresses its dissatisfaction. At that point, the system will not appear to be focused on the maintenance of the status quo but, rather, will appear to be in turmoil. *The Twenty Years' Crisis* documents a time when such a shift occurred. Observing the Great Power relations in the early 1920s, says Carr, led to the assumption that all powers had a harmony of interests between them in the maintenance of the peace. And for several years that was correct. In the early 1920s, France was interested in the maintenance of the Versailles agreement because its terms entrenched France in a position far superior to that merited by its conduct on the battlefield. Germany, although subjected by the peace to harsh disarmament terms, was equally anxious about maintaining the status quo because from its supine position things could certainly be worse. Indeed, they had been just two years before the signing of Locarno when France invaded the Ruhr Valley in order to forcibly extract payments from Germany. However, the impression that this state of affairs in the early 1920s was a perpetual condition discounted the underlying truth, which was that Germany was dissatisfied with the Paris peace and that, given the proper conditions, would seek to overturn it. By the mid-1930s, those conditions presented themselves and Germany took advantage of them.

The failure of the interwar period, claimed Carr, was that it had discounted power. It had presumed that you could wish the ugliness of war and power politics out of existence.

Whereas Carr deserves credit for pulling down the utopian edifice that had landed Europe in a catastrophe far more damaging than the one that had preceded it, accolades for the building of a new theory in its place go to Hans Morgenthau, a German expatriate living and working in the United States. Morgenthau is, more than Carr, responsible for the rise of realism as an organized theoretical approach to the study of international affairs. Morgenthau's main contribution can be found in two separate books. The first, *Scientific Man versus Power Politics*, establishes the microfoundations of realist theory. The second, *Politics among Nations*, explains the macrofoundations of international behavior as well as detailing the principles and practice of states in a realist world.

Coming during the height of World War II, before the tide had been turned either against the Nazis or the Japanese, *Power Politics* fills in some of the blanks from Carr's work. The book has two purposes. The first is to document how modern man had mistakenly grafted the principles that had given rise to middle-class liberalism in the domestic sphere on to estimations of behavior in the international sphere.[13] The second aim of the book was to establish the explicit base on which international relations is founded: power.[14]

As to the first task, in the same way that Carr had engaged in a lengthy discussion of the role of the ideas of Adam Smith and later Jeremy Bentham and James Mill in the misdirection of international relations, Morgenthau, too, expends great energy in showing how liberalism had been mistaken for a non-power-oriented approach to politics. Morgenthau denies this premise, arguing instead that liberalism, too, is, like all politics, a matter of power.

The more consequential contribution of *Power Politics* comes from Morgenthau's discussion on the nature of man. Reserved for the last several chapters of the book, it is in *Power Politics* that Morgenthau introduces the concept of the *animus dominandi* as motivating the actions of men.[15] Morgenthau asserts that all men possess an innate desire to dominate other men. In Morgenthau's theory, states emulate the behavior patterns of the men of which they are composed. Therefore, as all men seek to dominate; so, too, do all states seek dominance. That is not to say that a small state will seek to dominate a large one. Belgium will not necessarily seek to dominate Germany, but it will seek, or at least aspire, to dominate some other state or people.

Seeing as how the lectures on which *Power Politics* is based were given in the summer of 1940, a time when men such as Hitler, Stalin, Churchill, and Roosevelt were calling the shots on the world stage and where the appetites of single men such as Hitler and Mussolini came to be identified wholly with the ambitions of the states at whose head they stood, the conclusion of the existence of an *animus dominandi* is not particularly surprising.

With the war over and the immediacy of threat deferred, *Politics among Nations*, a longer and more considered work than *Power Politics*, became the standard text in the field of international relations theory. In the introduction, Morgenthau lays out in succinct terms what he believes the debate about political thought to be. In Morgenthau's estimation, the debate in international relations theory is a contest between two ways of thinking. The first, which had led to the debacle of the interwar years, suggested that human nature was infinitely malleable and capable of consistent rationality. Furthermore, that any time that social behavior deviated from rational expectations, such deviation could be traced back to mistaken understandings or to a unique depravity of individuals or groups.[16]

This approach is contrasted by Morgenthau's own, which is the second way of thinking. Morgenthau's approach sees outcomes in world politics as the result of forces that are inherent in human nature. Consequently, if change is to be achieved or quality of life bettered, the efforts to affect that change must not be expected to demand action that is contrary to the nature of man. Given Morgenthau's belief in the fixed and flawed nature of mankind, it is better and more realistic, in his opinion, to aim for the lesser of an evil than the attainment of an absolute good.[17]

Morgenthau saw international politics as a struggle for power, with power not as a material force but, rather, as a psychological relationship. Power is about control over the minds and actions of men.[18] Like the *animus dominandi* that makes a repeat appearance in *Politics among Nations*,[19] the drive to power and the elements that compose power in Morgenthau are almost exclusively ideational. Glory, prestige, and esteem in the eyes of other states are the "interests" of states that imbue power with meaning.

It should be clear that the conditions under which Morgenthau's approach to international politics can be employed require a great deal of understanding of the unique characteristics of each state, its leadership, and its history. While all states act in terms of interests, and those interests are always expressions of the desire for power, the specific way that that desire will be expressed is not easily predictable.

In other words, Morgenthau's theory is reductionist in the sense that it "reduces" explanations for international outcomes to the level of the state as animated by the people who compose it and their unique motivations. It was this factor in Morgenthau's thinking, coupled with the passage of time and the changing of the historical context, that brought on realism's first challenge.

INTERNATIONAL RELATIONS THEORY II: STRUCTURAL NEOREALISM

While Morgenthau and E. H. Carr had come of age professionally during a time when international relations seemed to be dominated by personalities, a new generation of scholars, including Kenneth Waltz, was educated in a different time. For Waltz and other scholars who had observed the end of World War II and the first four decades of the Cold War, the conflict did not seem to be about a quest for glory, prestige, or esteem. Neither did states seem very interested in expansion. Once the Korean War was settled, the remainder of the Cold War conflicts, at least until the Soviet invasion of Afghanistan in 1979, seemed to be about keeping things pretty much the way they were, about maintaining the status quo.

Neither did the Cold War seem to be about a clash of wills between leaders. In both the United States and the Soviet Union, successive generations of leadership, despite having widely ranging personality differences, behaved in essentially the same ways. Whether it was Truman and Stalin, Kennedy and Khrushchev, or Nixon and Brezhnev, there were recurring patterns in the interaction between the superpowers that seemed better explained by the conditions in which their interactions took place and less by who was doing the acting.

Waltz's main charge against realism, however, was not that it was outdated. Rather, it was leveled against the very reductionism that Morgenthau had claimed was necessary in order to make informed commentary on the behavior of states. Waltz found that focusing study on the role of either the individual person or the unique aspects of states failed to capture some of the dynamics of international relations that were caused by a variable that intervened between the specific actor's intentions and the outcomes of international politics. It is the question of why observed outcomes in international affairs appear to be at such a variance from the intentions of the actors in the system that impelled Waltz to offer a new theory.

Waltz observed that the best intentions rarely, if ever, translate into the best of outcomes. Particularly, states seem to strive for peace and security yet often find themselves embroiled in war. If, as Morgenthau suggested, international outcomes are the result of the intended behavior of states, unless a war is the result of a misunderstanding or an accident, it had to be intentional at least on the part of one party. Waltz argues that it is not just accidents or misunderstandings that can cause wars, even when no one intends them to occur. Waltz proposed that there is an additional variable that intervenes between the interacting units and the result that their acts and interactions produce, and that is systemic structure.

An international structure, says Waltz, is composed of two essential elements; an organizing principle on which the system is based and the distribution of the relative capabilities of the actors within the system. In Waltz's theory, the organizing principle of the international political system is one of anarchy. Anarchy in this sense refers to a condition wherein each of the actors in the international system is formally the equal of the others, where none is entitled to command and none is required to obey.[20] There is no overarching authority in the international system that provides security for all the actors or enforceably adjudicates disputes between them as exists on the domestic level.[21] This condition of uncertainty results in a self-help environment in which each state must perform similar functions to all the other states in the system if it is to ensure its own survival. Survival of the state is a motivation that Waltz assumes all states possess, although he admits that, in reality, some states may seek to amalgamate into larger units and achieve their security via that method. Excepting that circumstance, it is through the interaction of units in the system that patterns of behavior that reward or punish actors with either survival or destruction are developed.

Much of the visible behavior in the international system is derived from the condition of anarchy. Anarchy, for example, limits the ability of states to cooperate for two reasons. First, because even in the event that cooperation produces absolute benefits for both sides, each side will wonder if the relative gain of the other state will place them in a position to implement a policy that could damage or destroy the first state.[22] Second, even if states are inclined to cooperate, because they are the guarantors of their own security and existence, they shy from becoming too dependent on any other party for materials and services needed for their own survival.[23] This stands in stark distinction from both economic logic and domestic example wherein specialization is considered to create the greatest benefit for everybody. For states, however, specialization, if it comes at the expense of a reasonable expertise in producing the means of their own security, can spell disaster.

There are ways, of course, out of anarchy. One is for the distribution of capabilities in the system to become so inequitable such that one unit can, in effect, command, while others are compelled to obey. This is a condition of empire. A more genial solution would be to entrust managerial powers to a central agency. Such an agency would require sufficient powers so as to be able to protect its clients in the way the police protect the citizenry. Some of the clients, however, will be the most powerful members of the system, and to overcome the threat they pose, an even greater amount of power will have to be lodged in the hands of the central agency. The stronger the power of the center, however, the greater the incentive of states to engage in a struggle to control it.[24]

Because anarchy cannot be easily overcome, writes Waltz, states in the international system have developed an expertise at managing existence within it. The balance of power is the main mechanism that has evolved in the system. Waltz likens states to economic firms to explain how balances form. In economics, firms will emulate the successful practices of others as they seek to survive in a competitive environment. Thus, during the 1980s, for example, when Japanese corporations seemed to be increasing profits at the same time as American corporate profitability was declining, there was a rush among American companies to analyze and adopt managerial practices of Japanese firms in an effort to compete. In the 1990s, when American growth seemed to be the result of inflation control through monetary policy, other markets, like that of the Europeans, sought not only to emulate the American practice of low inflation but also codified it as a requirement of states to participate in the common currency. In international politics, states will observe what the strong states do and emulate them. This process of emulation will lead to a convergence of capabilities, which will result in a balance being formed between the Great Powers. No state need intend to "form" a balance as a matter of policy; it will simply occur as a result of the competitive drive toward convergence.

Waltz's structural neorealism proved alluring. Whereas Morgenthau (although not Carr) suggested that there was no such thing as a political science,[25] Waltz's theory held out the promise of turning international relations into a "real" social scientific endeavor with the ability to formulate testable hypotheses from its generalized assumptions. Because the root causes of international behavior could be found in the systemic level and not in the level of any particular state, deep knowledge of what any given state was like was unnecessary. All that was needed now was an understanding of the relative position of one state in relation to the others in the system in terms of its power capabilities in order to make predictions about the course of its behavior. This ability to make general predictions without reference to the particulars of a state's history and leadership promised to move the discipline of international relations away from the humanities with its emphasis on the role of history and philosophy and more in the direction of a social science, like economics, which appears to be governed by discernable and predictable laws.

Structural Weaknesses

There were, however, downsides to the new scholarship. For a theory that purported to explain reality, it did, at times, seem to be rather unreal. As an example, it was strongly implied in Waltz's theory that states balance against the capabilities of other states without regard to other factors. This seemed to be rather inconsistent with what observation of political life showed. For much of the Cold War, the powers of Western Europe sided with the United States despite the fact that the United States held, at times, the greater relative share of the power in the system. Such a condition would have suggested a move for Europe to ally themselves with the Soviets in order to balance U.S. power. More glaringly, Canada and Japan are dwarfed by the might of the United States and do not seek to balance against her as they should if mere capability is what motivates balancing behavior.

These shortcomings in Waltz's theory do not, in fact, bother Waltz at all. Predicting the behavior of specific states in specific situations is, he wrote, like "expecting the theory of universal gravitation to explain the wayward path of a falling leaf."[26] To understand why states do what they do in any specific case is, according to Waltz, to seek a theory of foreign policy not of international politics. Going even further, Waltz seems to acknowledge explicitly that while his theory predicts that balances will form, he cannot be expected to account for "the failure of balances to form, and the failure of some states to conform to the successful practices of other states."[27] The failure of a balance to form represents a deviation from his theory that can "too easily be explained away by pointing to effects produced by forces that lie outside of the theory's purview."[28] In other words, while Waltz has a theory of what will happen, that is, to states balancing, he cannot, nor does he even try to explain why they sometimes do not—even in epochal cases, such as the one explored here.

Not all scholars share with such equanimity the lack of specificity that comes from Waltz's "general predictions," especially when it comes at the expense of useful commentary on "real" international politics. Thus, Thomas Christensen and Jack Snyder, in an article to which we will refer back shortly, argue that many students of international politics expand Waltz's ideas, against Waltz's own admonition, in an attempt to integrate them into a "theory of foreign policy to make predictions about or prescriptions for the strategic choices of states."[29] The desire to expand Waltz's theory to apply to foreign policy predictions is understandable because, in the main, the behavior of specific states in any given situation is what really inspires curiosity. This need to expand Waltz's theory in order to enhance its utility is compelled all the more from the fact that, again in the words of Christensen and Snyder, "any foreign policy and its opposite can be deduced from Waltz's theory."[30] What good is a theory when everything and its opposite can be deduced from it? It is to several of these expansions on Waltz that we now turn.[31]

Supplements to Neorealism I: Balance against What?

Perhaps the most central concept in international politics is the balance of power. As Waltz writes, "If there is any distinctively political theory of international politics, balance-of-power theory is it."[32] The centrality of balance of power is consistently emphasized both by "old-school" scholars such as Henry Kissinger, and in the writings of newer ones such as Waltz himself.[33] Given the centrality of the concept, the predictive imprecision that results from the vagueness of Waltz's theory inspired a series of enhancements to neorealist theory whose purpose is to make structural neorealism more predicatively robust. While these corrections or amendments make neorealism more precise as an explanatory theory, they do so at a cost to the elegant parsimony that made Waltz's work so attractive in the first place.

One of the first issues to be explored and amended was the question of precisely what it is that states balance against. In Waltz's structure, the two factors that matter are the organizing idea (in this case, anarchy) and the distribution of *capabilities* (in other words, the distribution of power). It is against "capability" that balances will tend to form.

Stephen Walt challenges Waltz on this point. What Walt argues is that framing the question of balancing (and its corollary, bandwagoning[34]) solely in terms of power is "seriously flawed . . . because it ignores the other factors that statesmen will consider when identifying potential threats and prospective allies."[35] It is more accurate to say, according to Walt, that "rather than allying in response to power alone . . . states will ally with or against the most *threatening* [italics in the original] power."[36] The question then remains: how does one determine who is threatening? To answer that question, Walt proposes that the determination of threat comprises four different variables: aggregate power of a state, its proximity to the balancing state, its offensive capability, and the offensive intentions of the state. All four variables present certain problems. Only the second one, physical proximity, can be definitively measured. The aggregate power of a state is difficult to measure because it must include such factors as morale of troops and society as well as industrial capacity.[37] The extent of a state's offensive capability presupposes that a meaningful distinction can be made between different types of weapons with some being objectively "defensive" and others objectively "offensive." This supposition is dubious to say the least.[38] The least material factor that Walt mentions is the offensive intentions of the state. Understanding that some states mean to cause harm and some do not goes a long way toward bridging the gap between balance of power theory and the reality of observed politics. Thus, for example, the issue of Canada not balancing against the United States gets interpreted in light of the lack of a desire on the part of the United States to conquer Canada. The challenges inherent in employing this factor in a social scientifically rigorous way are daunting. How does one "know" the intentions of another state? Whose ideas matter? Those of the leader? Those of political elites? Walt's resolution to these problems is tautological and unsatisfying. We know the hostile intentions of a state from their hostile actions.[39] This may help states challenged subsequently to make decisions, but it does not assist the first state to be challenged to make a decision. Moreover, how are we supposed to distinguish meaningfully between "legitimate" actions and hostile ones? In this book, the question of when Hitler became hostile in a way that others should have understood is critical. When was the appropriate time to act? Was it in 1936 when both the Locarno and Versailles treaties were abrogated? In 1938 when Austria was annexed? Or was it in early 1939 over Czechoslovakia or the summer of 1939 over Poland?

It is precisely because of these ambiguities and complications that scholars such as Waltz eschew all but material variables.[40] These complications notwithstanding, Walt is to be commended for reintroducing this ideational element because the use of the ideational variable of offensive intention makes Walt's work jibe with the more intuitive understanding of international politics and, in fact, with observed outcomes as well.

Supplements to Neorealism II: The Structural Source of British Behavior in the 1930s

Neorealism's understanding of balance of power theory, whether the pure capability-based variety or the variant of it that includes the ideational elements introduced by Walt, is inadequate for explaining the years leading up to World War II. Whatever the variant, balancing is held to be in opposition to a parallel form of behavior generally called bandwagoning. Bandwagoning represents a choice to ally with the greater power rather than balance against it.[41] There are many reasons why a state would choose to bandwagon. Even as Steven Walt argues that balancing is far more prevalent than bandwagoning in international politics, he also posits that small states lying proximate to large ones may rationally choose to side with the state that may be the most threatening because of the futility of opposition—thus, for example, Finland's relationship to the Soviet Union during the Cold War.[42] Major powers, although generally not "Great Powers," also may choose this strategy. It is common to interpret the behavior of the United Kingdom in the years after World War II, and indeed up to the present, as reflecting such a choice. Whereas on Walt's scale the United Kingdom is not "afraid" of the United States, bandwagoning may allow Great Britain to exercise influence incommensurate with her material capabilities by being a confidant of the United States and thereby helping shape the latter's policies.

Regardless, neither balancing nor bandwagoning is what took place in the Soviet Union or Great Britain during the 1930s. Germany in the 1920s was not a threat to anybody. The Versailles treaty had dulled the fangs of the armed forces, rampant inflation crippled the German economy, and Germany's political leadership was far more concerned with easing the economic burden than in rising again to seek hegemony in Europe. So supine had Germany become that when France invaded the Ruhr Valley in 1922 in an effort to force the extraction of reparations payments, Germany was unable to offer any active resistance at all.

The mid- to late 1920s saw the rehabilitation of Germany's image under the leadership of Gustav Stresemann. The Treaty of Locarno, mentioned earlier, was an agreement between France and Germany finalizing their borders, which was guaranteed by Britain. Its signing paved the way for the entrance of Germany into the League of Nations, a move that signaled the return of Germany to the community of nations. By the early 1930s under the shadow of the global economic downturn of the year before, Stresemann succeeded in ending the payment of reparations fully and finally. The restoration of German stature during the 1920s and early 1930s did not take a military cast in the least. Indeed, only few hints of what lay ahead could be discerned. For example, Locarno only guaranteed the borders between France and Germany. It made no statement on the eastern boundaries of Germany. Even a moderate like Stresemann was not willing to concede that Germany's eastern boundaries would not require revision, albeit, if it were left to him, by peaceful means.

The ascendancy of Adolf Hitler to the chancellorship of Germany in 1933 took events in a different direction. From the start, Hitler tread far less softly than Stresemann. Where Stresemann worked subtly to overthrow the restrictive clauses of the Versailles treaty, Hitler repudiated them with brio. Where Stresemann was mainly interested in the restoration of Germany's economy, Hitler sought the restoration of German power and prestige. Within a few short years Hitler had commenced a rapid rearmament program, declared parity (falsely, as it turned out) with Great Britain in air power, introduced conscription, sent his army to occupy the Rhineland, effected a union with his native Austria, returned the ethnic German citizens of Czechoslovakia to the German Reich, occupied the remaining portions of Czechoslovakia, and brought the ethnically German city of Memel from Lithuania into Germany. He did all this before he was confronted in war by France and Great Britain over the issue of Poland.

If it was too complicated to try to infer Hitler's intentions from his actions, despite the list given here, he simplified the task by publishing *Mein Kampf.* As early as page 1, Hitler made clear his aim to expand the German Empire to encompass colonial possessions. "German-Austria must return to the great German mother country," he says in one place; "One blood demands one Reich," he says in another. "Only when the Reich borders include the very last German," he proclaims, can the German Empire begin its necessary expansion.[43]

Despite both the existence of clear expansionist rhetoric and the actions to back it up, Germany was not confronted until very late[44]— too late, in fact, to save France from defeat and nearly too late for Great Britain. German power grew rapidly, yet despite expectations drawn from international relations theory, balancing did not occur, despite the strong urging of some powers early on, especially France, that it should. Indeed, as the decade edged toward its end, the very powers that should have been confronting Germany made concession after concession, leading to both the aggrandizement and empowerment of their soon-to-be foe. The looming question is: Why did Great Britain not balance as international relations theory predicts that it should have?

INTERNATIONAL RELATIONS THEORY AND THE ORIGINS OF WORLD WAR II: I, BUCK-PASSING

In attempting to explain the events leading up to the Second World War, Waltz introduces the possibility that England's behavior was motivated by a desire to pass the costs of confronting rising German power from herself and France to Russia. Waltz writes, "As the German threat grew, some British and French leaders could hope that if their countries remained aloof, Russia and Germany would balance each other off or fight each other to the finish."[45] Christensen and Snyder make the argument in greater detail and with greater theoretical robustness. As mentioned earlier, Christensen and Synder were troubled by the lack of predictive certainty in Waltz's theory. Waltz posited that in a multipolar system states will either buck-pass, that is, externalize the costs of defense on to a second state or balance. Christensen and Snyder attempt to resolve which of those two policies states will choose and under what circumstances. They argue that marrying Waltz's ideas to Robert Jervis's writing on the security dilemma affords a more certain prediction.[46] In multipolar environments in which there is a perception that defensive weapons dominate the military scene, buck-passing will be more likely. Christensen and Snyder write, "The less the vulnerability of states, the greater the tendency to pass the buck. This is due to the expectation that other states, even singly, will be able to stalemate the aggressor without assistance and to the expectation that the process of fighting will be debilitating even for a victorious aggressor."[47]

Of course, as Christensen and Snyder acknowledge, even the marriage of Jervis to Waltz comes up short. The issue of defensive or offensive advantage turns out to be less of an uncontested material variable and relies rather more on perception. In both 1914 and 1940, states got it wrong. In the earlier war the assumption was that the offense would carry the day, when in fact it did not. In the later war, it was believed, so Christensen and Snyder argue, that the defense would dominate when in fact, as was shown so swiftly in May–June of 1940, that which could not be accomplished through four years of effort in the Great War took just six weeks in World War II.

For the leading theoretical explanation of the causes of British behavior before the Second World War, Christensen and Snyder's article suffers from some problems. For their approach to be valid, several conditions need to be shown to apply. First, it must be demonstrated that policy makers believed that there were operating in an era of defense dominance. After all, as the question hinges on *perception* of defense dominance, then it must be shown that the relevant policy makers held such a perception. Second, it must be demonstrated that the buck-passing state intended to pass the buck. The claim that Britain failed to balance effectively against the rising German threat is a fact. The very fact of what Randall Schweller calls "underbalancing"— that is, failing to balance adequately to the threat—however, does not mean that the state intended for someone else to rise to meet the challenger. In the case at hand, it must be shown that British policy makers during the relevant period were attempting to pass the buck to Russia or France.

Neither condition applies. A significant portion of this book is dedicated to showing that British policy makers in the 1930s saw Britain as being quite vulnerable to attack. During the 1930s, the concern in Britain was less about land warfare, in which perceptions of defense dominance may have prevailed, and more about attack from the air. In popular literature as well as in the military and political discourse of the day, the focus—indeed, the obsession—was on vulnerability to air attack.[48]

As for the second condition, that of intentionally transferring the war to Russia, it is true only to the extent that if there need be war, then better it be against Russia.[49] It is far more accurate to suggest that the British did not want war at all, not between themselves and Germany and not between Germany and Russia either.

The idea of passing the buck to France cannot be dismissed on its face as the idea of passing it to Russia can be. A significant portion of the remaining chapters of this book deals with the motivations and attitudes of the British leadership with regard to France. Although at times British leaders wondered to what extent French preparations would have the positive effect of aiding Britain, they always reached the conclusion: that Britain could not rely on France's efforts to provide security for Britain.

INTERNATIONAL RELATIONS THEORY AND THE ORIGINS OF WORLD WAR II: II, TRIPOLARITY

Randall Schweller rejects Christensen and Snyder's explanation of World War II as being the result of buck-passing because buck-passing depends on the system being multipolar, but Schweller sees the international system of the 1930s as being not multipolar but tripolar. Schweller argues that in any international system there are both poles, that is, states that possess a preponderant share of the total available military capacity, and lesser great powers. Lesser great powers (LGP) are, as their name implies, powers that while possessing formidable military and economic capabilities fall short of poles in terms of the total share of available capability they control. Schweller argues on the basis of calculations he made using the Correlates of War (COW) data set for 1938, that the international system of the time was in fact tripolar, with Germany, the United States, and the Soviet Union as the polar units, and the other future combatants, including Great Britain and France, ranking as LGPs.

Schweller further distinguishes between two types of behavior that, while appearing the same from the outside are actually quite different. The first is buck-passing, which was discussed earlier. The second is a new behavior that he calls "distancing." Among the variables that Schweller looks at is the potential strength of a coalition. If a potential coalition of two, for example, is strong enough to defeat an enemy, then buck-passing, which he defines as when "a threatened state attempts to ride free on the balancing efforts of other[s],"[50] may occur. If the potential coalition cannot defeat the enemy, then the behavior pattern, although phenotypically identical, is in fact distancing, not buck-passing. In a distancing situation, Schweller hypothesizes that "threatened status-quo states will not ally with each other when their combined strength is insufficient to deter or defeat the aggressor(s)."[51] What occurs in such a situation is that the "less directly threatened states will try to distance themselves from more immediately threatened states by refusing to coordinate their diplomatic and military strategies with the latter."[52]

Based on Schweller's calculations, as France and Britain did not have sufficient capability between them to defeat Germany, he expects to find behaviors consistent with distancing. According to this interpretation, Britain would choose to enhance its security at the expense France. Schweller finds that to have been the case, citing, for example, the Anglo-German naval accord of 1935 as a measure that would ameliorate specifically British concerns while at the same time leaving France even less convinced of the steadfastness of its potential ally.[53] In explaining why, after Munich, Britain became less conciliatory toward Germany and grew closer to France, Schweller suggests that the result of "Anglo-French rearmament [beginning to] closing the gap in Germany's military advantage" coupled with the fact that, at that point, "Britain saw itself and not France as the more immediate target of

German aggression" explains the shift in behavior.[54] In other words, after Munich, Britain and France neither buck-pass nor distance but, rather, strive to balance.

There are many points that bear examining in Schweller's analysis. A few of them are worth mentioning here. One problem is that Schweller analyzes the data from 1938 alone. Hitler rose to power in January 1933; by 1935, the signs were clear that the Germans were casting off the military restrictions of Versailles; by 1936, they had already made their first forceful demonstration in the remilitarization of the Rhineland. What would the COW data show those times? At what point does the balance tip in Germany's favor? Why did a balance not form before that tipping point was reached?

More fundamentally, however, the definition of the interwar system as tripolar is problematic. While as a material measurement of total available capability, it may be true, two of the poles were actively uninvolved in European affairs. The United States, second only to the Soviet Union in Schweller's calculation, had turned its back on Europe after its experience in the First World War. Two sets of neutrality acts, one in 1935 and the other just two years later, were a strong message to Europe about the intensions of the United States. It is not until war was declared on the United States by Germany that the former deigned to get involved. The statement could not have been articulated more forcefully than it was by President Roosevelt on May 11, 1940, the day after France and Belgium were attacked:

> Whereas a state of war unhappily exists between Germany, on the one hand, and Belgium, Luxemburg, and the Netherlands, on the other hand;
>
> Now, THEREFORE, I, FRANKLIN D. ROOSEVELT, President of the United States of America, in order to preserve the neutrality of the United States and of its citizens and of persons within its territory and jurisdiction, and to enforce its laws and treaties, and in order that all persons, being warned of the general tenor of the laws and treaties of the United States in this behalf, and of the law of nations, may thus be prevented from any violation of the same, do hereby declare and proclaim that all of the provisions of my proclamation of September 5, 1939, proclaiming the neutrality of the United States in a war between Germany and France; Poland; and the United Kingdom, India, Australia and New Zealand apply equally in respect to Belgium, Luxemburg, and the Netherlands.[55]

The Soviet case is, of course, more open to interpretation. From a geographic perspective, the Soviet Union during the period in question was buffered from Germany and from all of Europe by the *cordon sanitaire*, Poland, Czechoslovakia, and Romania, which formed a wedge between Russia and Europe.

> The British elite held the Red Army in great contempt and assumed that they would crumble in the face of a German attack. As A. J. P. Taylor notes, "Besides, there were in 1937 and the years immediately after it practical objections. Russia was in the midst of Stalin's great purge, and it was difficult to take her seriously as a military power when all her principal military leaders had just been shot. The British service chiefs rated Russia's power very low, and their opinion carried weight even if it sprang as much from political prejudice as from knowledge."[56] A direct quote from Neville Chamberlain makes the point even more succinctly: "I must confess to the most profound distrust of Russia. I have no belief in her ability to maintain an effective offensive, even if she wanted to."[57]

In any event, it scarcely matters whether the Soviet Union counts as a pole because the United States surely did not, rendering the system bipolar, at best.[58]

Finally, Schweller suggests that events bear out what he has claimed. Thus, "the very fact that Britain survived after France's defeat suggests that Anglo-French security lacked the property of jointness required of a collective good."[59] This is an unfair statement in that the British survived, but in many opinions, this was more the result of the *deus ex machina* of Hitler's decision to invade Russia in June 1941, his foolish decision to declare war on the United States in December 1941, and the willingness of the United States to negotiate the bases-for-destroyers deal in September 1940. To be saved by either the folly of your enemy or the magnanimity of your friend is no indicator of either wisdom or rectitude on your own part.

It is clear that Schweller himself is, in some ways, dissatisfied with the structural tripolar explanation that he offers, even as he views it as preferable to its buck-passing competitor. Hints to this dissatisfaction and later efforts to correct for it can be found in *Deadly Imbalances*.

In arguing against a "straight structural" explanation, Schweller comments, "The goals and policy decisions of statesmen, sometimes even those of extraordinarily unremarkable ones, can (and often do) exert a profound effect on the course of history and so human agency must be taken into account."[60] In that book, the comment serves as part of the justification for looking at the interests of states[61] but finds a more full expression in a recent one.

In his more recent book, Schweller again tackles the question of why Britain failed to balance against the rising German threat. Rather than focusing on the combination of structure and interests that he credited in *Deadly Imbalances*, Schweller now ascribes explanatory power to domestic level considerations of "elite consensus" among the British governing elites for explaining Britain's ineffective balancing.[62]

In driving yet another nail into the coffin of Waltz's purely structural explanation, Schweller observes, "From the policymaker's perspective, however, balancing superior power and filling power vacuums hardly appear as laws of nature. Instead, these behaviors, which carry considerable political costs and uncertain political risks, emerge through the medium of the political process," continuing a few lines later to suggest, "Leaders are rarely, if ever, compelled by structural imperatives to adopt certain policies rather than others; they are not sleepwalkers buffeted about by inexorable forces beyond their control."[63] As with his argument on tripolarity, here, too, Schweller is not arguing that structure does not matter at all. Certainly a part of the reason that Jamaica does not declare war on the United States, even if its leaders are inclined to such bellicosity, is the recognition on their part that the relative distribution of capabilities between the two states does not favor such a policy. Not all cases are so clear cut, however, and the crux of Schweller's latest thesis is that in cases in which there is no elite consensus on the nature of the threat, states will "underbalance," that is, inadequately respond to the external challenge.

In taking his research in this direction, Schweller is leading the vanguard in whose trail this project follows. Schweller is not wrong but, rather, in being right, he does not go far enough. Schweller's recent work is vague on what precisely the "elite" in "elite consensus" means. Although in building the theory he refers to the elite in a generalized, amorphous sense, when he deals with the nuts and bolts of his cases, especially the British in the 1930s, "elites" and "leaders" tend to get mixed up more intimately.

In hinting about the roles that specific leaders play, Schweller is creating a breach in the wall of reticence that exists on this topic in the international relations literature that we will now exploit. If Schweller posited that leaders are only one part of the elite whose consensus he believes is required for appropriate balancing activity, we will assert more forcefully that it is not the elites in any amorphous sense but, rather, the individual leaders, full on, that are the main determinants of whether or not an effective balance will be formed.

CHAPTER 2

LEADERS AND LEADERSHIP

A QUALITATIVE MODEL

To say that political science as a whole ignores the role of specific leaders is inaccurate.[1] To say, by contrast, that most modern international relations scholars tend to either ignore or disregard the role of individual leaders is, on the whole, true.[2] Undeniably, contemplating a role for the personality and abilities of any particular leader is difficult to reconcile with aspirations to scientific rigor. In one of the rare articles in the international relations literature that attempts to address the issue, the authors break down criticisms against consideration of the leader into two general varieties. In the first, they claim that "many political scientists contend that individuals ultimately do not matter, or at least they count for little in the major events that shape international politics."[3] Yet, as was suggested in the Introduction, the claim that individual leaders do not matter is simply inconsistent with the experience of most people and must be rejected because, as noted by Robert Tucker, "people as individuals, and particularly those who are leaders, often make a significant difference in historical outcomes by virtue of the ways in which they act or fail to act at critical junctures in the development of events."[4] The opening pages of this book suggested that it is hard to imagine the Second World War and its consequences without reference to Hitler. Hitler is not the only example that we can point to when suggesting that leaders matter. Would the Union have been restored if not for the tenacious leadership of Abraham Lincoln? Would the 1982 Israeli invasion of Lebanon have taken the cast it did if Ariel Sharon were not minister of defense? More recently, would the invasion of Iraq in 2003 have occurred if Al Gore had been in the White House instead of George W. Bush? The argument of this book ascribes crucial importance to the diagnoses that leaders make of a potential problem. During his campaign for reelection in 2004, President George W. Bush articulated his belief that after the attacks of September 11, 2001, the United States had to act peremptorily in the face of potential enemies. Bush diagnosed America's problem as that it had waited for provocation instead of acting in anticipation of it. Pursuant to that diagnosis he prescribed an attack on Iraq, a state that he believed was the probable nexus between dangerous capabilities and hostile intentions. Would all presidents have made the same choices as President Bush? If not, then what other than his specific leadership can explain American foreign policy choices between 2001 and 2008?[5]

In responding to the structuralist claim that leaders do not matter, Byman and Pollack suggest that "the goals, abilities, and foibles of individuals are crucial to the intentions, capabilities, and strategies of a state."[6] In other words, even for those who wish to factor only the capabilities of the state, the leader is part and parcel of those capabilities.

There is no question that a particularly gifted leadership can act as a force multiplier. In the military sphere this has been recognized for a long time. Few would argue with the suggestion that the unique abilities of Robert E. Lee played a significant role in allowing a decidedly materially inferior Confederate force to compete for as long as it did and as well as it did against the materially superior Union forces in the American Civil War.

Part of what goes into generating the power that is the main measure of state capacity is the ability to extract resources from society. One of those resources is the willingness of the nation to fight, that is, its morale. Even an act as materially insignificant as giving a speech can have a tremendous effect on the willingness of the citizenry to continue to fight. Examples of this abound, ranging from the ancient to the modern. The funeral oration of the Athenian statesman Pericles as documented by Thucydides helped, by Thucydides' account, to rouse the Athenians to continued action against the Spartan alliance. Of Winston Churchill, for example, President Kennedy offered praise, saying, "In the dark days and darker nights when Britain stood alone—and most men save Englishmen despaired of England's life—he mobilized the English language and sent it into battle. The incandescent quality of his words illuminated the courage of his countrymen."[7] Churchill's words alone did not win the war, of course, but they may have contributed to the moral fortitude that allowed Britain to endure the hardest years of sacrifice and privation before the Americans engaged.

The second criticism that is leveled at those who would consider the role of leaders is that "although individual leaders may matter from time to time, their influence does not lend itself to the kind of generalizations that political scientists seek."[8] Even if it is granted that the rhetoric of Pericles and Churchill drove their peoples on, how is that effect to be measured, quantified, or otherwise manipulated so that it can be used as a predicatively relevant variable? The latter third of the Byman and Pollack article is taken up with demonstrating that the attributes of leaders can in fact be framed in such a way so as to make them relevant for social scientific research. The first four hypotheses that they advance are theses on the relevance of leaders; the latter four hypothesize on how individual personality traits influence international relations. Thus, for example, they postulate that "states led by delusional leaders start wars and prolong them unnecessarily."[9] Such a hypothesis is quite vulnerable on its face. Although we may be able to both find correlation and make a good argument about causal links between delusion and propensity for war, we will still be at a loss to identify delusion *a priori*. It is a rare thing for contemporary observers to know that a leader is delusional. Moreover, how are we supposed to know when it is wise to fight a war and when prudence would dictate that a vulnerable position be surrendered? Would Britain have been wise to negotiate a peace with Hitler during the winter of 1940 when it stood alone against the Nazis? Was refusing to do so a necessary or unnecessary prolongation of the war? Was Churchill deluded in thinking that England could persevere?

While not denying certain weaknesses in Byman and Pollack's efforts to demonstrate the scientific efficacy of leadership as a variable, their statement on the merits of the consideration of leadership still gets to the heart of why such a pursuit is worthwhile. They claim, "Of greater relevance, however, we dismiss the contention that parsimony is somehow more important than accuracy when deriving political science theory. The field of international relations is an effort to explain the interaction of states and, ultimately predict their behavior. Consequently, realist (with a small 'R') is the best, and perhaps the only, determinant of the utility of a theory."[10] Even if consideration of the role of individual leaders is messy, if it impacts on international outcomes we would be wrong to ignore it simply because at present our efforts at dealing with it are clumsy. Byman and Pollack conclude that even if the factors they consider are "impossible to operationalize," such was said of "culture, ideology, ideas and norms" at one point and that "scholars over time developed methods to measure and weigh these concepts, greatly enriching the study of international relations."[11]

Some productive studies in leadership have resulted from the efforts of those political scientists with fewer scientific pretensions. Eliot Cohen, whose *Supreme Command* is a study in what makes for effective leadership of democratic states in wartime, and others appear to have willingly surrendered affiliations as a political scientist, adopting both the ambitions and method of a historian in building his case.[12] Other such political science renegades include Robert Robbins, who, in partnership with Jerrold Post, a psychiatrist, has coauthored a gripping study considering the role that the health of a leader plays in the politics that he or she makes when in the throes of illness or as a consequence of the confrontation that illness makes with mortality.[13] What distinguishes Robbins and Post is that as opposed to the vein of literature in psychology that overlaps with the politics of leadership, they look at physical, not just mental, infirmity.[14]

Closer to the political science heartland is Richard Samuels's *Machiavelli's Children*, which examines the role of particular leaders in late industrializing nations.[15] In explaining the motivation for looking at leaders in his work, Samuels writes, "In the real world, some leaders do little more than bob like corks on a restless sea. But others—many others—do much more. . . . And even those who are not revolutionaries, 'normal' politicians, will routinely select among equally plausible alternatives. In short, constraints may be greater in the historian's narrative than they are in the real world where social, political and economic forces can be tipped into the balance to abet the leader's scheme."[16] In other words, structure and the distribution of capabilities impact on outcomes but do not preordain them. Leaders have choices and opportunities, and the degree to which those opportunities are seized or otherwise made to conform to the desires of the leader determines how effective the leader is. Again, Samuels says,

> Leadership is that constrained place where imagination, resources and opportunity converge. The imaginings need not be original to the leader, but he is the one who can control their use for his ends. The resources need not be entirely of her making, but she must be able to commandeer them for her own use. Opportunities will flow past individual entrepreneurs from time to time, and the successful leader will seize them. Most important of all, the constraints need not be determinant and the change need not be serendipitous. Determined individuals will demonstrate a range of creative ways to combine resources and ideas, and to seize opportunity.[17]

The relevance of leadership is not limited by regime type, although certainly different leadership tasks are performed differently by leaders in different countries. Stanley Baldwin often drew attention to the fact that he believed that autocratic leaders could get more done faster than he could because of their control over the media instruments used for mobilizing society. Neither can leadership overcome all material realities. Robert E. Lee, who was mentioned earlier as a generally agreed-upon example of a force multiplier in the military sphere, was able only to prolong the American Civil War; he was never able to win it. That said, as Samuels suggested earlier, leadership is the place where material reality, fortune, opportunity, and imagination all converge. Some leaders are able to take those ingredients and do great things with them. Others are confronted with the same set of realities but founder, lacking the spark of imaginative leadership. In both cases, the leader matters because even the leader who lacks the capacity for creative action is determinative if only in providing the leaders of other countries with a window of opportunity for action that would have been impossible had a greater leader been in control.

For all stripes of international relations theorists, from structural neorealists to liberal institutionalists, leadership should matter because among the many tasks of leaders is their job as translators or mediators of inputs and constraints into policy outcomes. Structural neorealism in particular is in need of a mechanism that explains how the systemic constraints inspired by the distribution of capabilities get translated into its expectant policies, namely, balances of power. As discussed in the previous chapter, neorealist theory suggests that the formation of balances of power requires that only two conditions be met: (1) that the international system is anarchic and (2) that the states in the system wish to survive. Based on these two assumptions, we can expect that states will emulate the successful security practices of other states. The result of that process of emulation is the creation, intentional or otherwise, of a balance of power.[18]

That explanation is insufficient. The international system can be anarchic and states can seek to survive, yet a balance of power will still fail to form. The shortcoming of neorealism is that it is too vague in its understanding of what "power" is. Power can take many forms, even within so-called hard power elements. Power can be focused in the air, on the sea, on land, in space, or in some combination thereof. Power is not a Swiss Army knife, a tool that can be used equally well for a variety of tasks. States must first identify whom they are seeking security from in order to know what type of instruments of power to develop. Successful balancing, therefore, does not require states to emulate the behaviors of the strong states in the system. It requires, rather, a matching of capabilities by the balancing state to the vulnerabilities of the state from which it seeks to be secured. The proper balance of forces in any particular circumstance is not obvious, and there is not always a relevant great power precedent to follow as neorealism assumes there is.

What is required for the formation of an effective balance of power is a careful deliberative process geared to determining what the proper armament and political ratios are for a given rival. That process is carried out and mediated by national leaders. Predicting when balancing will be effective then, is not contingent on knowing whether the nation has the will to survive. It is rather dependent on the success of national leaders in their roles of diagnosis, prescription, and mobilization.

Waltz is correct that a balance of power need not be the intention of a state. It can form by accident if the balancing state happens upon an armament and political policy that succeeds in targeting the vulnerabilities of a second state. Failing that, though, and more often, it is the desire to prepare for a given set of contingencies that motivates states to pursue certain policies. When the process is successfully navigated by a skilled leader, two outcomes are possible. One possible outcome is that a balance will form that deters war. This outcome requires that the target state appreciates the exact nature of its vulnerabilities and understands how the strengths of the balancing state target and exploit those vulnerabilities.

A second possible outcome is war. This outcome may result if the target state either fails to appreciate its own vulnerabilities or fails to appreciate how the power of the balancing state exploits of those vulnerabilities. In such a case, we can expect the balancing state to acquit itself well on the field of battle because it has matched its capabilities to the vulnerabilities of the state with which it is now at war.

THE TASKS OF LEADERSHIP AND THE BRITISH CASE

British leaders during the years in question undertook the deliberative process of self-analysis that is required for the creation of an effective balance of power. However, the outcome of that process was the assertion of their preference for a focus on air power to the exclusion of land power despite the fact that their expert advisors informed them that a reliance on air power would neither limit their own vulnerability to German predations nor put Britain in a position to take advantage of German weaknesses. Britain singly failed to match its material capabilities to the strategic vulnerabilities of Germany during the 1930s and so no balance was formed, despite the fact that neorealist theory predicted that it would be. Britain was generating power. It was, however, generating the wrong kind of power. The power that Britain was generating did not create capabilities that would overcome its vulnerabilities. That failure to match capabilities to vulnerabilities cost Britain dearly in the fall of 1940, and nearly lost her the war.

As the extensive discussions in the following several chapters show, air power was, in the opinion of the experts qualified to understand it, unsuited to the task of balancing Germany. Their argument was simple and straightforward: British air power could not stop the German army from occupying positions in France and the Low Countries. Once the Germans were ensconced in France and the Low Countries, they could use those areas as bases from which to attack Britain both in the air and by sea. Britain would be hard-pressed to retaliate in kind because to do so would rain death on the peoples of France and Belgium while in no serious way hampering the German war effort. The key to British security lay in preventing Germany from reaching those positions in France and Belgium that would expose Britain to the greatest harm. To accomplish that required Britain to bolster and support Belgian and French efforts through the provision of a mechanized, rapidly deployable land army. The decisions on whether to create such a force, for such a task, are a main occupation of the remaining chapters of this book.

The reason that structural neorealism fails to capture the dynamic relations between Britain and Germany in the 1930s is because it does not account for the role that leaders play in choosing between various policy options. Leaders, writes Deborah Stone, tell causal stories that "describe harm and difficulties" and then use that story to "invoke government power to stop the harm."[19] Each leader can tell a different story, and those causal stories "continue to be important in the formulation and selection of alternative policy responses."[20] "Conditions, difficulties, or issues," writes Stone, "do not have inherent properties."[21] The way that they attain meaning is in being framed by leaders. "Frames help to render events or occurrences meaningful and thereby function to organize experience and guide action," write Robert Benford and David Snow.[22] What Stone does not know, she writes, is "what makes one side stronger than another. What accounts for the success of some causal assertions but not others?"[23] The answer is that some stories are told by leaders and others are not. The military experts in Great Britain told a causal story, which turned out to be correct, about the nation's vulnerabilities and what needed to be done to overcome them. That story was contrasted with one told by the politicians, particularly the chancellor of the exchequer, Neville Chamberlain. Chamberlain's story, which will be explored fully in Chapters 5 and 6, was translated into policy because as a leader he was able to get his preferences for action implemented over those of his underlings and rivals.

For liberals and institutionalists, too, the role of leaders in telling causal stories and being in a position from which they can translate those stories into policies should be more thoroughly examined.

There is a burgeoning literature on social movements that explores how idea get shaped and then diffused among a broader population. What is less well covered, even in that literature, is how those ideas, even widely held ones, get translated into actual policies, particularly in avenues of governmental activity that are neither open to the public nor transparent, such as national security decisions. Ultimately, beliefs about causal relationships, such as the widely held one about democratic regimes and pacific relations, get translated into actions by leaders. President George W. Bush, for example, used the logic of the democratic peace hypothesis to justify certain policies as a part of his Global War on Terror.[24] A different leader, one who was more skeptical of the causal link between regime and pacific relations, such as Henry Kissinger or Richard Nixon, would likely have chosen differently.

It is precisely because leaders who tell different causal stories craft and implement different policies that their role in policy outcomes must be reintegrated as a determinative variable in international relations theory. Alexander Wendt has famously argued that the condition of international anarchy, which is the underlying assumption of most of international relations theory, is "what you make of it." Wendt argues that anarchy by itself has no inherent meaning. It is the perceptions that states hold of each other as either enemies, rivals, or friends that shape how that condition of anarchy will impact on the conduct of international relations.[25] Anarchy, though, is not the only variable that is given meaning through ideas and perceptions. So are the requirements of security, ideas about which get translated into different policies by different leaders. In the case that we are dealing with, one causal story of threat, that told by the military, would have resulted in the production of tanks and a well-equipped land army, while the one told by Chamberlain and other politicians resulted in an almost myopic focus on aircraft production.

Modeling Leadership

Proving that leadership matters, however, is only one step of what is required for its reintegration as a determinative variable. A necessary second step is to create a model on the basis of which the performance of different leaders can be gauged. Although leadership performance does not lend itself to quantification except by the most arbitrary assignment of ordinal values to outcomes, a typology of the tasks that all leaders must perform allows for a comparative standard to be constructed. Robert Tucker has created a typology of leadership tasks that works well for this purpose.

In *Politics as Leadership*, Tucker distills the functions of leaders into three core tasks:

1. Leaders diagnose a problem. They are expected to define the situation authoritatively for the group they lead.
2. Leaders must prescribe a course of group action, or of action on the group's behalf, that will meet the situation as defined.
3. Leaders must mobilize the group to take the action prescribed in step 2.[26]

From Tucker's perspective, the aspect of leadership that is the most challenging is properly diagnosing the situation. The tendency is to view new situations as being parallel to earlier ones. Once a leader defines a situation in this way, the prescription generally will be drawn from the established repertoire that was used before. The challenge, according to Tucker, is to find a leader who is creative enough to understand the import of new situations. As he comments, "A crucial qualification for creative leadership is the capacity to perceive in group situations what makes them somewhat different from previously experienced ones which they may greatly resemble. Without such an ability, a leader is likely to rely on the repetition of policy responses that have proved successful in the past but may not be so in the present because they fail to take account of the elements of novelty in the situation currently confronting the political community."[27]

To apply Tucker's three-task typology usefully to the British case requires generating a null hypothesis of what a leader informed by the balancing logic of structural neorealist theory based on both capabilities and malevolent intention would have done. A specific set of hypotheses has been created for each task. Both of the leaders analyzed in this study then have their performance in each category of leadership measured against what a leader informed by the assumptions of neorealism would have done.

Given the threats it faced, as argued by its military leadership, the prudent path for Britain to have followed in the 1930s was to build an efficient, well-equipped, and rapidly deployable land army with independent armor units that would have been used to for the defense of northern France and the Low Countries, whose integrity was vital to British security whether by sea or in the air. The null hypothesis is that a British leader informed by the logic that states balance against capability paired with malevolent intention would have done the following in each core function area in order to meet the goal mentioned earlier:

1. **Diagnosis**—The leader would have broken down the task of diagnosis into two areas: political and strategic.

   a. *Political*—In terms of a political diagnosis, they would have recognized that the rise of a fascist, racist, and dictatorial Germany was an existential threat to the Britain and one that needed to be balanced against and resisted.

   b. *Strategic*—In terms of a strategic diagnosis, the leader would have recognized that with the development of air power as a credible arm, the British conception of border defense needed to be expanded in such a way that it would allow for an understanding that borders mark the perimeter of vulnerability, not just or even only, the physical boundaries of the state.

2. **Prescriptions**—On the basis of the diagnoses suggested earlier, the leader would develop prescriptions in two categories: political and military.

   a. *Political*—The leader would prescribe an explicit commitment to, and guarantee of, the integrity of the Low Countries and northern France so that Germany would be under no illusions about the extent of British interest in those areas.

   b. *Military*—The leader would prescribe that Britain raise a modern mechanized army with independently operated armor units that could be rapidly deployed to continental Europe either before the outbreak of war or immediately upon the outbreak of war. The purpose of that army would be to bolster the forward defense of Belgium, Holland, and northern France to keep Germany from acquiring air and sea bases in those countries from which to launch attacks against Britain.

3. **Mobilization**—The leader would mobilize both the people and the national governing institutions, the cabinet and Parliament, in support of the plan to develop an effective expeditionary army for the stated purpose of contributing to the defense of Western Europe.

In the following chapter, Stanley Baldwin's leadership is explored and then, in Chapter 4, evaluated to see how closely, if at all, it approximates the terms of the null hypothesis. The exploration of the leadership of Neville Chamberlain follows the same pattern in Chapters 5 and 6.

CHAPTER 3

LEADER

STANLEY BALDWIN

The previous chapter detailed a model of what a leader informed by the neorealist logic that states ought to balance against material capability paired with malevolent intention would have done in each of the core function areas of leadership: diagnosis, prescription, and mobilization. This chapter offers a detailed account of the tenure of Stanley Baldwin[1] as it relates to decisions on armaments and defense and compares his performance in practice with those of the leader informed by the terms of the null hypothesis presented in the previous chapter.

The historical material is complicated, as reality often is. In order to frame the information in the coming pages so as to make it useful for our purposes, the following points should be kept in mind as a guide when proceeding through the historical material: two core arguments need to be evinced from the record. First, the documentary record must demonstrate that the logic behind the structural neorealist theories on British behavior; buck-passing and distancing, were not in operation.[2] Second, the record should demonstrate how much of a role leaders play in translating their own preferences and ideas into policy.

In terms of the first, if either the buck-passing or the distancing arguments were correct, we should expect to see evidence of the intention on the part of the British leadership to either rely on France to confront Germany or to consider the placation of Germany at France's expense. The record for the tenure of Stanley Baldwin will show no such ideas. Indeed, to the contrary. Baldwin accepted the idea that neither France nor the Low Countries were strong enough to defend themselves against Germany without British participation. It should be observed that from as early as 1934, Baldwin accepted the argument presented to him by the military chiefs of staff that British security was contingent on the successful defense of France and the Low Countries. Note especially how Baldwin integrated that sentiment in his comments both before the ministerial committee in July 1934 and later that same month before the House of Commons. Baldwin excelled at articulating how the concept of British borders needs to be expanded from a reliance on the waters of the English Channel to a more encompassing vision of the requirements for defense. Evidence of that sentiment can be found in his speech to the party conference in 1935.

In terms of his prescriptive ability, take care to note the relative laziness that Baldwin applied to this task. The original contribution that Baldwin made to defense thinking was in his insistence that Britain should maintain air parity with, as he put it, "any country within striking distance of our shores."[3] Baldwin committed himself to that policy as early as March 1934 during the air estimates debate, before the specific recommendations of the Defence Requirements Committee were made in terms of armaments. Because Baldwin believed that defense against air attack was impossible, his insistence on parity was based on his idea that an aggressor might be deterred by the idea of a force equal in strength to its own. However, although Baldwin committed both himself and the country to air parity, it was never attained. Despite the fact that the commitment to parity was his idea, he allowed assertions by successive air ministers about Britain's inability to meet that standard pass without comment.

In terms of the type of prescription that would have been useful, namely, the creation and maintenance of an effective expeditionary force, Baldwin was less forceful. The record shows that rather than develop original ideas of his own in this area, Baldwin was content to accept the advice of those around him. And although he seemed to accept for himself the wise counsel of his military experts who suggested policies quite consistent with what was necessary for the defense of Britain, Baldwin's abdication of the role of developing concrete policies to his ministers should be observed. Particular attention ought to be paid of the extent to which Baldwin allowed his chancellor of the exchequer, Neville Chamberlain, to dominate the policymaking process.

Finally, take care to mark the difference between Baldwin's skill at mobilizing support among the people with his relative lack of skill at garnering support among his cabinet colleagues. Baldwin was a master orator, and his public speeches, both in Parliament and on the campaign trail during the election of 1935, constitute the bulk of the documentary record from which conclusions about his skills are drawn. Careful note of how determined Baldwin sounded in public versus the often hesitant tone he struck in committee discussions goes a long way to illuminating his shortcomings in terms of mobilization.

BACKGROUND TO THE PROBLEM: VERSAILLES

The Treaty of Versailles, which had formally ended the Great War, left in its implementation a great number of complicated problems, two of which, reparations and rearmament, towered high over the others. As for the first, the peace that President Wilson had promised would be one of "no victors and no vanquished" betrayed that noble sentiment by burdening Germany with billions of Reichsmarks of reparations to be paid, mainly to France. Time and the world economic collapse of 1929–31 would eventually solve the problem of reparations by mutual, if unpleasant, agreement between all sides.

Rearmament proved a more complicated problem. Although the treaty compelled a near total disarmament on Germany, it was based on the initial understanding, at least by the United States and Britain, that Germany's disarmament was a precursor to a global multilateral disarmament. Despite the protests of some high British officials, among them Sir Robert Vanssitart, permanent head of the Foreign Office, that "there is no real warrant for the theory that adequate equipment produces war,"[4] it was a common and widely held belief that the arms race of the late nineteenth and early twentieth centuries had contributed to the outbreak of the Great War. France, while agreeing during the negotiations at Versailles to the general notion of a global disarmament, did not, in fact, aspire in any way to realize that goal. Indeed, the French viewed Germany's relative weakness in arms as her strongest asset as it alone balanced Germany's lead in wealth, men and industry. It was the preservation of this relative strength that directed France to reject German calls for an "equality of status" in arms that was issued by the German government at the Geneva Disarmament Conference, before the rise of Hitler.

1932–1933: "THE BOMBER WILL ALWAYS GET THROUGH"

In the spring of 1932, Baldwin was presented with evidence about what future air warfare might look like. Middlemas and Barnes, Baldwin's most comprehensive biographers, summarize the effect that this presentation had on Baldwin, writing, "The evidence which he heard . . . gave Baldwin a horror of air warfare and bombing which became something of an obsession. His reaction to it was not always cool and logical and it shows more affinity with the sentiments of the later campaigns for nuclear disarmament than the technical approach of experts."[5]

During the summer of 1932 which Baldwin spent, like nearly all summers for almost twenty years, relaxing at Aix-le-Bain, he considered what he should do with the information that he had seen. The information about the future potential of air warfare when coupled with the fact of the rise of Japanese aggression against Manchuria, convinced Baldwin that the halcyon decade so nearly passed, in which war and the preparations for it seemed the furthest thing from the public mind was, or rather more, should be considered over. The twofold problem that Baldwin faced in asserting his new message was that for nearly all the previous decade, the governing approach in both official and public Britain was that the Treaty of Locarno, of which Britain was a guarantor, symbolized a reconciliation of sorts between Germany and France, the states whose rivalry was considered most likely, if anything could, to drag Britain into war. The second problem that needed to be overcome was that, as mentioned earlier, the very act of preparing for war by the building of weapons was considered by many to be itself a cause of war and, thus, forbidden. So entrenched had the belief become in the impossibility of war and the folly of preparing for it, that succeeding governments followed what was known as the "Ten-Year Rule." The Ten-Year Rule was an ongoing assumption made for the purposes of fixing the annual budget that there would be no major war for ten years from each new day. As a consequence of the operation of the Ten-Year Rule, almost no investment at all was made in developing new armaments or in building up large stores of existing arms and munitions from 1923 on.

The Japanese invasion of Manchuria caused the admiralty to request the suspension of the Ten-Year Rule. Japan, a rising naval power, was demonstrating its increased prowess and the sea lords, in surveying their position in the Pacific Ocean, deemed it too dangerous to continue to extend the assumption that no war would occur within the near decade. The naval position in the Pacific was extremely compromised with the fleet lacking both in ships and, no less importantly, in appropriate basing facilities. A base with extensive dry-dock and ship repair facilities had been planned for Singapore, but with the operation of the Ten-Year Rule, work had been suspended. A failure to address the issue of naval weakness in the Pacific would endanger the ability of Britain to protect its imperial assets not only in the colonies proper, such as India, but also in any imperial defense scheme that had to provide for the dominions of Australia and New Zealand.

The unhappy coincidence of the early displays of Japanese aggression when paired with the newly emboldened German demands for equality of status presented at the disarmament conference held in Geneva convinced Baldwin that he would have to undertake, in one of his favorite phrases, to "educate the Commons" and, through them, the public, about the true nature of the threats looming over Britain and what might need to be done about them.

The first such "educational" speech came on November 10, 1932, shortly after Baldwin's return from Aix-le-Bain. Baldwin rose to the rostrum to present the concluding remarks on behalf of the government during a debate about aerial warfare. He opened the speech by refuting the notion, asserted just minutes earlier by George Lansbury, leader of the opposition, that weapons cause war. "Disarmament," Baldwin claimed, "will not stop war . . . what you can do by disarmament, and what we all hope to do, is to make war more difficult. It is to make it more difficult to start: it is to make it pay less to continue."[6] Baldwin then set to explaining to the House wherefrom a new fear of war had arisen. It came from "the fear of the air. Up to the time of the last war civilians were exempt from the worst perils of war. They suffered sometimes from hunger, sometimes from the loss of sons and relatives serving in the Army, but now, in addition, they suffer from the fear, not only of being killed themselves, but, what is perhaps worse for a man, the fear of seeing his wife and children killed from the air."[7] And so that no one should have any illusions of safety, Baldwin continued, "in the next war you will find that any town which is within reach of an aerodrome can be bombed within the first five minutes of war from the air, to an extent which was inconceivable in the last war, and the question will be whose moral will be shattered quickest by that preliminary bombing? I think it is well also for the man in the street to realize that there is no power on the earth that can protect him from being bombed. Whatever people may tell him, the bomber will always get through."[8]

This last phrase became the one for which the speech and, indeed, Baldwin himself is most remembered. In some ways it proved to be an unfortunate choice of words because some listeners interpreted it- and the phrase that followed regarding the possibility of defense: "It cannot be done, and there is no expert in Europe who will say that it can,"[9] to suggest that investment in air defense would be futile. That is an interpretation that Baldwin would refute later. But his choice of words was intentional and served the higher purpose of shaking the Commons and the people out of their peaceful reveries and compelling them to recognize his belief that the future war would not spare them as even the previous one had.

Baldwin took the House through several issues in order to make his point. He tried to convince them that there was no purpose to be served by aiming for a limitation of size in airplanes or bombs; it would only lead to "making a high-explosive bomb about the size of a walnut and as powerful as a bomb of big dimensions."[10] Nor did he believe that there was much point in hoping for a limitation on bombing civilians. As Baldwin told the House, "If a man has a potential weapon and has his back to the wall and is going to be killed, he will use that weapon whatever it is and whatever undertaking he has given about it. The experience has shown us that the stern test of war will break down all conventions."[11] And lest the House think that a limitation on ghastly weapons is possible, he reminded them of how horrified they were when the Germans first used gas weapons in 1915 yet how quickly Britain in turn used them as well. Finally, and depressingly, Baldwin concluded that the only way to avoid this fate was through the abolition of all flying and that, he felt, would not happen. In ending his speech, Baldwin suggested, "Few of my colleagues around me here will see another great war. I do not think that we have seen the last great war, but I do not think that there will be one just yet,"[12] and so he admonished that it was up to the younger generation to find a way out of this fix: "As I say, the future is in their hands, but when the next war comes and European civilization is wiped out, as it will be and by no force more than by that force[air power], then do not let them lay the blame on the old men, but let them remember that they principally and they alone are responsible for the terrors that have fallen on the earth."[13]

From the 1932 speech, one could draw a faulty conclusion that Baldwin was setting the table in order to press forward with a full and complete rearmament. That was certainly not true at that time. Moreover, despite what he said on that day of the folly of the pursuit of limitation, he repeatedly encouraged the foreign secretary, Sir John Simon, to pursue the abolition of military aircraft, albeit in negotiation with Germany, France, and Italy, at the same time as he insisted that Britain begin a program to build up her own air forces.

In the meantime, however, Baldwin did take a first practical step, and that was to commission a report from the chiefs of staff in which they would make a statement on the deficiencies in men and materiel that they faced. The commissioning of the report was "the earliest indication of Baldwin's precept that if disarmament failed, Britain must look to her own defences."[14]

Baldwin's 1932 speech should also be recognized for what it indicates about the validity of Christensen and Snyder's theory of buckpassing. An essential condition for buck-passing is that there be a perception of the dominance of defensive weapons. It is only because states expect that they will suffer no serious or immediate harm because war will move so slowly, as it did in during the Great War, which facilitates the logic that others can be relied upon to provide at least initial security. Baldwin's speech is *prima facie* evidence that there was no such perception on the part of British leaders. Baldwin indicated not only that a fear of attack from the air gripped both him and the nation but also that he believed there was no defense against it.

Three months after the "bomber will always get through" speech, the situation in Europe, which had looked gloomy at the time, looked positively grim. In January, after General von Schliecher failed to form a government, the German president, von Hindenburg, appointed Adolf Hitler to the post. Within eight months, the Germans had both withdrawn from the disarmament conference at Geneva and announced their intention to withdraw from the League of Nations as well.

THE ANNUAL REVIEW OF 1933

The report commissioned by Baldwin from the chiefs of staff took its comprehensive form in the annual review of October 12, 1933. In that report, the chiefs made an extensive commentary on the political and military situation that Britain was facing. In terms of the political threat they wrote, "We should like to put on record our opinion that Germany is not only already starting to rearm, but that she will continue this process until within a few years hence she will again have to be reckoned as a formidable military power."[15] They continued,

> Since the war successive German Governments have pursued a logical policy with one object always in view—the revision of the peace treaties. It is not the policy which has changed with the advent of Herr Hitler, but only the methods. What was being done by stealth and subterfuge is now proclaimed in a most open manner. The first stage in the policy which has been consistently pursued by Germany was the elimination of the most objectionable clauses of the peace treaties—reparations and military occupation. This stage has been completed. The second stage is rearmament and the recognition of the German demand for equality in armament is undoubtedly a step towards the completion of this stage. The first two stages are stepping stones to the third—the revision of frontiers, particularly in Eastern Europe, and including, to judge by recent events, some kind of German control, direct or indirect, over Austria.[16]

After asserting that the political threat to be dealt with lay with Germany, the chiefs then turned to the military side of things commenting, "We feel that with the general instability of world conditions, we should be failing in our duty if we did not point out that, in say three to five years' time, when the anticipated military renewal in Germany may have been realized, we shall be in a worse position than to-day to implement the Treaty of Locarno, unless the unsatisfactory and inadequate means at our disposal are increased and the general position is rectified."[17]

As to precisely what the problem was in terms of the "unsatisfactory and inadequate means," the chiefs made the following points:

> The assumption that there will be no major war for ten years, ha[s] resulted in the reduction of the British Army to a force which is barely sufficient to provide for internal security in the Empire and on mobilization to form an expeditionary force which can only be mobilized gradually for a campaign in undeveloped or partially developed countries in the East. . . . Our present resources do not permit us even to aim at anything better than to place in the field single divisions in each of the first two months of the war . . . To launch so small a force into war on the continent would only be of value from the moral point of view, but most dangerous from every other aspect, since if it became involved in serious fighting we should be unable to reinforce it.[18]

Finally, the chiefs issued a succinct synopsis of the problem: "Serious deficiencies in all departments of our Defence Forces, to which we have drawn attention, cannot be made good in a hurry, yet the nature of modern weapons and scientific armament development renders surprise attack on a considerable scale and with weapons of great destructive power more possible than in the past."[19]

These deficiencies were allowed to accumulate because of the belief of British political leaders, based in large measure on their experience in the Great War, that military preparations and procurement could be dealt with ad hoc as and if, the need arose. The chiefs felt it their urgent responsibility to disabuse the political leadership of that notion and they warned, "The old idea that a nation can 'muddle through' possesses inherent dangers in light of the speed with which aggressive action can be initiated in these days."[20] In other words, the chiefs warned that, as opposed to during the last war when, for example, the crisis in shell production was able to be met at the time, the fighting in the next war may well be done by the time industrial production got going if arms production had to wait until the war actually started before it could begin.

As with Baldwin's "bomber" speech, the annual review also brings the assumptions of buck-passing into question. The chiefs seem dismissive of the prospect of being able to ramp up gradually for war. In an era of defense dominance, such a policy would be reasonable as it is expected that an ally would be able to hold off an adversary for at least as long as it took to get to the fighting. The chiefs indicate in their review, however, that they are concerned about the pace of modern war and that Britain needed to make drastic changes in order to meet the needs of such a war.

When the chiefs' review reached the cabinet and the Committee on Imperial Defence, it was met, as might be expected, with alarm. It was particularly the comments that the chiefs made about the significant lack of material readiness that inspired the cabinet to form a new subcommittee, called the Defence Requirements Committee (DRC), to issue a report as soon as possible. The DRC was instructed by the cabinet to make recommendations in order to "make good the worst deficiencies" in the defense services that had accumulated since the Great War. The committee comprised the three chiefs,[21] Sir Robert Vansittart, permanent head of the Foreign Office, Sir Warren Fisher, the secretary to the treasury and under the chairmanship of Colonel Sir Maurice Hankey, secretary to the cabinet and the Committee on Imperial Defence.

1934: THE DEFENCE REQUIREMENTS COMMITTEE

The chapters on Neville Chamberlain in this book will make far more extensive commentary on many of the specific elements present in the DRC report and in the meetings of the Ministerial Committee on Disarmament (DC[M]) to which the report was forwarded by the cabinet for discussion, particularly as it relates to the equipment decisions for the army. As far as it relates to Baldwin, however, the contents of the meetings of the DC(M) are considered by some to be of such critical importance to later events that Middlemas and Barnes claim that Baldwin's participation in the "hidden decisions of the summer of 1934," when the ministerial committee met to discuss the DRC report, largely exonerate Baldwin from claims of inaction in the face of a rising Germany. In fact, however, Baldwin was not present at the crucial meetings of the disarmament committee when they discussed the role of the army because he was compelled to appear before the Committee on Privileges to answer false charges raised against him by Winston Churchill. The minutes of the meetings that Baldwin did attend indicate only very infrequent participation on his part during the discussions. Despite both his absences and his taciturn demeanor, Baldwin clearly read the report, the minutes of the meetings that he missed, and perhaps more importantly, closely followed the responses of the chiefs of staff to questions that the committee had posed to them during its review of the role of the army.

The report itself in many ways picks up from the point at which the annual review from the previous October had left off. Like the chiefs, the DRC was deeply troubled by the lack of an effective expeditionary force with all that such a deficiency implied not only about the ability of the United Kingdom to meet its treaty obligations under Locarno and the Covenant of the League of Nations but also about the ability of the United Kingdom to defend itself from the new threats that all perceived would come from the air. Having agreed to "take Germany as the ultimate potential enemy against whom [their] 'long range' defence policy must be directed," the committee made the following comment about the extent and nature of their concerns over the state of the army:

> The most important deficiency, however, for the emergency in question so far as the Army is concerned, lies in the expeditionary force. . . . This is the big deficiency in the Army which it is necessary to make good, if this country is to be in a position to co-operate with others in securing the independence of the Low Countries. For centuries this has been regarded as vital to our safety, and it is certainly not less true to-day in view of developments in modern armaments. We have fought at regular intervals on the Continent in order to prevent any Power, strong or potentially strong at sea, from obtaining bases on the Dutch and Belgian coasts. To-day the Low Countries are even more important to us in their relation to the air defence of this country. Their integrity is vital to us in order that we may obtain that depth in our defence of London which is so badly needed, and of which our geographical position will otherwise deprive us.[22]

Despite the firmness with which the DRC expressed its belief that holding the Low Countries was a vital British interest and that an expeditionary force was needed to accomplish that task, the ministerial committee had some questions, many of them raised by the chancellor of the exchequer (this will be discussed in Chapter 5). For the moment, however, it should suffice to point out that the ministerial committee submitted a questionnaire to the chiefs after having looked at the report, which asked the chiefs if it would not be possible to forgo the expeditionary force and rely instead on other means, notably a strong air force, to secure the Low Countries. The chiefs answered the questionnaire submitted to them and denied that the tasks that they believed needed to be accomplished in order to secure Britain could be accomplished by air power alone. In addition to their answers to the questionnaire, they added an unsolicited comment on what they called the "Strategical Importance of the Low Countries." In their comment, the chiefs reminded the ministers that two factors now made the defense of the Low Countries more important then it had ever previously been. The first was the development of the submarine and the threat that this posed to commercial shipping. But, the chiefs continued, important as the Low Countries are to us in relation to sea power, they are even more important in relation to air power. War in the air, like war on land or on sea, is largely a matter of time, distance and administration. An important factor in determining the weight of attack which a given air force can deliver is the distance of its air bases from vital objectives. If the Germans were to succeed in over-running the Low Countries and in establishing air bases near the Dutch or Belgian coasts, not only London but the whole of the industrial centres of the Midlands and North . . . would be within effective and even decisive range of air attacks. The short range would enable those attacks to be heavy, continuous and sustained and would not allow time for the interception of the enemy's air forces.[23]

By the time that Baldwin was first able to attend the meetings of the disarmament committee on May 17, 1934, the committee had moved on from the discussion of the expeditionary force to discussing the role of the air force, a topic on which there was far greater agreement. The committee also discussed what sort of statement, if any, the government should make about British commitment to the integrity of northern France and the Low Countries.

At the meeting of May 17, Baldwin shared with the committee his thought, similar to the one expressed in November 1932, that "it was impossible to devise anything really practicable [in terms of air defence] unless flying was abolished, and that was obviously something that would not happen."[24] That being so, Baldwin was beginning to think that "in terms of air power, the north-west corner of Europe, and particularly the Low Countries, were vital to us . . . and the question to his mind was whether it might not be best to state frankly to the world that any hostile action towards France and the Low Countries could not leave us disinterested."[25] Baldwin then suggested that as Germany had left both the league and the disarmament conference, the chances of achieving some limitation of air forces now seemed impossible. That unfortunate truth led him to believe that "public opinion might be willing to agree to anything which would prevent foreign air forces from getting any closer than they were to-day."[26] Baldwin did not clarify what "anything" might mean. From the context of the discussion, it is probable that he meant any spending on the air and some new measure to guarantee France and the Low Countries.

These musings on the role of northern France and the Low Countries as integral to British security were followed by a long comment made by Baldwin at the meeting of the disarmament committee on June 11. During that meeting, Sir John Simon, the foreign secretary, reported on discussions held between the Belgian foreign minister, M. Heymans, and himself, Chamberlain, and the war secretary, Lord Hailsham. Heymans had come to London to request that Great Britain grant a new guarantee to Belgium that would supersede the guarantee in place under Locarno. Under Locarno, the United Kingdom was obligated to come to Belgium's defense after it considered the circumstances in which the request was being made. Heymans requested that the guarantee become "automatic," that is, operable at the instant of invasion, without the delay of consideration of circumstances.[27] Simon himself argued the merits both of issuing the guarantee as a new treaty or simply making a new statement in the Commons about it, along the lines of the one suggested at the previous meeting by Baldwin. Baldwin listened to the debate about what form a new declaration should take before adding his thoughts:

> It was essential that public opinion should be definitely instructed as to our real condition. At present the public were not in the least familiar with the position, and he thought it was time they were made aware what this position really was. From an air point of view our frontiers had been moved from Dover to the Rhine. When these fundamental things had been explained to the people and they understood, it might be possible to lead them on. He was nervous, however, of plunging the people suddenly into a situation, when they had not been educated gradually to appreciate it. One or two speeches would be very valuable, and the time for them was now. When the public had been made to consider the armaments position it was important that they should understand that we had left our armaments alone for a great number of years in the hope of achieving something which had now proved impossible [namely, disarmament].[28]

Baldwin's comments during the course of the ministerial committee meeting indicate that he internalized at least some of the recommendations of the DRC report. It is clear from these comments, for example, that not only did Baldwin accept that the defense of the Low Countries was a vital British interest but also that he held a more nuanced understanding than even the chiefs had offered. In Baldwin's thoughts, the borders of the United Kingdom had shifted. Modern weapons posed a threat that could not be countered as long as the concept of what was "Britain" was limited to the British Isles, and so he framed the borders of Britain as having moved to the Rhine.[29] It was a penetrating phrase to which Baldwin would return when the revised recommendations of the DRC report were presented to the Commons.

Although Middlemas and Barnes do not specify what actions of Baldwin's during the summer of 1934 provide the evidence that they consider to be exculpatory, they certainly must have in mind his comments made at the meeting of the ministerial committee held on June 25. Like Lord Hailsham, Sir Eyres Bolton-Monsell, the first lord of the admiralty, felt that Chamberlain's revision of the spending proposals made by the DRC was severely prejudicing the navy (and the army), on whom spending was to be cut by 64 percent and 50 percent, respectively, while spending on the air force was to be increased by 94 percent. The ailing prime minister, Ramsay MacDonald, solicited Baldwin's opinion on the chancellor's revised spending plan, and Baldwin agreed that he, too, felt that the key issue was one of balance. Baldwin felt that the DRC was an expert committee and that their recommendations reflected the best expertise on defense matters that Britain could muster. If the authors of the DRC report felt that it was equally important that the navy and the army be made good, that was something that was not to be lightly dismissed. The crux of the matter, according to Baldwin was this: "If the [Ministerial] Committee believed that the recommendations contained in the DRC Sub-Committee's Report were justified and essential to the safety of this country and the Empire, then the public ought to be educated" about the true nature of the situation that Britain faced.[30] Although he was a true conservative and was not keen to see spending outpace revenue, Baldwin concluded that "consideration ought to be given to a thing which had not been done for a very long time and that was an Imperial Defence loan."[31] This proposal was slammed immediately by the chancellor, who warned that even considering a loan was "the broad road which led to destruction."[32]

Baldwin's insightful comments on both June 11 and 25 notwithstanding, the fact remains that Baldwin did not attend the meetings of the committee at which the possible role of an expeditionary force was discussed. The DRC had strongly articulated their feeling that the means by which the Low Countries could be secured was through an expeditionary force alone. As we shall see in Chapter 5, the ministerial committee, under Chamberlain's influence, revised the DRC's recommendations about the role of the army so as to substantially undermine the aspects of the deficiency program that would remedy the shortcomings of the army as an expeditionary force. And while on June 25 Baldwin had argued strongly about not upsetting the balanced spending on all military forces suggested by the DRC, in the end he approved the revised spending on the army with all that it implied in terms of refusing, in fact, to sanction the creation of an expeditionary force that might participate in securing the Low Countries.

Perhaps the most peculiar outcome of the consideration of the first DRC report is the tension that exists between what the cabinet agreed should be done versus what the cabinet agreed would be done. Thus, in the revised draft that was circulated to and approved by the cabinet on July 31, 1934, the cabinet agreed, "We are forced to the conclusion that the Low Countries, whether considered in terms of sea power or air power, are vital to our security, and, in the opinion of our technical advisers, they can only be defended by the provision of military forces to co-operate with the other countries concerned."[33] Yet, at the same time, although the DRC had requested no less than £40 million for the army, that sum was halved by the cabinet and apportioned in such a way that almost no money would be spent that would make the military capable of precisely the type of cooperation that it suggested it had been "forced" to conclude was necessary.

When the government presented the spending plan that rose out of the revised DRC report, it was Baldwin who spoke on its behalf. The speech, the second great speech of the "educate the people" series to which he had alluded in his comment to the ministerial committee on June 11, is a masterstroke in attempting to deal with the criticisms of those who felt that the deficiency plan did too much, like the members of the opposition who felt that any armament at all was the road to hell and those who felt that it did too little, like Winston Churchill.

The speech was crafted around the new spending to be lavished on the air force. The Royal Air Force, as mentioned earlier, was given more money than the DRC had allotted to it, and, in some respects, more than it wanted.[34] The main purpose of the speech, however, was not to explain any specific policy but more to frame the discussion as to why this new spending was necessary. "The greatest crime to our own people," Baldwin said somberly, "is to be afraid to tell them the truth."[35] And the truth was that, as he had suggested to his ministerial colleagues earlier, "since the day of the air the old frontiers are gone. When you think of the defence of England you no longer think of the chalk cliffs of Dover, you think of the Rhine. That is where our frontier lies."[36]

What the speech pointedly did not do was make comment on the sorry state of the army, how it might be made good and, perhaps most important, what role the government conceived of the army playing in the grand scheme of defense. If Baldwin believed, as he indicated in his long comment on June 11, that once the people were apprised of Britain's "real situation" they could be led to taking the necessary steps, then the fact that he did not seek to, even gradually, introduce to the Commons the idea of an expeditionary force for use on the Continent (as opposed to Egypt, for example) is itself telling.

BALDWIN AND DETERRENCE

Stanley Baldwin was, as was shown as early as the November 1932 speech, a pessimist as regards to the possibility of air defense. "The only defence," he said at the time, "is in offence, which means you have to kill more women and children more quickly than the enemy if you want to save yourselves."[37] The more thought that he gave to the topic, the more he concluded that the best that could be hoped for in terms of air defense was not to focus on active defenses against bombing but, rather, to focus on deterring an opposing power from launching a bombing attack to begin with. The means by which a foe could be deterred, however, he perceived only dimly. Baldwin tried during the air estimate debate on March 8, 1934, to get a handle on the problem of how deterrence might work. Baldwin suggested to the House that the important thing was for Britain to achieve "parity" with other nations in terms of air armaments. What Britain had to attain was

> equality in air strength which I believe to be the first requisite for avoiding this danger. Why is it the first requisite? It is very simple. The great peril from the air, as all would admit in this House, is the attempt of any given nation, under any impulse, to get a knock out blow in early, and to decide the war as some people say. If you get equality, the chances of the knock out blow almost disappear and in any case it becomes so risky that people are going to think twice and thrice before they undertake it . . . the real danger to peace is a very strong air power on the one hand, and a defenceless city on the other hand.[38]

That fate could only be avoided, Baldwin continued, if Britain were not the "defenceless city." As such, he promised the House that "this Government—will see to it that in air strength and air power this county shall no longer be in a position inferior to any country within striking distance of our shores."[39]

He further clarified his thoughts on the topic during the July debate on the DRC proposals when he assured the House, "There is no deterrent to any country which is contemplating the use of the air like knowing that the other country which it may be thinking of invading is not going to sit shivering waiting for the invasion, but, while it knows perfectly well that it will suffer, is prepared to defend itself and to make it as difficult for the aggressor as possible. That is our position."[40] Or at least, that is the position that Britain hoped to attain.

The irony is that, as Michael Howard writes, "we need only point out that at no stage in this period did British air strength, existing or prospective, appear to have had the slightest influence on Hitler's policy or indeed on that of anyone else."[41] There was of course no way for Baldwin, or anybody else for that matter to know what was in Hitler's mind. Indeed, to the extent that Baldwin thought about Hitler's perceptions of British actions, his thoughts were likely in error since he, like many others, at least at this time, still presumed Hitler to be a force for peace.[42] What is more problematic is that precisely at the time that Baldwin was making this pledge, Britain was losing not only an *advantage* over Germany in the number of machines she had, but in fact, was losing even the pretense of parity. By May of the year following that in which Baldwin made his pledge before the House, Anthony Eden, the minister for League of Nations affairs, and Sir John Simon returned from their visit to Hitler in Berlin during the course of which Hitler had informed the ministers that Germany already had achieved parity in the air with Britain. Baldwin stood before the House and apologized for having gotten it wrong. In the end, we now know that Hitler's claim to Simon and Eden was a boast and a false one at that. Still, it was in short order to be true enough and, more importantly, Baldwin and everyone else accepted it to be true, yet British production was never boosted so high as to achieve parity with Germany.

This was an outcome that was entirely foreseen. Lord Londonderry, the secretary of state for air, had, in fact, informed the ministerial committee that they would not have parity with Germany if current plans were approved. On June 16 he had informed the committee, at a meeting in which Baldwin was in the chair, that the spending plan envisioned by the revised DRC report, even with the increased sums lavished on the Royal Air Force (RAF) would "not provide parity [with Germany] within the 5 year period."[43]

The following year, 1935, saw two major developments. The first is the presentation to the Commons of a White Paper on Defence in March. The second was the calling of a general election to obtain a new mandate.

1935: I—THE WHITE PAPER

The Statement on Defence, known as the White Paper, was presented to the Commons for debate on March 11, 1935. The document was initialed by the prime minister—although, as the leader of the opposition, Clement Atlee, pointed out in bringing a censure motion against it, the text bore little of his known flourish. During the debate that followed, the task fell once again to Baldwin to state the position of the government.

The White Paper laid out the nature of the challenge that Britain faced in a manner more explicit than the discussion of the previous summer. The problem was, as detailed in the paper, that "public opin-ion in this country has tended to assume that nothing is required for the maintenance of peace except the existing international political machinery, and that the older methods of defence—navies, armies and air forces . . . are no longer required."[44] "The force of world events," the writers of the paper continued, "has shown that this assumption is premature and that we have far to go before we can find complete security without having in the background the means of defending ourselves against attack."[45] It was, therefore, the feeling of "His Maj-esty's Government . . . that they would be failing in their responsibili-ties if, while continuing to the full efforts for peace by limitation of armaments, they delayed the initiation of steps to put our armaments on a footing to safeguard us against potential dangers."[46] The paper in general terms then called for an increase in the size of the air force and a formal recognition that "importance of the integrity of certain territories on the other side of the Channel and North Sea, which for centuries has been, and still remains a vital interest to this coun-try from a Naval point of view, looms larger than ever when the air defence is also taken into consideration."[47]

In defending the White Paper in Parliament, Baldwin picked up again on the theme that he had raised as part of the debate the previ-ous summer. It was his duty and the duty of the whole government to tell the people the truth. And the truth was, "in the light of the facts of the last two years . . . the disarmament which [they] hoped could be achieved"[48] was now impractical in the extreme. With that, however, Baldwin was at pains to stress that the only increase was in aerial arms and that with regard to the other services, particularly the army, it was simply a matter of outfitting them in such a manner that if called upon they could perform their task as intended.

The White Paper of 1935 is rather sparse on detail, but it is impor-tant if for no other reason than that it calls explicitly for rearmament and lays to rest the idea that Britain could or even should, consider disarmament when other Great Powers did not. With that, however, it was also an opportunity to which Baldwin did not avail himself, when he could have made a more firm statement about precisely what was necessary in order to secure those "vital interests" across the channel and the North Sea.

1935: II—THE GENERAL ELECTION

By 1935 Ramsay MacDonald's infirmities, both mental and physical, had become so glaringly obvious that it was clear that the time for him to be removed from office had come. There was some confusion in

MacDonald's own mind as to what would come next. He was under the impression that he and Baldwin would retire together and that Neville Chamberlain would become the prime minister. As it turned out, MacDonald simply switched places with Baldwin. MacDonald became the new lord president, though far less influential in the role than Baldwin had been and on June 27, 1935, Baldwin assumed the premiership for the third and final time.

The newly reconstituted cabinet decided to go to the people for a new mandate and an election was called for November 14. The record shows that Chamberlain suggested that the national government make the issue of rearmament the central theme of the campaign, mainly because he was concerned that the government was vulnerable on economic issues. The Conservative Party Central Office and Baldwin did not agree. Baldwin was very concerned that if the government made rearmament the focus of the campaign, then there was a chance that either the government would be turned out, or, at a minimum, lose a significant numbers of votes from its majority.

In part, as Baldwin would indicate later, he based that conclusion on the results of a by-election held two years earlier in East Fulham. As Baldwin himself recalled it to the House in November 1936, "You will remember the election at Fulham in the autumn of 1933, when a seat which the National Government held was lost by about 7,000 votes on no issue but the pacifist, and that the National Government candidate, who made a most guarded reference to the question of defence, was mobbed for it."[49] G. M. Young, the biographer whose work is based on discussions with Baldwin, reflected his opinion: "I have always felt that the nerve, injured in October 1933, the East Fulham nerve, never quite healed; he was afraid of the pacifists."[50] C. T. Stannage hesitates some in endorsing that conclusion, but even so, he admits, "It is generally agreed among historians that one of the most significant things about the result of the East Fulham by-election was the manner in which Stanley Baldwin reacted to it. It is claimed that Baldwin interpreted the result to mean that mood of the nation at large was pacifist and opposed to rearmament."[51]

Stannage argues, "Neither the National Government's foreign policy nor its defence policy was changed as a result of the East Fulham by-election. Its only effects were to confirm the Cabinet in its reluctance to rearm on a massive scale and to make it more aware of the need to publicize its peace efforts."[52] That conclusion provides a good frame for understanding some of the speeches that Baldwin gave during the 1935 campaign.

During the campaign, Baldwin did not pretend that Britain was not rearming at all. After all, the record was there for all to see. The air estimates had been increased in March 1934 and, as mentioned earlier, in July 1934 Baldwin presented the case for an expansion of the air force as a part of the DRC suggestions to the Commons. What Baldwin sought to do during the campaign was put the expansion of air force armaments in context and avoid all discussion of other types of armaments and the situations in which they might be used. As Stannage suggests, many of Baldwin's speeches try to strike a balance among affirming the need to rearm, lamenting the need to rearm, and assuring all that rearmament was not being carried too far. To achieve these three ends, Baldwin's speeches tended to vacillate between explaining why he and the government felt the need to rearm at all and emphasizing the ongoing efforts to achieve some sort of arms limitation with Germany—this last despite the fact that he had already come to the private conclusion that such an outcome was impossible.

Thus, for example, when Baldwin addressed the Evangelical Free Churches in April 1935, he began by affirming his pacifist credentials. He told the crowd, "You would like to see bombing abolished and so would I. . . . You would like to see arms reduced to a minimum and so would I. I have not yet lost hope of limitation."[53] Having thus reminded the people of his sincere desire for peace, he nonetheless beseeched them to be understanding of the task before him:

> It is an easy matter to say, 'I will have no armaments at all; we shall be all right.' If they knew what was going on; if they were in London: if they saw the millions of people there and thought of the women and children; if they knew that theirs was the responsibility as to whether any steps or none should be taken to try and protect those people from what might happen, they might perhaps judge more kindly than they would have done the decision a statesman came to on whom the responsibility to protect those people did lie, and they would remember the fearful dilemma in which he was placed. He might hate the prospect of an increased air force as much as any of them did, but he had to ask himself might this, or might it not, make the difference to the lives of those people who put him in power to do his duty? If he decided that it was his duty to see that a greater deterrent was put up and that the way of the aggressor was made harder, then he appealed to them to remember the dilemma he as a statesman had had to face and to respect his decision even though they might not agree with it.[54]

Baldwin reiterated his predicament of wanting peace yet being compelled to arm a little over a month later in his first speech as prime minister. He addressed a gathering in Worcestershire and reminded them,

You all know the anxieties of Europe today, and while we are still strug-
gling for peace we felt the time had come and we told the country that,
until you can get a limitation of arms—and what I say is with the particular regard to the air—we should not feel as a Government that we
were doing our duty to the people of this country, for whom we are the
trustees, if we did not tell them that until such limitation can be got we
are not satisfied with the defence of this country . . . We must safeguard
our own people as far as we believe it to be necessary.[55]

Baldwin assured the assembled group, however, that despite the
unfortunate need to rearm, the government was still "at the same
time . . . fighting hard for limitations and for disarmament."[56]

Baldwin took a less apologetic tack when he addressed the Conservative Party conference in October. He laid plain the facts as he saw
them: "The reduction of distance now that flying is making the strides
that it is . . . has an effect on this country, so far as its defence goes,
very much as though the land that was submerged in far distant geological ages and gave way to that stretch of water between us and the
Continent of Europe were once again rising and making an approach
over which people might pass, and on which we may well some day
have to defend ourselves. Let us never forget this."[57]

This new vulnerability should, Baldwin felt, compel the isolationists
within Britain and especially within the party to adjust their thinking.
Borrowing the words of Frederick Oliver, he warned the delegates,

If we allow prestige to become impaired, if we shirk responsibility and
let things of moment go by default—in other words, if we cease to care
where our strength lies—whether our voice is doubted or not in the
counsel of Europe where lies the chief security of our independence, we
risk our own ruin, we endanger the whole continental fabric. Confusion
and disaster will follow as certainly as if one of the planets in the solar
system should cease to pull its weight, and if aloofness is inconsistent
with our own safety it is equally inconsistent with public morality.[58]

As the election drew closer, however, Baldwin eased off the talk
of rearmament and of expressing the need for the United Kingdom
to be involved in the military goings-on across the channel. Baldwin
addressed the Peace Society on October 31, just two weeks before the
election. He sought to allay the concerns of those who had heard his
earlier speeches and reacted to their call for rearmament with alarm:

Do not fear or misunderstand when you have heard me say that we are
looking to our defences. It does not mean that we look upon force as
the judge and law-giver in the affairs of nations. We do not dedicate

ourselves to such evil, and there is here no spirit whatever of aggression. But weakness or wavering, or uncertainty, or neglect of our obligations—obligations for peace—doubts of our own safety—these things give me no assurance of peace. Believe me, it is quite the reverse. Do not fear a step in the wrong direction. You need not remind me of the solemn task of the League to reduce armaments by agreement. I know, and I shall not forget. But we have gone too far alone, and must try to bring others along with us. I give you my word that there will be no great armaments.[59]

Two weeks later, the government won reelection. Chapter 4 will evaluate what the speeches that Baldwin gave during the election say about his capacity for leadership and the fulfillment of the core tasks of a leader. At this point, however, it is enough to summarize the election by saying that while Baldwin did not shy away from acknowledging, with sorrow, the need to rearm, at least in the air, he was equally anxious that the public should not interpret his statements as a call for a massive rearmament. He was certain, in fact, that if he had called for such a rearmament, the government would have lost the election. As he explained it to the House a year later, "My position as the leader of a great party was not altogether a comfortable one. . . . Supposing I had gone to the country and said that Germany was rearming and that we must rearm— does anybody think that this pacific democracy would have rallied to that cry at that moment? I cannot think of anything that would have made the loss of the election from my point of view more certain."[60] Although the election gave Baldwin a mandate, it is not fully clear a mandate for what. Because Baldwin did not press the issue of large-scale rearmament, it is hard to argue that the people gave him a mandate for something he did not ask for. As the following sections will demonstrate, the leadership certainly did not consider that the election gave them a mandate for large-scale rearmament as new debates still centered on the old theme of what the public would be willing to bear.

1936: THE THIRD DEFENCE REQUIREMENTS COMMITTEE REPORT

The problems of German rearmament and signs of aggression were not going away. Neither was Germany showing much inclination to pursue serious arms limitation. By March 1936 German rearmament had advanced to a degree sufficient enough that the Nazis reoccupied the Rhineland in defiance of Versailles much to the chagrin of both France and Belgium, although in the end, without strong opposition from His Majesty's government.

When the cabinet had approved the first DRC report in July 1934, it stipulated that because the armament situation in Germany was so fluid, the issues involved, especially the ways in which the British armed services stood in comparison to Germany's, would be reevaluated periodically. The DRC undertook in the spring of 1935 a new review of the armed services, this time not merely with an eye to "making good the worst deficiencies" but to getting Britain onto a competitive footing.

When the DRC reconvened for the purposes of crafting a new report in May 1935, less than a year after the first one had been finally approved by the cabinet, they discovered, "the international situation had further deteriorated, and consequently, the defense programs, particularly of the Navy and the Army had become even less adequate to the defensive needs of the situation" than had been true just a year earlier.[61]

The third DRC report (there was no second report—the "second" report was an interim draft) is substantially different than its 1934 predecessor. It is far more detailed in terms of precisely the nature of the armaments problem that Britain faced. For example, the report details the problem of artillery in the British army. The British field artillery pieces were all of a 1905 design whose *maximum* range was nine thousand yards while the newer German guns had an *effective* range of twelve thousand yards, leading to the nightmare scenario in which British counterbattery units would have to face at least three thousand yards of punishing fire before they could even get their guns in a position from which it would be theoretically possible to take on the German guns.

The report summarized the problem in no uncertain terms: Even if the July 1934 DRC program were completed in its entirety, the situation would still be unacceptably grim. As the report commented, "Whatever means we adopt to forward our main policy of preserving peace, there is no alternative to our raising our armaments to a far more effective standard than they will attain when existing approved programmes are completed."[62]

As with the previous report, the DRC concluded this time as well that the army must be reconditioned and a field force created that would be able to deploy rapidly to the Continent and participate in the "occupation for ourselves and the denial to the enemy of advanced air bases in the Low Countries."[63]

Baldwin himself, as prime minister, was sufficiently alarmed by the implications of the report that he formed a select committee of ministers arranged as the Defence Policy Requirements (DPR) Committee, with himself in the chair, which would meet to discuss the report and make recommendations to the cabinet. Baldwin moved the third

DRC report forward far more quickly than MacDonald had done with the first report. The report was dated November 25, 1935, and by the second week of January 1936, the DPR was discussing it.

As with the previous report, there was little disagreement over increasing spending on the air force. This report also acknowledged that with events trending as they were, it was possible that Italy might become an enemy, which was a change from the assumption in the first report that Italy would be either an ally or neutral. The report called for increased naval spending to defend the home waters and the Mediterranean in the event of a war, which would also draw ships to the Far East, and this was approved easily. Like the first DRC report, this new one got hung up on the issue of the army. Unlike the first report, this new report also spent a great deal of time in considering the industrial reorganization that Britain may have had to undertake in order to meet the production targets the report envisioned. To that end, Lord Weir, who had served in the cabinet during the Great War, was brought in at Chamberlain's behest to advise the DPR on industrial matters.

The issues of the funding for the army and its future roles were first raised during the second meeting the DPR held. That meeting opened with a prolonged comment by the chancellor to the effect that, if he understood the warnings of the military chiefs correctly, modern war would move so fast that there was a real possibility that whatever the British land contribution might be, it might not arrive on the Continent in time to be of any use. If that understanding was correct, he thought it best for the committee to consider "whether, from the point of view of a deterrent, a strong offensive air force was not more effective than a field force which could not be put in the field for two weeks."[64] In addition to that, Chamberlain noted, "there was the political difficulty that proposals for the re-constitution of the Field Force were not likely to get such public support as the proposal for the renovation of the Navy or the expansion of the RAF."[65]

Baldwin noted the chancellor's concerns over the political difficulties involved in funding the army for the purposes envisioned in the report, but as with the considerations of the first report, he believed that it could be done. Baldwin commented, "On the political side it would be necessary to carry conviction with the House of Commons and the country, and that might not be easy with some of the recommendations made, although anything which was considered essential would have to be carried through."[66]

Colonel Hankey, who was both the chair of the DRC that had issued the report and present at the meetings of the DPR that discussed it, was deeply alarmed to see the question turn once again away (as it had in July 1934) from serious consideration of the role of the army and instead to a confidence on the deterrent capacity of the air force. That confidence was not shared by himself or the military chiefs, including the chief of the air staff. During the January 14 meeting and in a private letter to Baldwin dispatched the following day, Hankey was far more vocal than was his custom in battling against this trend. At the January 14 meeting, Hankey reminded the committee that "to-day Germany and Japan were arming to the teeth. If we did not build up our strength and were not in a position to resist them we should incur defeat, nor should we possess the strength necessary to deter war. Perhaps the nature of armaments might change some day, but that was a matter for the future. If our forces were to provide a deterrent, therefore, our armaments must broadly be on the same lines as those of other countries."[67]

The events of the following day, January 15, bear particular attention. A third meeting of the DPR was held with only the ministers and Lord Weir in attendance. Colonel Hankey, the chiefs, and the various and sundry others who occasionally attended meetings of this nature were excluded from participation. No record exists of what was discussed nor of the conclusions reached. What makes this meeting interesting is what can be inferred about it from a rather bold and highly unusual letter that Colonel Hankey wrote to the prime minister on the day of the meeting that begged Baldwin to find the time to read it immediately, before that day's meeting. It can be inferred from Hankey's letter that the DPR was going to discuss the issue of the field force, its use on the Continent and the possible public statements that might be made by the United Kingdom to clarify the strength of its commitment to France and the Low Countries. Hankey wrote,

> The issue before the (Committee) is a tremendous one, for we may well be at one of the turning points in the history of the world. The fundamental issue is between the authoritarian system of civilisation, as represented by Germany and Japan, both arming to the teeth, and the democratic system of which the United Kingdom and France both ill-armed, are the champions.
>
> 2. The wrong decision to-day will result in a force which will neither deter war nor avert defeat.
>
> 3. War can only be averted by a combination which includes at least France and Belgium. These States as well as other Continental States are not satisfied that aircraft can defend them against invasion and still look on armies and fortifications as their mainstay. If we have no efficient army they will feel that we do not mean business. Without some

aid from us France will not help Belgium; Belgium will collapse; London will be exposed to the worst horrors of aerial bombardment; and we shall not have an effective base from which to retaliate on Germany. The deterrent effect of our air forces will thus be largely reduced.

4. In a word, an efficient army, if only a small one, is essential to reassure our potential allies, to put heart into them to make the necessary effort, and to deter war; and, on the day of battle, to cover our offensive air forces.

5. Aircraft, in spite of their vast potentialities, have never yet proved a decisive factor in war even against second rate forces. . . . Armaments may be in a state of transition, but the period may be long. To be too futurist is as dangerous as to be too archaic . . .

9. If we have the will and the leadership we can do it [raise an army and equip it], and so prevent a war. If we fail to make the effort at this turning point in the world's history we shall perish.[68]

As Brian Bond has concluded, Hankey's letter was "the best defence of the Army's continental role" offered during the 1930s.[69] What Baldwin's personal reaction to this letter was, we cannot know. What we do know is that when the DPR reconvened the following day, this time with Hankey and the others once again in attendance, Baldwin went on record with his comment; "He was . . . inclined to recommend to the Cabinet that, so far as the Field Force was concerned, the Army should be authorised to make all preparations that could be completed within the five year period. This should admit bringing up the existing Army to the highest point of efficiency, and the preparation of the Regular contingent of the Field Force of the strength recommended in the Report with all its necessary personnel, equipment and reserves of all kinds."[70] Where Baldwin was less committed was on the issue of the equipping of the Territorial Army (TA), which he acknowledged would be the force from which later contingents, beyond the initial field force, would be drawn. Although he did not reject the DRC's call for equipping the TA, he simply concluded that it was a moot point at present because the industrial capacity to equip them at the same time as equipping the regular force did not exist. In this conclusion he was supported by Field Marshal Montgomery-Massingberd and by Alfred Duff Cooper, the secretary of state for war. What Baldwin suggested, therefore, was that rather then deciding either way about whether the TA should be equipped in a like manner to the regular field force, the whole issue should be "held in abeyance, and the whole question of these later contingents should come up for review in three years time,"[71] which was the earliest point at which the industrial capacity would be able to undertake such a task anyway.[72]

The final issue in the DRC third report that needs to be addressed is Baldwin's position in regard to interference in industry. In the very first meeting that the DPR held in which it reviewed the DRC report, Lord Weir made it clear that "the programme could not be realised without disturbing industry."[73] What he meant was that if business was left to its normal course, it would not be able to meet the production demands of the DRC. To meet those demands, some type of national interference in industry would be required for tasks as varied as the creation of new plant for building munitions and armaments, directing labor into certain industries, and so on. Baldwin, as usual sparse on detail, replied to Weir's comment with a vague "it has always been assumed that industry must be interfered with to a certain extent."[74] Baldwin, however, did not clarify what he meant by that, what level of interference he was talking about, or the extent to which he was willing to consider allowing the rearmament schemes to disrupt the "normal business" of Britain.[75] By the time the issue reached the cabinet for a decision on March 2, 1936, it was concluded, "the plan of defence requirements must be carried out without restrictions on the programme of social services and that the maintenance of the general industry and trade of the country must be maintained."[76] In other words, there was to be no real interference in industry at all.

Baldwin's involvement with defense planning ends, essentially, with the third DRC report. In the waning days of his premiership, the issue of the TA was revisited because industrial capacity had expanded in such a way that it was now reasonable to consider that which was held in abeyance, upon Baldwin's suggestion, a year earlier. But the issue was shunted to a side committee, and by the time any decisions were reached regarding it, Chamberlain had succeeded Baldwin as prime minister, and Baldwin had moved to the House of Lords.

The remainder of Baldwin's tenure in office after the third DRC report was taken up, in the main, with the death of King George V; his succession by King Edward VIII; the abdication of King Edward, whose intention to marry his recently divorced American mistress, Wallace Simpson, nearly tore the empire apart; and finally, the coronation of the new monarch, King George VI, Edward's brother and father of Queen Elizabeth II. When those tasks were completed he stepped down, as he promised he would, so that Chamberlain could establish himself in the lead with a good two years to spare before the next general election.

CHAPTER 4

LEADERSHIP EVALUATED

STANLEY BALDWIN

In light of the account of Baldwin's tenure presented in the previous chapter, this chapter looks at how well Stanley Baldwin performed the core tasks of leadership and how closely his choices reflect the terms of the null hypothesis presented in Chapter 2. Baldwin's performance in diagnosis, prescription, and mobilization will be evaluated, and some conclusions about both Baldwin's role in history as well as what his tenure teaches us about how effective balances of power form will be drawn.

DIAGNOSIS

The null hypothesis contends that a leader informed by the structural neorealist logic of balancing against capability and intention would have broken down diagnostics into two broad categories: political and strategic.

Political Diagnosis

In terms of a political diagnosis, the leader would have diagnosed the rise of a fascist and racist Nazi Germany as an existential threat to the United Kingdom. Colonel Hankey had summed up the situation well in his letter of January 15, 1936, in which he had written, "The fundamental issue is between the authoritarian system of civilization, as represented by Germany and Japan . . . and the democratic system of which the United Kingdom and France . . . are the champions."[1]

Did Baldwin share that sentiment? Baldwin probably did not feel as strongly as Hankey did, although he did comment as early as February 1934 to his friend Tom Jones that he viewed the United Kingdom as "the only defenders of liberty in a world of Fascists."[2]

Baldwin's diagnosis of the political problem was not specifically that fascism was a threat but, rather, that British unilateral disarmament was creating unnecessary vulnerabilities. Already in November 1932, three months before Hitler assumed the chancellorship in Germany, Baldwin argued that Britain's unilateral disarmament had gone too far and that rearmament was an urgent, if unfortunate, necessity. That diagnosis was one to which Baldwin would frequently return. Baldwin returned to that theme in 1935 when he defended the government's White Paper on defense and again during the election campaign of the same year when, even as he promised "no great armaments," he also warned that Britain had "gone too far alone" in terms of unilateral disarmament.[3]

Strategic Diagnosis

Where Baldwin comes closest to emulating the terms of the null hypothesis is in his strategic diagnosis. A leader informed by neorealist balancing logic would have understood that the advent of air power had introduced a new vulnerability to Britain that could only be met by expanding the concept of defensive borders. Keeping Britain secure meant keeping other nations from having the ability to cause serious damage to it. In terms of aerial warfare, that meant keeping enemy aircraft so far away from Britain that the challenges of overcoming the distance would be so great that an enemy would not be able to bring effective force to bear. Baldwin both saw this and articulated it in an outstanding manner. At the meeting of the ministerial committee on June 11, 1934, Baldwin first explained his diagnosis to his ministerial colleagues. He said, "From an air point of view our frontiers had been moved from Dover to the Rhine."[4] He used the same phrase in the speech to Parliament in defense of the Defence Requirements Committee (DRC) spending plan. On that occasion Baldwin was even more explicit. He said, "When you think of the defence of England you no longer think of the chalk cliffs of Dover, you think of the Rhine. That is where our frontier lies."[5] And, finally, during the election campaign of 1935, Baldwin told the Conservative Party conference that, as he saw it, the effect of flying on the defense of England was "very much as though the land that was submerged in far distant geological ages . . . were once again rising and making an approach over which people might pass."[6]

PRESCRIPTION

Stanley Baldwin was able to carry his astute diagnostic understanding into the first of the two required prescriptive tasks. The appropriate prescriptions can, like with diagnosis, be broken down into two categories: political and military.

Political Prescriptions

In terms of the political prescriptions, a leader who understood the logic of balancing against material capability and malign intent would have translated a diagnosis of aerial vulnerability into an explicit commitment to, and guarantee of, the integrity of the Low Countries and northern France so that Germany would be under no illusions about the extent of British interest in those areas.

Certainly the most forceful way to make such a commitment explicit would have been, as the Belgian foreign minister had requested of Sir John Simon in 1934, to issue a new treaty making British involvement in a war automatic upon the violation of Belgium. That did not happen. Baldwin did, however, make clear his feeling that "in terms of air power, the north-west corner of Europe, and particularly the Low Countries, were vital to us" and that it might be "best to state frankly to the world that any hostile action towards France and the Low Countries could not leave us disinterested."[7] Baldwin reiterated that sentiment publically in October 1935, calling Europe the place "where lies the chief security of our independence" and that a Britain that was not involved in the balance of power in Europe would be as if "one of the planets in the solar system should cease to pull its weight."[8]

Certainly, Baldwin could have been more strident in his prescription of a political commitment to France and the Low Countries. The fact is, at all times, both Belgium and France pressed Britain for closer military cooperation, and that cooperation was denied. Baldwin's vague phrases about events in Belgium not leaving Britain "disinterested" hardly had the immobilizing and sobering effect on German policy that he wished they would. Furthermore, a true translation of the correct diagnosis that Baldwin made in terms of the consequences of vulnerability would have meant the permanent garrisoning of troops in France and the Low Countries, assuming that those nations were willing, and not just a readiness to deploy them when hostilities commenced. The United States, for example, implemented precisely that kind of prescription during the Cold War as it translated its diagnosis that the integrity of a West Germany free from Soviet communism was vital to U.S. security into a prescription to make the American commitment to the forward defense of Germany no less clear than America's commitment to the defense of the U.S. homeland. Baldwin came nowhere near that type of prescription.

Military Prescriptions

Baldwin's military prescriptions were even weaker. Baldwin's original contribution to defense thinking lay in his insistence that the secret to the deterrence of Germany lay in achieving air parity with her. Baldwin had made clear his belief that in the age of air power the only defense lay in inflicting equal or greater damage to a rival than they could inflict on you in his November 1932 bomber speech. On that occasion, Baldwin had insisted that defense lay in the ability to "kill more women and children more quickly than the enemy."[9] By 1934, Baldwin had refined that idea to a demand that Britain attain "equality in air strength" and guaranteed that in terms of air power Britain "shall no longer be in a position of inferiority to any country within striking distance of our shores."[10] Baldwin, however, did not ever make that prescription a reality. Baldwin was informed by Lord Londonderry in 1934, by Hitler in 1935, and by Londonderry's successor, Lord Swinton, in 1936 that Britain was not holding parity with Germany in airplanes, yet Baldwin did not press to have his public guarantee of equality made good.

There is sufficient reason to doubt whether air parity would have had the type of deterrent consequence that Baldwin thought it might. The null hypothesis here echoes Colonel Hankey, who argued that the necessary prescription was for "an efficient army, if only a small one," which would "reassure our allies, to put heart into them to make the necessary effort, and to deter war; and, on the day of battle, to cover our offensive air forces."[11] Such a course of action had been suggested by each annual review since 1933 and by all three reports of the DRC. It is fair to say that Baldwin accepted, in theory, the suggestion for an expeditionary force for use on the Continent. During the discussions of the ministerial committee regarding the first DRC report, Baldwin was troubled by the chancellor's eviscerating of the army sections of the proposals, which included the spending on the expeditionary force. Baldwin told his colleagues that he considered the DRC a committee of experts and that if they considered it necessary to make good the army in the manner prescribed in the report, than he was inclined to agree with them. In 1936 Baldwin was clearer on that point. He spoke to the committee considering the third DRC report: "He was . . . inclined to recommend to the Cabinet that, so far as the Field force was concerned, the Army should be authorized to make all the preparations that could be completed within the five year period. This should admit bringing up the existing Army to the highest point of efficiency, and the preparation of the Regular contingent of the Field Force of the strength recommended in the Report with all its necessary personnel, equipment and reserves of all kinds."[12]

Ultimately, however, Baldwin's commitment to this most necessary prescription must be called into question. Baldwin not only allowed but also affirmed the spending plan that the chancellor created in 1934 that reduced spending on the army by half. That plan, which will be discussed in great detail in the next chapter, limited army spending to port defense and antiaircraft materials and pointedly left very little for the creation of an effective expeditionary force. And, whereas the air parity prescription, while not carried out in practice, was strongly defended by Baldwin in public, the same cannot be said of whatever conviction Baldwin had for the field force. On every occasion on which he spoke in public about rearmament, he ignored the role of a land army and chose to focus instead on the preparations being made for war in the air. In the debate on the first DRC report in July 1934, in which Baldwin represented the government, he limited his comments to the expanded air force spending and neglected to mention the army at all. Baldwin also passed up a golden opportunity to speak in defense of the role of the army during the debate on the 1935 White Paper on defense. Rather than expand on the need for an effective army, Baldwin limited his comments to a vague suggestion that they ought to be outfitted in such a manner that would allow them to perform their task as intended. Given the lavish words Baldwin used in defending expenditure on the air force, it is hard but to conclude that his commitment to this more necessary prescription was far weaker.

MOBILIZATION

Finally, then, it remains to evaluate how Baldwin performed the core task of mobilization. In some senses, to talk now of mobilization after having established how inadequate and nonspecific Baldwin's prescriptions were may seem odd. Yet, Baldwin as lord president and prime minister was the public face of the government, particularly in light of the ever-deteriorating mental and physical capacities of Ramsay MacDonald. It was Baldwin who rose in the House to speak in defense of the air estimates and the revised DRC spending plan. It was also Baldwin who defended the White Paper of 1935 that issued the clear call for rearmament, at least in the air. Finally, it was Baldwin who as the prime minister seeking reelection in 1935 gave most of the important addresses during that campaign season.

Although his oratory would be decidedly unsuited to our modern age, in his own time he was an unqualified master. Baldwin's speeches were well crafted and his choice of phrase was almost always deliberate. The question then is, How well did Baldwin use these gifts to mobilize Britain? The answer to this can only be: in those areas in which he sought to mobilize support, he did well.

Baldwin excelled at finding the phrase that people could remember. His 1932 speech, "The bomber will always get through," can be credited with bringing the issue of British vulnerability to the fore in a way that it had not been before. It also should be counted as the beginning of British interwar rearmament. Baldwin's 1934 speech, including the phrase, "When you think of the defence of England you no longer think of the chalk cliffs of Dover, you think of the Rhine," served to put both the House of Commons and the people on notice that developments in Germany were dangerous and that Britain had to reconcile itself to the prospect of war in near future.

By 1932 Baldwin had already accumulated a significant record in being able to mobilize support for some rather difficult scenarios. Baldwin's rise from a nobody to the leadership of the Conservative Party was on the basis of his ability to convince others to abandon Lloyd George's coalition. Baldwin survived subsequent attempts on his political life in 1924 and again in 1930. On the latter occasion, Baldwin overcame serious opposition to his stance on trade and got himself reconfirmed in the leadership despite having seriously bungled—indeed, lost—the General Election of 1929. By far Baldwin's greatest success at mobilization lay in the successful passage of the India Bill of 1935. Baldwin led the effort to get the government to aspire to an eventual dominion (as opposed to colonial) status for India. It was over this very issue that he broke with his former chancellor (the still very popular Winston Churchill), who rejected the proposed grant of dominion status.

Indeed, knowing that Baldwin clearly possessed the capacity for effective political mobilization, the question of why in the case of defense matters he proved so unable to translate his own preferences into government policy becomes both more urgent and more vexing. The answer may be that whereas Baldwin did well in large gatherings and national speeches, he did less well in the smaller, more intimate environment of the cabinet and its subcommittees. There, his ponderous manner was inconsistent with the quick flow of discussion and exchange of ideas. It was his habit, as we have seen, to intersperse an occasional vague and general thought into the debate, but he very rarely spoke at length or in detail. This inability to mobilize support within the cabinet fatally undermined his ability to translate his own thoughts and beliefs into policy. Baldwin had prescribed a need for air parity with Germany yet was unable to induce the cabinet to push for it. Baldwin supported the creation of a field force and its proper equipment as suggested by the military experts, but he never saw it created.

The more basic reason why, even as prime minister, Baldwin was unable to get his way is because he, more than any of his successors, viewed his own role as *primus inter pares*. And, as opposed to later prime ministers, he took the *pares* aspect of the phrase far more seriously than they would. Roy Jenkins argues, "Partly as a reaction against the restless interference of Lloyd George, he [Baldwin] believed in giving his ministers the maximum freedom. He was always available for consultation, but rarely forced it upon them."[13] Thus, for example, although his preferences may have leaned one way, he allowed Chamberlain to revise the spending plan on the armed forces in 1934 as he saw fit. As the next chapter will show, Chamberlain used that authority to forward his own prescriptions for defense, which did not include spending on the army almost at all.

Baldwin also did not believe in dismissing or sidelining ministers simply because he disagreed with them, a behavior that would likely have made gathering support for his preferred policies easier. Baldwin's successor, Neville Chamberlain, for example, had no qualms about moving recalcitrant ministers to posts where their obstructionism would be less felt.

Baldwin was a success at mobilizing the people, and indeed the Commons, but only for the more limited task of aerial rearmament that, with the exception of only the smallest of Labour Party oppositions, they were well disposed to anyway. The challenge would have been to mobilize the House and the people to large-scale land rearmament and renewed commitment to France and the Low Countries. This Baldwin did not do. In fact, despite his talk in the summer of 1934 and the spring of 1935 of the worst peril to democracy lying in the fear of telling the people the truth, Baldwin himself gave in to that very fear. If we give Baldwin the benefit of the doubt and assume that he really wanted to see his prescriptions made good, both those he conceived of himself, like air parity, and those he agreed with others upon, like the creation of an expeditionary force, then his efforts at mobilization must be considered a rather abject failure. The final outcome of the policies that were enacted on his watch had the effect, again from the words of Colonel Hankey, of creating a force "which will neither deter war nor avert defeat."[14] And, in fact, they did not.

HISTORICAL CONCLUSIONS

When historians study Stanley Baldwin, the question that they all struggle with is: To what degree is Baldwin culpable for the state of British armaments in the late 1930s?

Leaders are the mediating agents that are responsible for the successful formation of effective balances of power. Wise, strong, and effective leaders are able to do great things for their country, often overcoming material disparities that would ordinarily work to the advantage of rival states. Foolish, weak, and ineffective leaders often squander valuable years and resources taking policy in less productive directions. Leaders who do some tasks well but others poorly will, obviously, have a mixed record to show for it.

Stanley Baldwin is, as this chapter has shown, a leader of the latter variety. He was a keen diagnostician of the nature of the crisis that Britain faced, yet unoriginal and underspecified in terms of suggesting corrective measures. Although he was a great orator, Baldwin was less skilled at getting his way in smaller groups and effectively was outmaneuvered by subordinates who were both more combative and assertive.

Brian Bond sums up the situation that Britain faced during the years in question succinctly: "Britain was at a disadvantage in several respects in rearming in competition with Germany. Germany began her effort two years earlier (in 1933) and between then and 1938 spent approximately three times as much on rearmament as Britain. In some vital areas such as the production of steel and machine tools she possessed a stronger industrial base."[15] To overcome those advantages would have required a leader who understood what needed to be done, which Baldwin did but only vaguely. It also would require a leader who was willing to lead a reluctant nation in the direction in which it may not have wanted to go. Stanley Baldwin, despite his good intentions, was too hesitant to be that leader. Baldwin believed that if properly informed, the British people would allow what was necessary to be done, yet when it came to it, he was willing to share with them only so much of the "truth," the withholding of which he had called a "crime" during his speech in support of the first DRC program. As was cited in Chapter 3, when the opportunity came for gaining a real mandate for the type of rearmament that may have either produced the effective deterrent that Britain sought, or, more likely, would have produced the kind of military force that could have been a more effective and perhaps even decisive participant in the defense of France and the Low Countries, Baldwin did not press his advantage. He became gun-shy after the East Fulham by-election, and when his back was against the wall during the 1935 campaign, he backed off from an urgent call to arms and assured the Peace Society that there would be "no great armaments" when great armaments were exactly what was needed according to the counsel of the expert advisors he trusted.

A final summary of what was needed from Stanley Baldwin borrows from the words of Winston Churchill, who, in 1934 during the debate on the air estimates, rose before the House and said the following:

> I address myself particularly to the Lord President. . . . He alone has the power not only because of the confidence which is placed by large numbers of people in the country in the sobriety of his judgment and in his peaceful intentions, but also because as leader of the Conservative party, he possesses control of overwhelming majorities of determined men in both houses of the Legislature. . . . The Lord President has the power, and if he has the power, he has also what always goes with power- he has the responsibility. Perhaps it is a more grievous and direct personal responsibility than has for many years fallen upon a single servant of the Crown. He may not have sought it, but he is tonight the captain of the gate. The nation looks to him to advise it and lead it in this dangerous question, and I hope and believe that we shall not look in vain.[16]

Churchill did not get the leadership he hoped for from Baldwin. When the time came, during the election of 1935 when he could have sought the mandate that would have allowed him to lead the Commons and all of Britain to a significant rearmament, he balked. As Baldwin recounted in his "appalling frankness" speech in November 1936, "I asked myself what chance was there—when the feeling that was given expression to in Fulham was common throughout the country—what chance was there within the next year or two of that feeling being so changed that they would give a mandate for rearmament?"[17] Neither he, nor we, will ever know.

CONCLUSIONS ON LEADERSHIP AND INTERNATIONAL RELATIONS THEORY

The overarching purpose of this book is not to add one more opinion to that of the existing biographers of Stanley Baldwin. It is, rather, to see what the leadership of Stanley Baldwin tells us about the validity of existing theories of international relations and what directions it suggests for new ones. Structural neorealist theory has its own expectations about what Great Powers will do. One of the most basic expectations is that Great Powers will form balances between them. That expectation was not met here. There was no secret about the extent of German rearmament. Nor, in fact, in light of both his public rhetoric and his published writings, was there any real doubt over Adolf Hitler's expansionist and bellicose intentions. If ever there were a case that seems tailor-made to test structural neorealism's predictions about balancing behavior, it is this one. If states balance against either capability alone, as Waltz implies, or even if they balance against capabilities paired with malevolent intention as Stephen Walt has suggested, than Britain should have balanced against Germany, which possessed both.[18] Yet it did not.

Structural neorealism has attempted to deal with this disconfirming example to one of its most basic predictions by offering two subsidiary structural explanations for the phenomenon of British underbalancing. The first is Christensen and Snyder's buck-passing argument and the second is Randall Schweller's theory of distancing.

If Christensen and Snyder's argument were true, there are certain hallmarks that we would have expected to see. We should expect to see evidence of the perception of defense dominance, which is the necessary *sine qua non* for buck-passing to be considered a reasonable menu option. Given Baldwin's comments on the fear of aerial attack and the lack of defense against it and the tenor of the times with regard to that threat, it is hard to argue that the British leadership held strong ideas of defensive dominance.

Beyond that, even though buck-passing is a response to a structural stimulus; multipolarity, the response has to be mediated through some kind of agent. Somewhere in the discussions that the British government held about the German threat, therefore, we would expect to find evidence of reliance on France.

Evidence of the logic of tripolarity should likewise be present in the discussions of the British government if we are to be accept the distancing argument advanced by Randall Schweller that also purports to explain the behavior of Great Britain. Schweller disagrees with Christensen and Snyder's characterization of the international system of the time as being multipolar, arguing instead that the system was tripolar and that in such a situation a less threatened state will seek to offer up a more threatened state in an effort to pacify the potential enemy.

In this case, the idea is that Britain perceived France as being more threatened by Germany than she was and therefore sought to turn its back, in essence, on France in the hope that France's weakness would satisfy Germany's appetites. As with buck-passing, the documentary record should show some evidence that this logic was perceived and understood by those in charge. Again, responses to structural inputs, even if conditioned by the structure, still have to be mediated through an agent before outcomes can be discerned.

As the previous pages have shown, however, the documents do not support either conclusion. Nowhere in the discussions of any of the plans on how to deal with Germany is the idea of abandoning France or expecting France to bear the burden on Britain's behalf in evidence. Indeed, the evidence is far more to the contrary. As both DRC reports conclude and as Baldwin himself reminded the delegates to the Conservative Party conference during the 1935 campaign, France could not hold out alone against Germany, and Britain's security was tied inextricably to France's. The record shows that it was generally agreed upon that Britain would sink or swim with France, not separate from her.

Because it is acknowledged that Britain did not balance effectively and because the documentary record does not substantiate either of the subsidiary structural neorealist explanations that purport to explain that outcome, the key to British armament behavior must lie elsewhere. Richard Samuels was cited earlier as writing about leaders that "even those who are not revolutionaries, 'normal' politicians, will routinely select among equally plausible alternatives."[19] That is certainly true of Baldwin. The correct prescription for Britain, including the need to develop an efficient army, was one of the "equally plausible alternatives" that was on the table at all times. It had been articulated as early as the October 1933 annual review and reaffirmed in each year subsequently until after Baldwin left office. The military chiefs, Colonel Hankey and Sir Robert Vansittart, had all provided strong justifications for why Baldwin should pursue that very option. And although it is fair to conclude that Baldwin accepted that prescription, his own particular leadership skills were not sufficient to translate his theoretical acceptance of that prescription into practical policy. Leaders matter not just when they succeed in doing something spectacular, but when they fail to do something spectacular as well. It is the fact that Baldwin made the wrong choices about what was necessary to balance German power and that he was unwilling, or perhaps even unable, to lead his ministerial colleagues to support whatever prescriptive choices he did make, that pushed the interwar European system out of balance. The fact that leaders through their relative skills are able to impact the material distribution of capabilities in the system in so profound a way indicates both their importance and the importance of including them as a determinative variable in international relations theory. If Baldwin had been a different kind of leader, if Baldwin had been a leader who was decisive in what he wanted and determined in getting it, it is likely that the security situation for Britain and all of Western Europe would have looked much different.

The experience of Stanley Baldwin's role in the armaments process exposes one of the most deep and fundamental flaws in the structural neorealist theory of international relations—its underspecificity of power. Power can take many forms, some of which will prove effective in balancing against rivals and some of which will not. The secret to an effective balance of power is matching the power capabilities of state A with the strategic vulnerabilities of state B and vice versa. During the Cold War, for example, both the Americans and the Soviets employed teams of academics and strategic thinkers to figure out which weapons systems were likely to promote stability and therefore balance and which were likely to lead to an offensive advantage and thereby throw the system into imbalance. Baldwin, it turned out, had a clear understanding of what Britain's vulnerabilities were, but not Germany's, and that had an impact on the prescriptions he gave. The creation of national power is the outcome of a policy process that is dominated by leaders. Different leaders may have even given the same sets of systemic and institutional constraints, made different choices, and achieved different outcomes. The recognition of the validity of that argument and what it implies about the role that leaders play as an intervening variable between intention and outcome as it relates to the formation of an effective balance of power was, hopefully, evidenced in these pages.

This chapter and chapter 2 have shown how leaders constitute the variable that intervenes between intentions and outcomes. Waltz has suggested that power balances are the result of converging capability through a process of emulation. Britain faced a new vulnerability with the advent of air power and there was no model to emulate. The experts counseled in one direction, the chancellor in another, and Baldwin landed in the middle. It was the pusillanimity of one national leader who refused to insist that his subordinate ministers submit to his policy preferences instead of their own that contributed to the lack of an effective balance being formed against Germany more than any structural feature of the international system.

Waltz expects that states will either comply with the dicta imposed by the anarchic, self-help nature of the international system or be punished for not doing so. The concomitant implication is that states that do comply with the logic of self-help will not suffer unduly. It turns out in light of Baldwin's experience that those states are not fully representative of all possible outcomes. Britain could answer the call of self-help in defense yet still suffer because her choices of how to arm were so poor.

Baldwin's experience teaches an important lesson about neorealism's shortcomings. Neorealism has no mechanism to explain how states balance save emulation, and as emulation is either not always possible or desirous, depending on which rival a state is attempting to balance, neorealism fails to capture the real-world dynamic of how balancing actually occurs and loses both subtlety and nuance in appreciating the difference between ineffective and nonbalancing behaviors.

CHAPTER 5

LEADER

NEVILLE CHAMBERLAIN

Neville Chamberlain bears a large share of the responsibility for the deviation of British policy from that which would have created an effective balance to that which resulted in the near destruction of British forces in May 1940 and that nearly cost Britain the war.[1]

The decisions taken during the crucial years 1934–36 made the events that came later, including the policy of appeasement for which he is best remembered, almost inevitable. Of particular interest to this chapter is the role that Chamberlain, then chancellor of the exchequer, played in the deliberations on the report of the Defence Requirements Committee (DRC) during the late spring and early summer of 1934. The DRC was charged with creating a plan to "make good the worst deficiencies" in the armed forces of the United Kingdom that had accumulated during the decade and a half since the Versailles treaty formally ended the First World War. The decisions taken during that fateful summer reverberated for years and set the table for the events to come. It is, as one historian has commented, "sensible to conclude that the circumstances of the late 1930s were the nearly inevitable result of the decisions that Chamberlain was instrumental in making at the DRC."[2]

Neville Chamberlain was more than just the chancellor; he was also by far the most important minister and, from very early on, the heir apparent to Baldwin. In his own diaries and correspondence, Chamberlain made clear the degree to which he actually controlled policy. Chamberlain was charged with the most crucial of armaments decisions, namely, the task of deciding how much money each military arm would get and what they would spend it on. As he wrote to his sister during the height of the discussions with which this chapter will deal in great detail, "I have practically taken charge of the defence requirements of the country" or, a year later, "As you will see I have become a sort of Acting P.M."[3] Chamberlain was convinced that he was the architect of rearmament and the true leader of the government who was tragically fettered by the need to exercise his power through the agency of the "actual" prime minister until such a time as the post was his.

This chapter shows how Chamberlain's participation in the armament process demonstrates the role of leaders as the variable that explains the divergence between intentions and outcomes in international politics. In so doing, it not only highlights the problems in Kenneth Waltz's canonical statement of neorealist theory but also addresses the subsidiary structural theories of balance of threat, buck-passing, and distancing that attempt to explain the particular outcome of ineffective British balancing during the 1930s within the structural framework.

Chapter 2 laid out a model for what an effective leader, informed by the logic that states balance against capability and malevolent intention, as neorealism suggests they do, would have done for each of the three core tasks of leadership: diagnosis, prescription, and mobilization. Chamberlain's behavior is not fully consistent with what an effective leader informed by the terms of the null hypothesis would have, or, moreover, should have, done.

The rest of this chapter provides an account of Neville Chamberlain's role in the armament decisions during the years in question. Because we look to Chamberlain for further evidence of the decisive role of leaders in the formation of effective balances of power, a reading of his part in the process must meet the same standard as did Baldwin's. The record must demonstrate, as it did with Baldwin, that the logic that underpins neorealist structural explanations for British behavior was not applicable to Chamberlain. It also must show, of course, that it was Chamberlain himself whose skills and limitations most explain the failure of Great Britain to arm itself appropriately. To understand Chamberlain's role in the armament process the following points should be kept in mind.

Chamberlain was an active diagnostician. There were three diagnostic elements that appeared repeatedly in Chamberlain's performance. The first is the extent to which Chamberlain believed that the probability of public support should be a key consideration of defense requirements. Chamberlain strongly doubted whether a plan for the creation of an expeditionary army for use on the Continent would be able to garner public support, and he diagnosed that lackluster support as one of the key features of the political reality that impacted on his armament decisions. Chamberlain brought this point up at nearly every opportunity. A strong example of this element can be found in his comments to the ministerial committee discussing the first DRC report, particularly in his response to the concerns of the first lord, Sir Eyres Bolton-Monsell, on the stationing of aircraft in Malta and Gibraltar. Evidence of the impact of this diagnosis can also be found in his memorandum to the ministerial committee, at the meetings of the Defence Policy Requirements (DPR) Committee on the third DRC report, and finally, in his reply to the memorandum of the secretary of state for war, Alfred Duff Cooper, from December 1936.

The second diagnostic element that should be noted is Chamberlain's diagnosis of the timing of the German threat. The councils of experts whose various reports are mentioned in this chapter all envisioned Germany as a threat within five years of 1934. Chamberlain was dubious of that assessment and did not believe that Germany would be ready for war by 1939. Chamberlain let that timing assessment shape his prescriptions.

Finally, Chamberlain did not believe that Hitler himself was either a threat or untrustworthy. The kind words that Chamberlain spoke regarding Hitler at a time when all others, including some of Chamberlain's closest political allies, had lost faith in the German dictator are telling and should be carefully noted for what they imply about Chamberlain's overall diagnostic skills.

The first task that a leader must fulfill for the formation of an effective balance of power is to identify the potential rival against whom balancing is to occur and recognize them as a threat. As will be seen, Chamberlain accepted the idea of Germany as a threat in a general sense, but much of his hesitancy over endorsing the more assertive recommendations of his advisors may have been caused by his more positive perceptions of Hitler.

A careful reckoning also should be made of Chamberlain's prescriptive skills. As opposed to Baldwin, whom as was seen in the previous chapter was quite lazy in this regard, Chamberlain was both active and imaginative in his prescriptions. One of the key features of Chamberlain's prescriptive program is how he continually overruled the counsel of experts about the need for balanced armed forces and demanded instead that attention be focused on creating a strong air force, which he believed would deter Germany. This focus on air power was to come at the expense of a well-equipped army. In reading the documentary record, Chamberlain's dedication to this idea can be observed in several instances. Chamberlain's dedication to air power appears first in 1934 and again in 1936; it persisted despite its explicit rejection by the professionals best suited to evaluating its potential for success.

The relative weakness of Chamberlain's willingness to make explicit commitments to France and the Low Countries also bears consideration. An effective balance of power reflects not only a military capability but also an expression of political will. An effective leader would have strongly endorsed a commitment to France and the Low Countries. Although Chamberlain did endorse such a commitment, he did it in a manner so vague that it lends itself to a corroboration of both the logic of buck-passing and distancing, whose refutation is a key aim of this project. A later section of this chapter shows why that is nonetheless a erroneous interpretation, but for now it is sufficient to note how feeble his acceptance of the political prescription for a close alliance was.

Finally in terms of mobilization, the extent to which Chamberlain was active in gathering support within the closed forums of the cabinet and its subcommittees should be observed. As opposed to Baldwin, whose comments were both cryptic and infrequent, Chamberlain was vocal in committee meetings and prolific in his written contributions to the debate. Particular attention should also be paid to the arguments presented in his memoranda and in his comments both to the ministerial and the DPR committees because they serve as windows into Chamberlain's thinking. It should be observed, for example, how Chamberlain sponsored Lord Weir's participation in the DPR, which debated the third DRC report, and then supported Weir's position on the need for an offensive air force, which was a close echo of his own in subsequent discussion. Finally, it should be noted how Chamberlain's attempts to gather support often took the form of pushing holders of contradictory opinion out of positions of influence and how that facilitated action on his prescriptions that may otherwise have been delayed.

CHAMBERLAIN AND THE DEFENCE REQUIREMENTS COMMITTEE: 1934

Chamberlain's first, and in some ways most decisive, involvement in the question of defense planning came with the evaluation of the DRC report of 1934. The DRC had been commissioned by the powerful Committee on Imperial Defence (CID) in the wake of the rather scathing annual review of the chiefs of staff from October 1933. That review, covered extensively in Chapter 3, had warned that Germany was already in the processes of rearming, that Germany's revisionist goals were open and declared, and that as a consequence of both of these, the state of British arms was wholly inadequate to the challenges that lay, in their estimation, three to five years in the future. The chiefs' review summarized the challenge: "Serious deficiencies in all departments of our Defence Forces, to which we have drawn attention, cannot be made good in a hurry, yet the nature of modern weapons and scientific armament development renders surprise attack on a considerable scale and with weapons of great destructive power more possible than in the past."[4]

When the CID considered the annual review in November 1933, they recommended to the cabinet that a committee be created that would examine the worst deficiencies in British military readiness that the annual review had warned of and offer suggestions on how they could be made good.[5] That committee, the DRC, comprised the three chiefs of the defense services; Sir Robert Vansittart, permanent undersecretary of the Foreign Office; Sir Warren Fisher, the permanent secretary to the treasury and head of the civil service and Colonel Sir Maurice Hankey, secretary to both the cabinet and the CID. Hankey served as chair of the DRC.

The report of the DRC was submitted to the cabinet in early 1934, where it languished for months until, finally, under pressure from Sir Bolton Eyres-Monsell, the first lord of the admiralty, and Lords Hailsham and Londonderry, ministers of war and the air, respectively, to have the report urgently considered, it was forwarded to the important Ministerial Committee on Disarmament (DC[M]) for consideration and review.[6]

It is important in the context of reviewing Neville Chamberlain's involvement in the evaluation of the DRC report to highlight the portions of the report by which he was most exercised and to which he dedicated most of his vast energies. The DRC provided the detail of the nature of the deficiencies in the equipment of the armed services that the annual review of October 1933 had hinted at. All three defense services had fared badly during the previous decade during which the Ten-Year Rule had been in effect. That rule posited that for budgetary purposes it should be assumed that there would be no major war for ten years, the counting of which would renew each day. The operation of the rule had the effect on all services of stunting research on new weapons and, in most cases, even the production of existing ones. Plans, for example, which had been approved in 1923 for the expansion of the air force, were held in abeyance during the operation of the rule, such that measures that had been considered necessary for British defense at a time in which Germany was indisputably supine remained unrealized years later when the threat of a resurgent Germany loomed larger. Similarly, the navy found that construction of the Singapore base, which was to have been the lynchpin of imperial defense in the Pacific, was incomplete and inadequate for the needs it was envisioned to meet. But, the DRC wrote, the gravest deficiencies lay in the army's ability to execute the tasks that it was charged to fulfill. Within the shortcomings of the army, the following was most grievous:

> The most important deficiency, however, for the emergency in question so far as the Army is concerned, lies in the expeditionary force. . . . This is the big deficiency in the Army which it is necessary to make good, if this country is to be in a position to co-operate with others in securing the independence of the Low Countries. For centuries this has been regarded as vital to our safety, and it is certainly not less true to-day in view of developments in modern armaments. We have fought at regular intervals on the Continent in order to prevent any Power, strong or potentially strong at sea, from obtaining bases on the Dutch and Belgian coasts. To-day the Low Countries are even more important to us in their relation to the air defence of this country. Their integrity is vital to us in order that we may obtain that depth in our defence of London which is so badly needed, and of which our geographical position will otherwise deprive us.[7]

Building on the chiefs' annual review, which had argued that the German threat would be acute within "three to five years' time," the DRC laid out a plan for the remediation of the most glaring deficiencies for all three services within five years such that the military would find itself in a greater state of readiness precisely at the time in which it was reasonable to expect that they would be called on to practice their craft.

The idea that these deficiencies should be remedied within a period of five years was the first assumption that Chamberlain questioned when the ministerial committee convened to discuss the DRC report on May 3, 1934. At that meeting, Chamberlain took the puzzling stance that "he was quite agreeable to accepting the suggested 5 year period, provided it was understood that it did not necessarily mean that we were tying ourselves down to complete the programme in 5 years."[8] In other words, Chamberlain both accepted and rejected the idea that deficiencies would have to be made good within five years. The foreign secretary, Sir John Simon, pointed out to Chamberlain that the DRC was not talking about making the military perfect, a project that perhaps could reasonably be expected to take longer but, rather, to only making good the worst deficiencies that would need to be done with all due speed. Chamberlain was taken aback by the foreign secretary's comment and asked if that meant that the DRC's recommendations were "only a beginning from the defence requirements point of view"?[9] Whether Chamberlain was genuinely confused on this point or not is unclear but, as events would show, the idea that the DRC report was "only the beginning" was in fact exactly true. When the DRC was charged with writing a new report less than a year after this first one was approved, it was tasked with providing for more than just the remediation of the worst deficiencies but, rather, with correcting for all deficiencies.

Lord Hailsham, the war secretary who would clash mightily with Chamberlain over the course of the few weeks that the ministerial committee met to discuss the report, tried to relieve Chamberlain's concerns by suggesting that the DRC report was only giving a guide to making good that which the government had already committed to doing. The effect of Hailsham's remarks was precisely the opposite of what he intended. Rather than soothing him, Chamberlain revolted at Hailsham's suggestion that "an Expeditionary Force had been approved"[10] by the government. He certainly did not recall authorizing any such thing. Hailsham explained that the large sum of £40 million allotted to the army in the DRC scheme "would not produce a bigger army, nor would it have the effect of creating a new force. It would only provide the weapons which were necessary to give our soldiers reasonable protection against a modern foe."[11] In other words, all that was changing was the equipment and training of the army, not its size or purpose. Chamberlain did not have an immediate response but found one the next day when he pressed Hailsham to explain why, if he had said that the size of the military would not increase, the DRC report providing for the recruitment of an additional fifty-six hundred men. Hailsham did not consider such a small rise in personnel to constitute an increase, but even so, he explained that these new personnel were not combat soldiers but, rather, support staff like lorry drivers and fuelers, who would ordinarily be recruited and trained upon the outbreak of war. However, as the expeditionary force was slated for immediate deployment the moment hostilities commenced, troops, even those in combat support roles only, had to be held in readiness at all times. It was the same with the demand of the DRC that three months' worth of munitions be held in stock based on the idea that such a reserve would be the stop-gap between the time that hostilities commenced and the time that wartime emergency production would come online. Chamberlain pressed on that point and wanted to know more about why wartime production could not be relied upon to produce arms sufficiently in any coming emergency. In other words, Chamberlain wanted to know why any advanced production was required at all. The point, not immediately responded to at the meeting, had in fact already answered by the chiefs in their annual review. The chiefs had argued that modern weapons could not be created on the spur of the moment, as they required careful planning and dedicated production facilities. The risk of being defeated before such production operations could be put in place under conditions of modern war was too great for the military to chance.

The second meeting of the ministerial committee concluded with the remark by Chamberlain that while he clearly did not agree with the perspective offered by the chiefs, "he did not wish to urge the Government to adopt a line which was not recommended by their technical advisers."[12] It is crucial to keep this seemingly level-headed statement in mind because at the very next meeting of the ministerial committee Chamberlain lambasted the same technical advisers—namely, the chiefs—for the answers that they provided to a questionnaire that had been sent to them by the ministerial committee after its first meeting on May 3. The point of the questionnaire was to ask the chiefs to clarify the logic that lay behind their call for an expeditionary force.

The questionnaire that was sent to the chiefs asked pointed questions about precisely why an expeditionary force was required. Chamberlain, in particular, questioned "whether the best role for the army was deployment on the Continent" and argued with his colleagues that a "better means existed to deter Germany."[13] Chamberlain was under the impression that air power could achieve a greater deterrent effect than land power and, in so doing, also spare Britain "the kind of trench warfare that had featured in the First World War, a repetition of which he believed would be the result of providing sufficient funds for the army to prepare an expeditionary force."[14]

The questions that were sent to the chiefs by the ministerial committee clearly reflect Chamberlain's bias against a land commitment. They asked, for example, if a British "contribution to an alliance against Germany necessarily involve[d] an expeditionary force? Could it not be limited to air and naval forces?"[15] In their answer, the chiefs tried to explain to the ministers that there was a twofold problem with the idea of only a naval or air commitment. One problem was how the continental nations, both allies and putative enemies, would react. The second was what Britain's defense position would be if "Belgian and French resistance proves inadequate as it did in 1914?"

The chiefs held that the integrity of northern France and the Low Countries was crucial to the defense of Britain both from the sea and the air. If those countries could not be held, as the chiefs feared they could not without British land-based involvement, then British security would be compromised. More critically, they argued that even if the expeditionary force was created, that did not mean that it needed to be deployed. However, if one were not created and properly equipped then all would know, including Germany, that Britain *could not* intervene and that inability would be factored into the plans of both would-be attackers and would-be allies who would discount the British commitment to their existing alliances like the Treaty of Locarno or the Covenant of the League of Nations, the latter of which had an ostensible military component to it.[16] That same point was made by Sir Robert Vansittart, the permanent head of the foreign office. Vansittart wrote to the ministers, "It is widely thought in France and elsewhere that we are in no position to execute even those [commitments] which already bind us; and we cannot quarrel with the supposition for it is a perfectly correct one in every respect. Our moral stature is the highest; but . . . our physical stature, and with it our moral influence has been shrinking steadily."[17]

What the ministers also had difficulty in understanding was why, if the loss of the Low Countries would be so injurious to Britain, could Britain not make the Low Countries equally untenable for the Germans? The ministers also wanted to know why the French could not be relied upon to defend the Low Countries if their integrity was so clearly vital to defense. In essence, the ministers were asking whether buck-passing was a practical policy under the circumstances.

As to the first question, the chiefs answered in no uncertain terms that while the integrity of the Low Countries was vital to the defense of the United Kingdom,

> there are no places in the Low Countries which are vital to the Germans. If we make no effort to prevent the Germans establishing air bases in the Low Countries, we give away all the advantage of position to the enemy. The Germans could in that case develop intensive and continuous short range air attacks on our shipping and cities, whereas vital objectives in Germany are so far away as to make effective attack difficult. Air attack on German forces located in Belgium would not be decisive in forcing a disciplined Army to withdraw while the disadvantages of air bombardment of an allied country are obvious.[18]

With regard to the second question, beyond the unwise policy of relying on others to do what is critical for your own security, the chiefs explained plainly that the assumption that what was vital for Britain must also, perforce, be vital for France was in error: "The Low Countries are vital to us but not to the same extent to France," they wrote to the ministers, in the hope that that would settle the matter.[19]

The chiefs were not oblivious to the underlying theme of the ministerial questionnaire. Clearly, the ministers did not fully understand why the Low Countries were of such importance to the defense of Britain and, moreover, why that defense necessitated a land-based commitment. Even though they were not directly asked that question, they undertook nonetheless to answer it in the hopes that once the ministers understood the military position they would be able to have a greater appreciation for the requirements that were needed to meet it.

In an unsolicited three-page memorandum titled "The Strategical Importance of the Low Countries," which they attached to their response to the questionnaire, the chiefs explained that the integrity of the Low Countries had been, historically, a crucial British defense interest and that "we have fought at regular intervals" in Europe in order to prevent any other power "from obtaining possession of the Low Countries."[20] That traditional requirement of British defense had only become more acute with the advent of the submarine, which could interdict British shipping, the free navigation of which was critical for keeping the British Isles both supplied and in communication with her empire. But, the chiefs explained, "important as the Low Countries are to us in relation to sea power, they are even more important in relation to air power."[21] If excluded from the Low Countries, German planes would have to start their attacks from some three hundred to five hundred miles from London, and further than that even to the industrial midlands. To overcome that distance would require fuel loads that would severely restrict the weight of bombs that they could carry. In addition to that, the need for German planes to cross over the Low Countries would provide greater warning of impending attack, which would allow civil preparation to be made, antiaircraft gun batteries alerted, and interceptor planes to be scrambled. Loss of the Low Countries would erase all those factors likely to ameliorate the severity of German attacks. British security would be further weakened if the Low Countries were not held because in addition to increasing British vulnerability as specified earlier, any advantages that Britain would have had in launching an aerial attack against Germany would be likewise squandered as it would now be British planes whose bomb loads would be reduced and vulnerability to interception increased. In short, the chiefs argued, "it is vital to the security of this country both at sea and in the air" to hold the Low Countries, and that to accomplish that "we should be prepared to send a contingent, if necessary, to the Continent." The defense of the Low Countries, the chiefs argued, "could be ensured by diplomacy in peace but must be secured, if necessary, by armed forces in war. The only certain method of preventing this in war would be by the action of land and air forces acting in close co-operation."[22]

Despite the forcefulness with which the chiefs expressed their professional assessment of the situation, Chamberlain remained unconvinced. At the meeting of the ministerial committee on May 10, he did not endorse the idea that the nature and timing of the threat necessitated its being addressed within five years but, moreover, "he was not satisfied that it would be a necessary concomitant of war against Germany that we must immediately despatch an expeditionary force." In addition, "he felt doubtful if the air situation had been sufficiently examined."[23] Even if Chamberlain conceded the vital importance of holding the Low Countries, he still wanted to know why Britain could not prevent their being overrun by the use of air power against them. Lord Londonderry, the air minister, replied to Chamberlain's question, saying "he did not think the air had ever made any specific claims that they could stop armies on the march."[24] Chamberlain, however, would not take the word of the civilian air minister, and it was decided to solicit from the chiefs a further statement that would address precisely what British air power could be used for. It was also decided to ask why the extensive fortifications being constructed in France were not sufficient to free up enough French troops from defending France who could then go off and defend Belgium leaving Britain unentangled on land.

The task of replying to the chancellor's questions fell to Field Marshal Sir Archibald Montgomery-Massingberd, chief of the imperial general staff (CIGS), and Air Marshal Sir Edward Ellington, chief of the air service (CAS).

Montgomery-Massingberd addressed the issue of French fortifications on May 14. The goal of the French fortifications was not to prevent Germany from attacking France, Montgomery-Massingberd wrote to the ministers. The goal, rather, was to "force the German General Staff to consider a repetition of Germany's violation of Belgium and even of Holland." The nature of the fortifications was such that they would free enough men to hold the Germans back, but the aim of the French was not to hold Belgium but, rather, to "preserv[e] French territory inviolate." What they did not aim to do was "to ensure the integrity of Belgium, far less that of Holland."[25] The holding of both Belgium and Holland was critical to British security. It was crucial, Montgomery-Massingberd argued, that the ministers understand that, as the chiefs had already written to them previously, "French interests . . . unlike would own, do not make the security of the Low Countries a vital factor for her."[26]

The above notwithstanding, the CIGS took pains to explain to the ministers that the French fortifications, no matter how strong, would not hold forever. Germany would, he was sure, use the time during the prelude to war to build weapons that could breach the fortifications. In this he turned out to be mistaken. He also surmised that the Germans would develop tactics to overcome the Maginot fortifications and in this he turned out to be correct. In either case, Britain could not, the CIGS asserted, depend on France to do for Britain what it was not in France's interests to do for herself.

The more critical document that was provided to the ministerial committee for consideration was the written answers of Ellington, the air chief. The ministers, particularly Chamberlain, clearly hoped that air power would serve to defend Britain and repulse Germany without the need for British soldiers to once again fight on French or Belgian soil. The responses of the chiefs to the questionnaire from May 3 had discounted this possibility, but Chamberlain had demanded a detailed accounting from the CAS as to why this would not work.

Ellington's memo of May 14 is the answer to the question that the ministers had decided to ask a few days earlier, about whether "superior [British] air forces prevent the Germans from operating air attacks against us from the Low Countries." Among the notions that Ellington sought to disabuse the ministers of was the idea that the British could do unto the Germans in the Low Countries as Germany could do unto Britain from them. "If retaliation in kind was attempted," he wrote, "our attacks and the consequent suffering would fall on the Dutch and Belgian people who would be unable to bring any effective pressure on their conquerors to stop the war."[27] The bombing of so many allied people would only be conceivable if doing so meant that all German air operations would then be paralyzed. To sustain sufficient attack over German positions in the Low Countries so as to paralyze them, the CAS commented, "would require a twelve-fold superiority"[28] in terms of aircraft over Germany. Such a production figure was beyond even the realm of British fantasy, which was finding itself eclipsed by German productive capacity already at that time.

The crucial point that Ellington wished to convey to the ministers was that the successful air defense of Great Britain would not be attained through the interdiction of German aircraft, which would reduce but a small fraction of the incoming planes, but rather through crippling German industry's ability to replenish such losses to material as they did experience. To accomplish the goal of disabling German industry, Ellington wrote, meant that the British must hold the Low Countries themselves because a failure to do so "would provide for [Germany] . . . the most effective means of defending their own vulnerable centres, particularly the Ruhr, from our counter-air attack."[29] Without holding the Low Countries, the Ruhr Valley and its industrial targets would require over 240 miles of flight, including no less than 120 miles in which British forces would be over hostile territory. Thus, not only would occupation of the Low Countries by Britain make German targets nearer, it would force the Germans to have to fly over at least three hundred miles of British-held territory, in addition to the short sea crossing if they wished to hit British targets. All of this, when considered together, suggested to Ellington that "the occupation and successful defence of the Low Countries against German invasion would be the most effective means of mitigating the severity of German air attack on London."[30]

Even that assessment by Ellington was optimistic. Ellington neglected to mention that while "British targets were concentrated and with easy reach, German targets were diffused over a wide geographical area. The same weight of bombs, ferried over the same distance, could do far more effective damage to the British economy, and probably British morale as well, than it could to the German."[31]

The argument embedded in the presentations of Montgomery-Massingberd and Ellington were enough to sway some ministers who had been hesitant about the whole idea of an expeditionary force for involvement on the Continent. Sir John Simon, the foreign secretary, had commented at the third meeting of the ministerial committee that he was "shaken as regarding the . . . assumption that such an action would be necessary."[32] Five days later though, after digesting the reports of the chiefs, Simon had concluded that "we should have to have these forces [land-based expeditionary] because at some time or other we might find it essential to despatch them to the Continent."[33]

Chamberlain, however, does not seem to have been similarly swayed. Rather than address the reports of the CIGS and the CAS directly, Chamberlain exposed his leanings during the second half of the May 15 meeting when he pressed a rather confused Lord Londonderry on the air portion of the DRC scheme. Chamberlain suggested having the air elements increased substantially over what had been recommended by the DRC. Londonderry can be forgiven for his confusion, as, having already witnessed the withering beating his colleague Lord Hailsham had taken at the hands of Chamberlain who had questioned even the need for ammunition, he could not have expected the largesse that was to come to his air service. When Chamberlain asked Londonderry if he was comfortable with the recommendations of the report, Londonderry replied that they were "considered an adequate measure of defence."[34] Chamberlain, however, did not think so. He was, rather, "inclined to think that they had been asking for too little. He would like to get a definite assurance that this [current allotment] was the considered opinion of the Air Force." Londonderry again insisted that the provisions of the DRC were not merely adequate but that the air force was willing to see the spending spread over ten years instead of the five recommended in the report. The logic of the air force was that too much spending too early would simply produce aircraft whose design would be obsolete by the time the true test of war came. They would rather have had an air force that was gradually ramped up such that its most honed capabilities would coincide with the time when it was expected to be called to duty. Chamberlain resisted that logic and asked "whether part of the programme could not be expedited" so that results could be seen more quickly. Chamberlain wanted to show publicly that he was responding to the panic over the air threat.[35] Indeed, it can be inferred that he was really more concerned with public perception than with any firm understanding of the needs of defense. When the first lord suggested, for example, that perhaps some of the air forces should be stationed at Malta and Gibraltar where they could secure the shipping and lines of communication to ships navigating the Mediterranean, Chamberlain retorted, "To have Squadrons at places like Malta and Gibraltar would not meet the public view. The public would want to see the squadrons actually housed in this country."[36] At several points in the meeting, Chamberlain suggested that he really would like this issue of spending on the air to be reconsidered as he wanted to "arm himself against probable criticism on this point,"[37] that is, that he was not doing enough to secure Britain from air attack. It is likely that comments such as this, which appear to completely discount the opinion of experts such as Ellington, direct Keith Neilson to the conclusion that Chamberlain's approach to the DRC recommendations had "little to do with strategy . . . and much to do with Chamberlain's concern for his career."[38]

As the meeting of May 15 adjourned, Chamberlain was charged with creating revised proposals for spending. Chamberlain told his colleagues that it would take him a month to do so. In the meantime, the committee discussed a proposed guarantee to Belgium.

Chamberlain executed his charge to revise the DRC spending recommendations in a memorandum that he circulated to the ministerial committee members on June 20. The memorandum encapsulates Chamberlain's approach and highlights the twin pillars of

Chamberlain's logic. The first is that all plans must be made with an eye to what the public will accept. The second is that the secret to publicly acceptable defense measures lay in emphasizing the air force over the other services.

Chamberlain introduced his changes by suggesting to his colleagues that the DRC spending recommendations, as they currently stood, "appear hardly likely to command popular support" because, he continued, "Expenditure on the Army, even if no mention be made of an expeditionary force, bulks so largely in the total as to give rise to the most alarmist ideas of future intentions or commitments. On the other hand, the Air Force proposals for home defence, in which public interest is strongest, contemplate no more than the completion of a programme which was developed so long ago as 1923."[39] These proposals, Chamberlain felt, would be shocking to the public, and "proposals which too deeply shock public opinion might lead to a revulsion of feeling."[40]

Chamberlain suggested that two facts were informing his thinking on the defense situation: "First, that the danger to this country lies in attacks by air. Second, that the exclusion of Germany from the Low Countries is essential to our security." Based on these facts, Chamberlain proposed the following:

> Our best defence would be the existence of a deterrent force so powerful as to render success in attack too doubtful to be worth while. I submit that this is most likely to be attained by the establishment of an air force *based in this country* [emphasis in original] of a size and efficiency calculated to inspire respect in the mind of a possible enemy. We must, however, contemplate the possible failure of such a Force to act as a deterrent, and we must provide the means of defence in that event. Such defence would be found partly in the enlarged Air Force, partly in the completion of anti-aircraft equipment, and, finally, in the conversion of the Army into an effectively equipped force capable of operating with Allies in holding the Low Countries and thus securing the necessary depth for the defence of this country in the air.[41]

Chamberlain's words are soothing enough, but a cursory glance at the revised spending chart that the chancellor attached to the memorandum shows more of his true sentiments. Funding for the navy was reduced by 64 percent from what the DRC had recommended, spending on the army cut by 50 percent but monies flowing to the air force, despite the protests by Lord Londonderry that the air force found the DRC proposals adequate, were increased by 94 percent, nearly double what the DRC had recommended.

Those who suffered most from Chamberlain's decisions were not shy about expressing their dissatisfaction. Both the first lord, Sir Bolton Eyres-Monsell, and the secretary of state for war, Lord Hailsham, expressed their opposition to Chamberlain's cuts. The first lord complained, truthfully enough, that Chamberlain's decision meant, essentially, a surrender of position in the Far East. Chamberlain did not see it that way, but the sea lords did. True, the Singapore base would be completed under Chamberlain's proposal, but as new ships would not be built, it was a lasting question as to what the base would do.

The cuts to the army, while proportionally less than those the navy endured, were, in absolute terms, enormous. Where the DRC had allotted £40 million to making good the deficiencies of the army, the chancellor had cut that amount to just under £20 million. It is worthwhile to quote the objections of Lord Hailsham at length, if only because his commentary on Chamberlain from a seat just across the table from him are no less valuable, and perhaps through deep acquaintance even more so, than those of later scholars. Hailsham noted that the chancellor

> accepted that the exclusion of Germany from the Low Countries was essential to our security. That was a point which had been clearly brought out in a number of papers which the Chiefs of Staff had submitted to the Committee. It was true to say that the integrity of the Low Countries was more important to us now than it ever had been before, owing to the advent of aircraft. . . . In order, therefore, to reduce the air menace it was essential to keep Germany out of the Low Countries. But, having accepted that, the Chancellor . . . reduced the proposed expenditure of the Army . . . He [Hailsham] fully appreciated the need for economy, but the DRC had given what, in their opinion, was the lowest possible figure to meet the worst deficiencies of the Army. Nevertheless, the Chancellor had reduced that figure by more than half. . . .
>
> The Chancellor had urged that a deterrent was necessary, mainly provided by a strong Air Force. That was quite true: but a strong Air Force operating from this country would not constitute a strong deterrent. If air attack on Germany could be launched from forces operating from Belgium, that threat would be very powerful, and the deterrent correspondingly strong. . . . But there would be no deterrent . . . if we were unable to prevent Germany from invading Belgium if she wished to do so, and it was therefore essential to have an Army capable of putting the declaration [of a guarantee to Belgium] into effect. . . . The Army, in fact, was necessary in order that Belgium should be available as an air base for ourselves, and not as an air base for Germany.[42]

The problem, Hailsham said, was that while the chancellor paid lip service to the idea of a force equipped to aid in the defense of

Belgium, an examination of his spending proposal revealed that he had not "altered the amounts suggested for the provision of anti-aircraft defences at home, or for the defense of Singapore."[43] Adding those numbers to what he had decided to allot to the air and naval arms, left a "small residuum" from which "the Army [was] to meet all its other requirements," including the equipping of an expeditionary force.[44]

Chamberlain responded to Hailsham's vitriol and claimed again that "he did not wish to put up his opinion against that of the experts" but that it "had been necessary to make some sort of arbitrary cut in order to bring down the totals to a manageable size." In addition, he assured Hailsham, "he did not contemplate any alteration to the Army programme except from the point of view of time, and that his proposal was that instead of the Army being ready to field an Expeditionary Force five years from now, the process should be delayed until the end of a longer period."[45] Whether this statement reflects his true intentions at the time cannot be known. What is known is that in the following years he repeatedly deprived the army of funds, until, finally, once he had assumed the premiership, he denied the role of the army as an expeditionary force at all.

It was not only those who felt shortchanged by the proposals that found fault with them. Lord Londonderry, whose air service stood to gain the most, commented that "he regarded the Chancellor's proposals as being better designed for public consumption than for real utility. An Air Force built up on the lines suggested by the Chancellor . . . would very soon be destroyed in war, as adequate provision was not made for the reserves in order to keep the original force in being, which otherwise will be decimated."[46] More critically, Chamberlain's thoughts on the deterrent powers of a large air force were seriously underdeveloped. His plan, as Londonderry pointed out, "did not provide parity" with German air power, which would be the absolute minimum standard for a deterrent. The idea of deterrence achieved through air power was, in any event, one that the "Air Ministry did not accept."[47]

Even Baldwin, who had great confidence in Chamberlain, expressed some reservations about the chancellor's conclusions. "The point on which he was the most apprehensive," Baldwin said, "was the upsetting of the balance which, as a result of the most careful examination, had been evolved for our defence situation as a whole." He preferred, rather, that even if financial realities forced some scaling back of the original spending proposals, any reductions should be careful to "preserve the balance between the three Defence Services which had been most carefully examined and agreed by the experts."[48]

Baldwin articulated his long-held position that if the need was true, then the public could be educated to understand it and that they would approve anything that was necessary. The chancellor, however, rejected both claims, telling Baldwin that to say that "it was necessary to educate the public and to carry out the Government policy regarding defence, whatever the public might think was treating the question in a lighthearted spirit."[49] He also demurred from Baldwin's claim that the "report of the DRC should be accepted as a balanced document which could not be upset. Chamberlain was not able to accept that view. It was not," he claimed, "an entirely military question, but very largely political in the broadest sense."[50] That is true, of course, because all politics is about the allocation of scarce resources, including money. What cannot be denied, however, is that this "political" decision would have very real military consequences for which Chamberlain is largely responsible.

The meeting of the ministerial committee on June 26, discussed earlier, marks the turning point of the debate on the DRC report. Although meetings would continue for another month, Chamberlain's spending plan was accepted, a fact that would allow him to boast later on that in defense policy, the fate of the country was "guided by me."[51] The service ministers were directed to draft new plans in accordance with the revised figures as the chancellor had presented them in his memorandum of June 20. In the final meetings, the secretary of state for war, although complying with the directive to cut back spending by £20 million, went on record warning his colleagues that after spending on antiaircraft supplies and port defense for Singapore, there was essentially nothing left over to make good the deficiencies in the expeditionary force. If his colleagues accepted the chancellor's claim that "he could not think that in five years from now Germany would be ready for a war," then Hailsham wanted it understood that "the War Office were absolved from responsibility for the risk which was being run. The War Office had no margin in their figures which could be cut; indeed, their estimates of costs had been extremely conservative and only the essential minimum had been put forward."[52] Hailsham made a similar warning for the record at the meeting of the full cabinet, which approved the revised DRC report on July 31.[53]

THEORETICAL IMPACT: CHAMBERLAIN, THE DRC, AND THE CREATION OF POWER

How does Chamberlain's role in the discussions of the ministerial committee on the DRC report contribute to the theoretical arguments of this chapter on the creation of the power and policies necessary for an effective balance? It does so by showing how a political leader, Chamberlain, overruled the advice of experts who had been tasked with providing precisely the kind of self-diagnosis about national vulnerability that leaders are supposed to consider when they decide on policies of national security. The DRC report is tangible evidence that an appropriate diagnosis was in place and that the adoption of policies in light of it may have served to create the power resources that could have been an effective balance against Germany's rising ability to rapidly take ground in Western Europe and hold it, thereby establishing convenient bases of attack to use against the United Kingdom.

The DRC, which comprised professional military officers representing each of the three combat arms, put their heads together with the leading civilian experts in the foreign office and the treasury to craft a plan whose explicit purpose was the identification of Britain's worst vulnerabilities. They identified those vulnerabilities as lying in Britain's inability to take and hold ground in northern France and the Low Countries. Holding those territories was necessary to keep Britain from having its trade interdicted as well as keeping German air power at a distance sufficient so as to substantially weaken its ability to play a decisive role in war.

Chamberlain did not disagree with their diagnosis of Britain's vulnerabilities, but he did disagree over what should be done about them. Where the DRC had recommended a broadly balanced armament program that would include the development of a mobile, rapidly deployable expeditionary force for use on the Continent, Chamberlain insisted that Britain's resources be marshaled for the building of aircraft. Chamberlain argued that not only would aircraft suffice to deter Germany but also that it was all Britain could afford and all that the British public would support.

Whether either of those beliefs was true is impossible to tell. As to the issue of affordability, that depends on whether Britain was willing to run a deficit to pay for arms or to borrow for that purpose. Baldwin suggested taking an imperial defense loan at the meeting of June 25. Chamberlain reproached the lord president for even suggesting it and called the proposal "the broad road which led to destruction."[54] Was the sum of £40 million available in the budget? Not without reducing spending elsewhere or increasing revenue through taxation or borrowing. Chamberlain opposed all three of those options. To the extent that Britain could not afford to rearm in the manner envisioned by the DRC, it is more because the chancellor refused to prioritize that spending than because the money could not be found.

As to the second issue—whether the public would have stood for it—that, too, cannot be known definitively. Certainly Baldwin indicated, albeit vaguely, that he thought that the Commons and the nation could be relied upon to approve whatever was necessary. Chamberlain, however, never indicated that he believed that people could be led by leaders, only that the decisions of leaders needed to be guided by what the people would bear. In the end, of course, when war did come, the British people gave their very last energies in defiance of Hitler. Could they have been motivated similarly to make an effort that might have made later sacrifice less necessary? Chamberlain was not willing to see.

Regardless of whether Chamberlain's assumptions about finance and public opinion were valid, they nonetheless guided his hand. Chamberlain as leader interposed his own opinion on the security requirements of the nation in such a way that the completely ignored the military reality on the ground. Both Ellington and Montgomery-Massingberd warned that Chamberlain's strategic vision did not accurately factor in the invulnerability of Germany to the air weapons that Chamberlain had in mind. More than that, too, it would not protect Britain from her own weaknesses. Chamberlain did not agree, and a policy that would have been consistent with that needed to form an effective balance was cast aside in favor of one that had no chance at achieving that outcome.

Chamberlain's role in the discussions of the DRC report is evidence of the idea that it is individual leaders who intervene between intentions and outcomes in international politics. The logic behind the creation of the DRC was that it should find ways to make good the British armed forces so that they might be effective in balancing or deterring Germany. Its creation reflects the intention to balance. Chamberlain's foisting his vision on the cabinet through his control of the budget shows not only the impact that a domestic institutional arrangement can have on outcomes but also how individual leaders can direct policy in a manner consistent with their opinions. The end result of Chamberlain's spending decisions was the creation of a military force that was poorly suited to compensating for British vulnerabilities and exploiting German ones. The intention to balance inherent in the creation of the DRC failed because of Chamberlain's control of the armament process.

THE THIRD DEFENCE REQUIREMENTS COMMITTEE REPORT—1936

During the 1930s, the international situation in Europe was, as Chamberlain had described it in his memorandum from 1934, "kaleidoscopic." Even though the cabinet and the House of Commons had approved the revised DRC plan in July 1934, by May of the following year the international situation was deemed to have changed sufficiently so as to warrant the commissioning of a new report by the DRC to revaluate, on the basis of these new realities, how things stood in terms of defense requirements.

As opposed to the first DRC report whose terms of reference asked for only the remedying of the worst deficiencies, the new terms of reference called for "programmes on the assumption that by the end of the financial year 1938–39 each Service should have advanced its state of readiness to the widest extent in relation to the military needs of National defence and within the limits of practicability."[55] As a consequence of those new, more encompassing, terms of reference, the new report, issued in November 1935, is far more detailed than its predecessor in terms of specific armament requirements and suggestions for policy changes.

Among the changes that the new report called for was the increase of the naval standard from that which required the ability to fight only one other major naval power to the ability to fight two such powers more or less simultaneously. The shift to a "two power standard" reflected the reality perceived both by the chiefs and the representatives of the treasury and the Foreign Office that efforts that had been made to ameliorate tensions with Japan were not succeeding and that, consequently, the need to prepare for naval engagement against both Germany and Japan was very real. Likewise, whereas the first DRC report had taken it for granted that Italy would not be a belligerent hostile to the interests of the United Kingdom, this new report bowed to the growing closeness of Mussolini's Italy to Hitler's Germany. The growing closeness of the two would mean real trouble for the British fleet in navigating the Mediterranean and through Suez.

While the authors of the new report were troubled that British aircraft production targets would need upward modification in light of German industrial achievements, the real trouble was that "the defence programmes, particularly of the Navy and the Army had become even less adequate to the defensive needs of the situation" than they had been even a year before.[56]

As opposed to the first DRC report, which had languished unlooked at for months after its submission to the cabinet, this one, on Baldwin's instruction, was handled more swiftly. A special constellation of ministers, organized as the DPR Committee under Baldwin's chairmanship, was charged with the task of discussing the report and preparing it for the approval of the cabinet.

In the intervening year since the first DRC report, the government had been reconstituted. Baldwin was now the prime minister and MacDonald, increasingly senile and absent, the lord president. Hailsham, who had been instrumental in seeing that the position of the war office was well articulated in the ministerial committee, had been replaced by Alfred Duff Cooper, who was less expressive than Hailsham and who would, ultimately, resign after Munich.

An additional change that allowed Chamberlain to have his strategic vision reinforced in the DPR as it had not been in 1934 was the appointment, at the chancellor's urging, of Lord Weir, a former secretary of state for air to the DPR.[57] Weir, as will soon be shown, submitted a memorandum that, while bearing his signature, was a very loud echo of the positions taken by Chamberlain at the ministerial committee meetings in 1934 and that allowed Chamberlain to build on it in his own arguments in front of the DPR.

Lord Weir, brought in ostensibly as an industrial advisor, cautioned the members of the DPR at its first meeting that there was simply no way to meet the production targets that the new DRC report envisioned within the three years specified in the terms of reference. Weir suggested, rather, that it may be better to consider gearing the programs toward completion in five years. Anthony Eden, who had succeeded Samuel Hoare as the foreign minister, suggested that "it was not clear that we could afford to wait for 5 years."[58] When Chamberlain asked Eden what he meant about not being able to wait five years, Eden responded that the dispatches from the embassy in Berlin indicated that Britain could expect a "challenge by Germany . . . within 5 years."[59] As with his position taken during the first DRC discussions in which he doubted that the German threat would be ready in five years, Chamberlain must have expressed similar reservations now, because within four days of the meeting, Eden circulated a memorandum to the cabinet in which the reports of the various ambassadors to Berlin that had been submitted over the last years were collected. The collection represented, in Eden's words, "clear evidence . . . of the steady and undeviating development under Hitler's guidance of German policy along certain definite and pre-ordained lines."[60] Among the German goals developing on "definite and pre-ordained lines" was "economic and territorial expansion so as to absorb so far as possible those of German race who are at present citizens of neighboring states, to acquire new markets for German industry and new fields for German emigration."[61]

Chamberlain's response to the evidence the Eden presented is difficult to comprehend. On the one hand, he seemed to deny the imminence of the danger. On the other, he argued, "Germany was a potential enemy who was re-arming quickly. It would take a long time to catch up with her even with exceptional measures. Chamberlain therefore considered the question of finding a deterrent to be vitally important."[62] This comment, about the need to find an effective deterrent, served as a good segue within the DPR to a discussion of the rather lengthy memorandum submitted by Lord Weir.

THE WEIR MEMORANDUM

"I think it will be admitted," Lord Weir wrote, "that Air attack is now firmly fixed in the public mind as the major menace."[63] The question, however, was how best to defend against that menace. The trend as identified by Weir had been to seek to actively defend against air attack by the use of such devices as searchlights, antiaircraft guns, and the like. What Lord Weir suggested was that rather than defend against incoming German attacks, consideration should be given to the use of the air force as an offensive weapon, a striking force, which would either deter Germany from launching an attack against the British Isles, or punish her mercilessly for so doing.

Weir wrote at great length about the folly of investment in a field force (the term coined to replace the more historically evocative "expeditionary force") for Great Britain. As near as he could understand it, "the main object of the Field Force is to support our Air strength, both offensive and defensive, rather than to act in co-operation with our Allies in normal land warfare." Germany, however, was "unlikely to be seriously deterred by the development of our Field Force," as the British field force, comprising only four divisions such as had been approved of by the first revised DRC report, would be dwarfed by "a nation like Germany with ample and docile manpower." Although British land forces may not succeed in overawing the Germans, "it is reasonable from the practical and psychological standpoint, to appreciate Germany being very powerfully deterred from aggressive action by the existence of very powerful British Air strength as a striking weapon."[64]

More fundamentally, however, Weir argued that the DRC had misunderstood how collective security would, or rather should, work. "What then is the true conception of the part each country should play in a collective effort," Weir asked. "Is it not that in the aggregate we should together present the greatest possible deterrent, and if that fails, then the most effective fighting force? Is that really secured by each country producing something of each arm for the general effort, or is it not rather secured by the various contributing those elements which industrially, economically and geographically they are best fitted to contribute and make immediately effective?"[65]

As an extension of Adam Smith's logic of specialization in commodity production, Weir's memorandum is right on, but in terms of its applicability to defense matters, it provoked a rather serious response by both General Montgomery-Massingberd and by the normally reserved Colonel Hankey.

The attack by the military professionals was not just against Lord Weir but in fact against the chancellor as well. In the revised version of the first DRC report, Chamberlain had proposed a scheme that "contemplated the creation of some kind of international partnership in Europe under which each signatory would undertake to supply a specified force, but with limited liability, for use against an aggressor."[66] The idea of limited liability and specialized contribution was a pet of Chamberlain's and it will be seen that he enthusiastically supported Weir's suggestion before the DPR.

Montgomery-Massingberd replied to Lord Weir's suggestion to create an "offensive air force," arguing, "no margin of superiority in bomber aircraft can compensate for the situation in London. London combines in one target objectives that in Germany are spread over Berlin, Hamburg and the Ruhr. Further, German war reserves will be so large that she can dispense with industry for some months and it is difficult to see ourselves in such a position. To challenge Germany to a type of warfare in which we must be in an inferior position would appear to be sheer folly."[67]

What really infuriated the CIGS, however, was the whole premise of Lord Weir's memorandum—namely, that Britain could inflict significant damage by bombing Germany. That premise had been rejected by General Ellington, the chief of the air staff, a year and half earlier when Chamberlain had essentially suggested the same thing and the CIGS took Weir to task for having not read the CAS's treatment before writing his memorandum.[68] The crisis was plain, at least in Montgomery-Massingberd's eyes: "Germany with her ever-increasing population and with the huge army which is now taking shape will be a more formidable opponent than ever upon the ground. It is vital to our security that France and Belgium should not be defeated on land and a war lost in the first round. For this reason we cannot afford to concentrate on our Navy and Air Forces and to neglect the provision of a Field Army, attractive as the proposition may be from many points of view."[69]

The CIGS's memorandum seems to have fallen on deaf ears, as least as far as the chancellor is concerned. Chamberlain took advantage of the second meeting of the DPR, held on January 14, to support Weir's idea of using the air force as a deterrent at the expense of a field force. Rather than argue against the need for a field force as he did in 1934, Chamberlain argued now that even if a field force was desirable, he had been given to understand that with the speed of modern warfare, a German attack might be successful within a week. If that was so, then the field force envisioned, rapidly deployable as it may be, was not sufficiently fast to get there in time to make a difference. Therefore, "it was for consideration whether, from the point of view of a deterrent, a strong offensive air force was not more effective than a field force which could not be put into the field for two weeks."[70] There were additional factors that, in Chamberlain's mind, militated against moving forward with the army recommendations as presented. As he told his colleagues, "there was the political difficulty that proposals for the re-constitution of the Field Force were not likely to get such public support as the proposal for the renovation of the Navy or the expansion of the RAF [Royal Air Force]."[71]

Although his ministerial colleagues did not deny the veracity of that last assertion, the military experts in attendance became exasperated at the need to explain yet again why what Chamberlain and Weir were suggesting was simply not possible from a military perspective.

Colonel Hankey, the ever-present secretary to both the cabinet and the Committee on Imperial Defence, had been silent, at least publicly, during the first discussions of the first DRC report, even when those had turned the focus away from the recommendations of the committee that he had chaired.[72] Now, however, he was sufficiently troubled by the direction that the ministerial discussion was going in that he chose to remind the ministers using the same exact language as in the report itself, that "the defence programmes, particularly of the Navy and Army, had become even less adequate for the defence needs of the situation. In fact the RAF had been given a start, but not the other two services."[73] Indeed, Hankey went further. Where Montgomery-Massingberd had written in his response to Lord Weir that "the experience of air warfare . . . does not justify the belief that air forces will be able to achieve the decision which in the past has always rested with armies,"[74] Hankey made an impassioned plea:

> Perhaps the nature of armaments might change some day, but that was a matter for the future. If our forces were to provide a deterrent, therefore, our armaments must broadly be on the same lines as those of other countries . . . the Report, had considered what other nations were doing in the West and in the Far East and had drawn up a balanced scheme which took account of all relevant factors. The Report was therefore based on a considered and balanced plan for the three Defence Services calculated on the needs for the whole Empire and was the best his Committee had been able to devise.[75]

In the end, it was Baldwin who suggested a compromise solution to the question. At the fourth meeting of the DPR, Baldwin suggested that plans for the provision of the regular field force go forward as suggested by the DRC report. The part of the plan that called for the enlargement and equipment of the Territorial Army, from whence reserves and later contingents would come, should be held in abeyance for three years. Baldwin was not arguing that equipping the territorials was a bad idea; rather, that a decision on that precise subject did not have to made right then because it had been indicated that production could not commence within the next three years on equipment for the later contingents anyway. Neither the secretary of state for war nor the CIGS denied that nothing concrete could be done for the territorials now and both accepted the idea of revisiting the issue three years hence or at such a time as the industrial situation might allow it to be reconsidered.

Baldwin's suggestion was accepted and in the final decision of the cabinet to approve the third DRC report, it was concluded, "That in approving the sixth recommendation referring to the Territorial Army, the Cabinet should take note that if, contrary to expectation, it should be found possible to make a start with the Territorial Force side of re-equipment before the end of 3 years there would be no objection to a re-opening of the question with a view to a fresh decision."[76] Chamberlain, however, had no intention of ever seriously considering equipping the field force, let alone reconsidering the issue of equipping the territorials. The issue would rise again at the end of 1936, and by then Chamberlain found sufficient ways to stall it until such time as Baldwin and his stubborn willingness to support the idea of continental commitment were retired.

THEORETICAL IMPACT—CHAMBERLAIN, THE THIRD DRC, THE WEIR MEMORANDUM, AND THE CREATION OF POWER

Because the financial blueprint for the defense spending that impacted on armament readiness in 1939 was crafted during the 1934 meetings of the ministerial committee, later events, such as the consideration of the third DRC report and the Weir Memorandum, are, in some ways, merely addenda. That said, Chamberlain's role in these events lends further evidence to the claim that leaders are the variable that intervenes between intentions and outcomes in international politics, particularly with relation to the formation of effective balances of power.

During the meetings of the DPR, Chamberlain clearly articulated his desire that Britain should be in a position to either deter Germany or to repulse it, both of which he insisted, in tandem with Lord Weir, could best be accomplished by focusing energies on what he called an "offensive" air force. In so arguing, Chamberlain turned the logic of the chiefs against them. The chiefs had written in 1933 that modern war moved quickly. Chamberlain inferred from that that British land support, even if desired, might not arrive in time to make an initial difference. The chancellor's argument was that an air force could operate against Germany directly if France fell and the fight had to be carried on alone.

Chamberlain's continued insistence on that strategy, when coupled with the passage of more than a year and a half between the two DRC reports with so little to show for it in terms of new weapons creation, caused, as we have seen, the military experts on the DRC to vent their frustration with their civilian overlords. The meetings of the DPR in which the third DRC report was discussed contain some of the clearest statements by the military professionals of the risk involved in relying on an aerial approach. The CIGS warned the DPR that their obsession with air power was at a complete disconnect between the vulnerabilities of Britain, the capabilities of air power, and the weaknesses of Germany. As quoted earlier, the CIGS cautioned that "no margin of superiority in aircraft can compensate for the situation in London."[77] All of Britain's power centers, political, military, and industrial, were concentrated in and around Greater London and the midlands. That degree of concentration, the CIGS argued, made Britain vulnerable to a massed aerial bombing campaign that could paralyze Britain by bringing industry to a halt for a period greater than the British war effort could endure. Germany, he wrote, was not similarly situated. Britain's vulnerabilities were not the same as Germany's. To defend Britain required that German forces be kept behind the Ruhr so that the weight of bombs that they could ferry to the United Kingdom would be so severely reduced so as to make them a far less relevant consideration.

Both the first and third DRC reports when considered by the ministers reflect a clear lack of imagination on the part of the civilians, particularly Chamberlain. Their comments and his own during the relevant committee meetings indicate that he experienced great difficulty in understanding that that which impacted Britain did not necessarily impact France or Germany the same way. France, as had been explained to him in 1934, did not have the same defense requirements as Britain did with regard to Belgian territorial integrity and so could not (and in any event, should not) be relied upon to secure it. Germany, he was told repeatedly, was not vulnerable to air attack in the same way that Britain was. To restrain Germany would require a land army, so the experts told him, yet he continued to choke off the provision of funds for that purpose, limiting spending in such a way that arms producers would not bid for contracts so small so as to make profitable production impossible.

It is important to note that the accuracy of the need for a land-based army is not just true in hindsight but, rather, was known at the time. The strategy that Chamberlain was suggesting had not worked in the few places where it had been tried, such as in Abyssinia. Chamberlain was made aware of that during the discussions on the third DRC report, but he chose to ignore it. Chamberlain never offered a narrative of how he expected the air force to be able to overcome the weaknesses that the chiefs insisted that it had. Nonetheless, he controlled the purse strings and, in many ways, the cabinet. Britain bought an air force that, as the chiefs warned, failed to have the balancing deterrent effect that the chancellor thought it would. An effective balance was there for the taking if Chamberlain would have recognized what it required and funded policies consistent with it appropriately. Chamberlain did not, and in so doing, once again demonstrated the role of an individual leader in creating the material realities of power that skew outcomes in international politics from the intentions of those who craft them.

CHAMBERLAIN ON DEFENCE COORDINATION

In both the first and third DRC reports, there was one thing that frustrated Chamberlain, and that was that the service chiefs continued their unanimous insistence on the need to balance defense spending among air, land, and naval forces. Chamberlain had tried, unsuccessfully, to get the chiefs to turn on one another and to have the air service give a more forceful advocacy of their own arm to the exclusion of the others, but to no avail. Under direct questioning the air service insisted that it could only perform its tasks if the army was equipped to hold the Low Countries, which would require a land-based commitment to Europe, which Chamberlain wished to avoid.

Chamberlain had exposed, from the very first meeting of the ministerial committee in 1934, his hostility to the idea of the army playing a continental role and thwarted efforts in that direction through whatever budgetary tools were at his disposal. After having to endure yet another report in which all the chiefs agreed on the urgent necessity of properly outfitting and equipping the field force, Chamberlain changed tack in his effort to force diversity of opinion between the services.

In a memorandum that the chancellor wrote in February 1936, immediately after the third DRC report had been discussed, he argued that a minister should be appointed in order to "coordinate" defense matters. Chamberlain wrote to his colleagues that the problem was that he could "not see how under present arrangements a completely objective view can be taken by the men [the Chiefs] who are themselves heads of Services, each with specific and sometimes diverging responsibilities."[78] What is perplexing about that observation is that, given the traditional selfishness of each of the services, one would expect that each chief would argue for the equipage of their own service at the expense of the others, not that they would produce a string of unanimous reports for three years in a row advocating a balance of forces. Chamberlain provided evidence of what he believed to be the glaring shortcomings of the existing system when he wrote:

> It will be remembered that in November, 1933, the DRC was desired by the then Cabinet to submit a programme for making good the deficiencies of our Defences and that this programme was duly submitted. . . . The proposals of the Committee were thereupon examined by a Ministerial Committee which came to the conclusion that, while parts of the programme, notably those concerning the Army, could properly be spread over a much longer period than that contemplated by the Committee, their proposals for the treatment of the Air Force were seriously under-estimated and must be substantially increased.
>
> It will be observed that in this case the amendments of the Defence Requirements Sub-Committee's plan made by the Ministerial Committee were based not on political but on military considerations, and that they were right has been proved by what has happened since.[79]

The chiefs, to be sure, would take exception to the entire final paragraph. The "proof" of the wisdom of the ministerial committee that Chamberlain found has to do with the relation of front-line aircraft, which was the only dimension in which he was disposed to think. The disparity between the growing capabilities of the Germans and the diminishing capabilities of the British in terms of taking and holding ground, for example, was not a marker to which Chamberlain assigned any weight.

The suggestion that Chamberlain made about the motivations of the ministerial committee in revising the first DRC report being based on a military calculation are either revisionist self-delusion or a lie. Chamberlain had on that exact occasion, after all, chastened the lord president when Baldwin had suggested that the military logic should carry the day. At that time, Chamberlain had said, "It was not an entirely military question, but very largely political in the broadest sense."[80]

As further evidence of the shortcomings of the unsupervised chiefs, Chamberlain referred to the more recent DRC report and the fact that "the conversion of the Air Force from a defensive organ into a weapon of aggression with unprecedented powers of destruction did not form part of the plan submitted to the Ministerial Committee [DPR]."[81] Although it is true that the service experts had not made that suggestion, it was only because the suggestion to do so was without any justification militarily. As the CIGS had written in response to the suggestion of such a conversion by Lord Weir, overwhelming Italian air power had not succeeded in cowing the rather less advanced—from a military perspective—Abyssinians when Mussolini had set it upon them in 1935; and if air power had failed under conditions of maximum superiority, how could Britain expect that its air forces, which would never attain a similar level of superiority over Germany, could fare better?[82]

Chamberlain was, as usual, successful in his bid to have a minister for the coordination of defense appointed. The post went to an attorney, Sir Thomas Inskip. Inskip was a proficient civil servant who deserves more credit for his role in preparing Britain for war than he generally receives. Inskip pushed the air service to continue the production of the fighter-interceptors that played such an important role in the Battle of Britain when others, including Chamberlain and Weir, were advocating in favor of a bomber force.

THE ARMY'S LAST CHANCE

The last chance for the army to get progress made in authorizing a real commitment to equipment and a continental strategy came at the end of 1936, just a few months before Chamberlain assumed the premiership. During the discussions of the DPR, which had considered the third DRC report in January, Baldwin had suggested that decisions to outfit the Territorial Army be held in abeyance until such time as any decision to equip them could be meaningfully implemented. At the time, it was believed that it would take at least three years to get to that point. When the cabinet had approved the third DRC report, however, it did also stipulate that if, by some chance, industry had advanced at a faster pace than had been imagined, the issue could be revisited prior to the three years' expiration.

By December 1936 Duff Cooper, the war secretary, reached the conclusion that the idea that industry was not in a position to supply equipment to both the regular and territorial contingents at the same time was no longer valid. Duff Cooper wrote, "It now appears that not only can both operations proceed simultaneously . . . but also that the lack of a decision with regard to the equipment of the Territorial Army is definitely delaying the equipment of the Regular Army."[83] Chamberlain, however, would have none of it. In a memorandum written a few days earlier, the chancellor had again argued that the army was simply the wrong branch to which funds should be provided. Chamberlain argued that "only [by] building up an Air Force capable itself of dealing a powerful attacking blow, and therefore affording a strong deterrent against any attack upon us, that we can ever hope to provide a real measure of security for these islands."[84] Chamberlain also urged his colleagues again to remember that "in making our choice of the relative sizes of the three arms of our Fighting Services, we should not lose sight of the fact that the political temper of the people in this country is strongly opposed to Continental adventures."[85] Chamberlain acknowledged that "opinions will, no doubt, differ as to whether or not this almost instinctive aversion from large scale military preparations corresponds with a sound perception of the principles upon which our foreign policy should be founded. But at least it is a factor which can never be ignored by those responsible for framing our policies."[86]

The war secretary implored his ministerial colleagues to approve spending on equipment. Duff Cooper circulated a memorandum to them in January 1937 in which he argued, "I must point out the danger in delay from the point of view of production of material. If we are to get within the next two years any substantial quantity of major equipment . . . it is essential to take the necessary steps to provide at once for their production. Even now it is difficult to see how this can be done with any reasonable economy; and in a few months' time, under normal conditions and with the usual limitations, it will probably be impossible."[87]

Duff Cooper cautioned his colleagues, "I cannot proceed with schemes which are now becoming very urgent without such approval as will satisfy the Treasury."[88] The war secretary's protests notwithstanding, the cabinet decided in February that the territorials should only get enough equipment for training, not for deployment.[89]

When the issue was raised yet again in April, the cabinet decided to delay discussion until May. By the end of May, Baldwin had retired and Chamberlain kissed the sovereign's hands. Duff Cooper, who in many ways had been less articulate in defending the role of the army than his predecessor Lord Hailsham had been, was moved to the admiralty, where he would be less irksome to Chamberlain. In his place, the prime minister appointed Leslie Hore-Belisha, a Chamberlain apprentice, whose only previous claim to fame was the endorsement of the crosswalk lamp (still called "Belisha Beacons"), as the new war secretary. Within a few months, Chamberlain had broken ways with Anthony Eden as well, allowing Lord Halifax, who was more sympathetic than Eden to appeasing dictators, to become the foreign secretary. Sir Robert Vansittart, the arch-enemy of appeasement, who had sat as the permanent head of the foreign office for nearly as long as anyone could remember, was pushed out by the new prime minister, and Andrew Cadogan, a Chamberlain sympathizer, was appointed in his place.[90] Even Colonel Hankey, who had been the memory of both the cabinet and the Committee on Imperial Defence, was put out to pasture and, with him, his passionate views on the immaturity of the air service as a decisive weapon.

With this new, fully cowed cabinet, Chamberlain was able to practice appeasement unchallenged until after Munich when the first lord quit and Halifax who had to that point been his strongest ally in the cause, withdrew his support.

Once Chamberlain assumed the premiership, bolstered by the fawning support of Hore-Belisha at the war office, all talk of a continental role for the army ceased until well after the Munich settlement. The idea of an expeditionary force for use on the Continent was quashed, and by the end of 1937 Chamberlain had rescinded the approvals such as they had been for the field force that had been passed during the years of Baldwin's leadership.[91] Within a year, the definition of the role of the British army was, as it had been at the time of the annual review of 1933 that had started the whole ball rolling, reserved for use in "an eastern theatre"—in other words, not Europe.

THEORETICAL IMPACT: CHAMBERLAIN, DEFENCE COORDINATION, AND THE ARMY

Chamberlain's memorandum on defense coordination provides outstanding evidence for this chapter's claim that Chamberlain's diagnostic and prescriptive skills were decidedly inadequate to the needs of Britain at the time. In his memorandum, cited earlier, Chamberlain actually credits himself with saving Britain from certain peril by his insistence that aerial forces be the backbone of British defense. In that memorandum, Chamberlain argued that it was the military experts whose conception of vulnerability was so off that they were actually willing to see fewer aircraft produced and money spent on land forces instead. It was only because he intervened to reassign spending priorities that Britain was so close to Germany in terms of front-line aircraft capability.

The irony, of course, is that all the aspects of the performance of the military experts to which Chamberlain points as being evidence of their shortcomings are in fact evidence of his own.

CHAPTER 6

LEADERSHIP EVALUATED

NEVILLE CHAMBERLAIN

This chapter aims to evaluate how closely Chamberlain's leadership approximates the expectations of the null hypothesis about how a leader informed by the logic that states balance against capability and malevolent intention would choose to secure Britain. First, however, and as was done with Baldwin, the historical data presented in the previous chapter will be evaluated to see if it lends confirmation to either of the prevailing structural theories: buck-passing and distancing.

In the chapters on Stanley Baldwin, the matter of proving that the logic behind either buck-passing or distancing was being completely absent from Baldwin's considerations was a relatively simple matter. Baldwin had articulated on many occasions his sincere belief that Britain would rise or fall with France and not separate from her. Chamberlain's behavior, by contrast, does seem to have a great deal motivating it that can be interpreted as evidence of either buck-passing or distancing logic. However, although the behavior is grossly consistent with the expectations of buck-passing, the logic behind it is not, and that is not without relevance. More to the point, however, a reading of Chamberlain's policies as being consistent with buck-passing, although plausible, is in fact an error. Chamberlain was not trying to pass the buck of defense to France but was, rather, trying to develop a theory of collective security in which Britain would play a part—a part different than she had in the Great War. More specifically, Chamberlain was motivated by a belief, rooted in economic logic, that Britain's contribution to defense should be a part of the allied effort but distinct in nature from the contributions of Belgium and France.

Buck-passing theory postulates that in a multipolar international system in which perceptions of the superiority of defensive weapons dominate, states will seek to pass the responsibility for confronting a common threat from one to another in an attempt to ride free on the security producing efforts of others. In this specific case, the claim is that Britain sought to have France bear the brunt of the cost of confronting the Nazis.

Most, if not all, of the biographers of Neville Chamberlain agree on one thing, and that is that he was not seeking to abdicate responsibility for the security and defense of the United Kingdom. Although his particular choices both in terms of armaments and general strategic outlook proved to be horribly in error, his intentions were good. Chamberlain, as near as can be discerned, genuinely believed that an exclusive focus on air armament would produce a strong deterrent effect on Germany. The fact that he held this opinion despite being counseled to the contrary by the military experts does not mitigate the extent to which the aim of securing Britain was a relevant calculation for him. Chamberlain believed that the advice that he was getting from the military experts was of a kind that would weaken rather than strengthen the defenses of Great Britain. As he wrote in the memorandum mentioned in the previous chapter in favor of creating the post of minister for the coordination of defense, the advice of the chiefs for a force balanced between army, navy, and air force with so much of the absolute available money going to the army, misperceived wherefrom Britain's security would come. Chamberlain believed that because a British land force would not, of itself, be sufficiently strong to repel Germany, the key to British security lay in creating negative inducements against a German attack to begin with. Chamberlain felt passionately that the best way to cause Germany to not attack was to be able to threaten an overwhelming response by aerial attack. The problems inherent in the fact that Chamberlain insisted that such a posture was possible absent a British land contribution directed toward securing France and the Low Countries will be dealt with in the following section. For now, however, it is enough to make clear that the idea that Chamberlain expected France and Belgium to defend the United Kingdom is not true.

More to the point, if buck-passing theory is correct, then we would expect to see evidence of two of three ideas. First, we should expect to see evidence of a perception of defense dominance. Without a perception of defense dominance, buck-passing is not a predicted outcome. Beyond that, we should also expect to see either that Chamberlain did not believe that the integrity of France and the Low Countries was vital to British security, or that he believed that France and the Low Countries were capable of holding out on their own. If Chamberlain did not believe that they could, then he could not be relying on them to provide security for Britain.

It is very hard to argue that a perception of defense dominance predominated during the period in question. As Lord Weir wrote, "Air attack is now firmly fixed in the public mind as the major menace."[1] The fact that the obsession in the British mind was of air attack against which there was believed to be no defense whatsoever makes it hard to accept the claim that the system was pervaded by a sense of defense dominance. Given the sheer amount of time that the various committees spent in consideration of air power and how little was spent of naval or land warfare indicates its relative ranking in terms of concern as well.

Even if one were to focus on land warfare for which it has been argued that a perception of defense dominance did exist, there is ample evidence to indicate that this perception was less pervasive than might be imagined. For example, a memorandum issued by the war office in 1935 forecasting the opening stages of a war with Germany suggested, "Either side may gain a great initial advantage by mobile operations conducted principally by mechanised forces and aircraft." Or elsewhere, "The value of mechanisation as an aid to the offensive is generally recognized."[2] These citations show that military thinkers, at least, recognized that the creation of mechanized forces restored the offensive to at least a credible option. That idea was accepted by Chamberlain himself who used its logic to argue that British forces might not even be able to arrive quickly enough to forestall a French and Belgian defeat because of the pace of the modern mechanized offensive.[3]

Beyond the issue of defense dominance remains the question of how Chamberlain perceived France and Belgium. Did he believe either that their integrity was unnecessary to British security or that they were sufficiently strong so as to defend themselves without British aid? As to the first, it is a mistake to infer from Chamberlain's disdain for a land-based commitment that he did not accept the fact that the integrity of France and the Low Countries was vital to British security. In his memorandum of June 1934, the then-chancellor had accepted that "the exclusion of Germany from the Low Countries is essential to our security."[4] Additional evidence of Chamberlain's acceptance of the need to assist in the defense of France and the Low Countries can be found in his willingness to endorse the statement made by Sir John Simon in the House of Commons, that any compromise to the security of Belgium could not, in Baldwin's phrase, leave Britain disinterested.

As to the second idea, that Chamberlain believed that France and Belgium could hold their own against Germany, the record shows that Chamberlain was quite convinced of their weakness and used his belief as to their inability to hold out as a justification for his own choices. Chamberlain wrote in several places, cited in the previous chapter, that he believed that any British land contribution would arrive after those allies would have already collapsed leaving Britain to stand alone and fight from bases on the British Isles proper, which he believed could only be done by air. This, indeed, was the spirit of the comment that he made in support of the Weir Memorandum at the meetings of the Defence Policy Requirements Committee in 1936. At those meetings, Chamberlain had said that because "it was not contemplated that the first proportions of the Field Force would be disembarked on the Continent in less than a week, and the remainder a week later . . . he questioned whether, in modern war, so considerable a lapse of time was acceptable. If Germany were to attack in the west, she, presumably, would not attempt to overcome the French line of fortifications, but would seek to encircle them by a mechanised force, and it might well be that that operation would be completed in less than a week."[5] In fact, it was Chamberlain's expectation that France and the Low Countries could not hold out that led him to suggest that "whether, from the point of view of a deterrent, a strong offensive air force was not more effective than a field force which could not be put in the field for two weeks," by which time they would not be landing in support of an ally but assaulting a position already held by the enemy.[6]

DISTANCING

All the evidence that argues against the validity of the buck-passing explanation is equally valid against the distancing argument that also purports to explain British behavior. In Schweller's conception, it is the unique behaviors of states in a tripolar international environment that explains British armament behavior. In Schweller's theory, the state that perceives a threat to be less imminent to itself will attempt to sacrifice a state against whom the threat is more imminent in an effort to either forestall completely or significantly delay the hour of its own reckoning. In this case, Schweller claims that Britain sought to betray an alliance with France because France lay more immediately vulnerable to Germany than Britain itself did. If this were true, we would expect to see some evidence of Chamberlain's willingness to see France come under the German boot.

There is a fair amount of truth in the claim that Britain sought to appease the German appetite for expansion at the expense of other states. What is not true, however, is that it was at the expense of France or any other great power. When the ministerial committee was discussing the talks between the Belgian foreign minister Heymans and his British counterpart, Sir John Simon, Chamberlain did not demur from the overall feeling of the committee that the integrity of France and the Low Countries was vital to British security. In fact, he suggested that as long as it was clear that the committee was speaking of France and Belgium then he believed such a statement of support would win public backing. All he cautioned his colleagues was that "if we were to propose an arrangement which might lead into war over an obscure cause in a remote part of Europe, then he thought we should find no support at all."[7] "A remote part of Europe" to Chamberlain meant eastern Europe. Indeed, Chamberlain's belief that eastern Europe was not worth fighting for was a theme to which he returned in explaining why he did not believe that Britain should take up arms over the Czechs. Importantly, by contrast he did, in the end, stand firm next to France when the latter was invaded in 1940. Chamberlain may have felt that the British contribution to the collective cause against the Nazis should be different than what the French themselves may have wished for, but there is no evidence that he was ever willing to see Britain secure at the cost of a permanently defeated France.

Chamberlain even took pains to explain that behaviors that later scholars, such as Barry Posen, have taken to be evidence of buck-passing, such as the 1935 Anglo-German naval treaty, were not intended to weaken the commitment of Britain to France.[8] Despite noting in a letter to his sister Hilda that the treaty had annoyed the French, he went on to write that the British would be able to show the French that "the Treaty is good not only for us but for them."[9] By reducing Britain's naval anxieties, the treaty would allow Britain to marshal more of its resources into other arms that would be part and parcel of the British contribution to the limited liability scheme.

CHAMBERLAIN AND THE NULL HYPOTHESIS

To merely indicate that the current explanations on offer from structural international relations theory are inadequate is only half the task. The other half is to offer an explanation that is both more compelling and more consistent with the documentary record in order to explain why Britain failed to balance effectively during the years in question.

The more compelling explanation for British behavior comes from a two-step understanding of the role that leaders play in creating effective balances of power. The metric that we have been using gauges leaders against their ability to accurately diagnose threats, prescribe correctives that minimize those threats, and mobilize support for those prescriptions. As with Baldwin in the previous chapters, Chamberlain's performance in those categories will now be evaluated.

DIAGNOSIS

A leader seeking to create an effective balance against Germany and guided by the logic that states balance against capability paired with malevolent intention would have broken down diagnosis into two areas. In terms of a political diagnosis, the leader would have diagnosed an ascendant, fascist, racist, dictatorial, and well-armed Nazi Germany as a threat that should be balanced against. From a military-strategic perspective, a leader would have appreciated the impact that the rise of aerial warfare demanded on how Britain's borders for security needed to be conceived. Chamberlain fulfilled neither diagnostic task well.

Political Diagnosis

The most troubling aspect of Chamberlain's diagnostic abilities lay in his complete misjudgment of Hitler personally and of Nazism generally. While it is true, as Tom Jones commented in 1934, that "all sorts of people that have met Hitler are convinced that he is a force for peace," as the years went by fewer and fewer people held that position.[10] Yet, as late as Munich, Chamberlain would insist that he had looked into Hitler's eyes and "saw in his face . . . that here was a man who could be relied upon when he had given his word."[11] Or, as he told the cabinet when he returned from his meeting with Hitler at Bad Godesberg, "he [Hitler] would not deliberately deceive a man whom he respected and with whom he had been in negotiation, and he [Chamberlain] was sure that Herr Hitler now felt some respect for him."[12] What Chamberlain based these "gut" feelings on is hard to tell. After all, Hitler had affirmed all manner of treaty and previous commitment only to shred them moments later. By the time that Chamberlain was having his positive experience with the German dictator, Hitler had already broken all the armament clauses of the Versailles treaty, annexed Austria in contravention of the treaty, introduced conscription, and pushed forces all the way forward to the border with France. Why Chamberlain chose to ignore those truths in favor of an uncertain promise remains a troubling aspect of his diagnostic skills.

Where Chamberlain fundamentally misdiagnosed the situation was in his assumption that all statesmen were as equally set against the prospect of war as he was. That assumption was false and could have been known to be so beforehand. Unlike Baldwin, who made frequent comments on how he saw Britain as "the only defenders of liberty in a world of Fascists," Chamberlain believed that a general European settlement was attainable despite all the evidence that accumulated over the years to the contrary. And where Baldwin had kept irksome colleagues and those with dissenting views within the cabinet, Chamberlain slowly but surely isolated himself such that opinions differing from his own were kept far away. By the time that Chamberlain was to face Hitler at Berchtesgaden, Eden, Hailsham, Montgomery-Massingberd, Hankey, and Vansittart effectively were gone, or nearly so. And soon afterward, Halifax, who had been Chamberlain's faithful partner early in the appeasement process, lost the faith and withdrew support as well, which saddened Chamberlain but did not dissuade him from persisting in his plans.

Instead of looking at the arming Germany and deriving policy from the armament requirements necessary to respond to that threat, Chamberlain instead focused on domestic issues and used them as a guide for his armament policy. Chamberlain broke down his political diagnosis into two elements. The first was that Britain could not afford a massive rearmament program. The second was that Chamberlain was convinced was that the British public would not stand for a rearmament program that included any significant measures that signaled an intention to use the army in a war on the Continent. Both of these diagnoses impacted on the prescriptions that Chamberlain would offer.

Chamberlain's steadfast belief that strict financial rectitude on the part of the United Kingdom was more important than a universal rearmament effort led to a great deal of disgruntlement on the part of the military. Ministers within the cabinet who were, like Chamberlain, quite sensitive to the exact status of British finances still thought that perhaps some loosening of the purse strings now would save even more money in the end. The first lord of the admiralty, Sir Eyres Bolton-Monsell, had suggested as much during the deliberations of the ministerial committee. The first lord had told the chancellor that "admittedly, the question of financial provision was very difficult, but it was far cheaper to find the money for defence services in peace than it was to finance a war."[13] Baldwin had intimated something similar at the previous day's meeting. At the meeting of the ministerial committee on June 25, 1934, Baldwin had suggested that perhaps the time had come to consider a defense loan in order to finance the necessary armament purchases. Chamberlain responded to that suggestion with regret, calling the idea of borrowing money for defense needs "the broad road which led to destruction."[14] To the military professionals, the chancellor's policy preferences seemed so out of synch with the urgency of the strategic situation that one of them commented that "the Government seemed less concerned to set the national defences in order than to have enough money to pay an indemnity to a victorious enemy after the war had been lost."[15]

No one can deny the reality of the financial straits that Britain was under. The global economic crisis of 1929–31 had only just recently passed and the chancellor was worried that such recovery as had yet been experienced was fragile and could be easily lost. Chamberlain worried, too, that in choosing armaments spending, he would be breaking a pledge to the voters to cut taxes. Chamberlain told his colleagues on the ministerial committee in 1934 that "it had been hoped to giver further [tax] relief in succeeding years, but that it was now found impossible to do so because the deficiencies of the Defence Services were so great that the money had to spent on them. We might be forced into taking this action, but he did not think that public would be easily reconciled to the idea."[16] It is comments like that which leads historians such as Brian Bond to conclude, "The predominantly Conservative Government is open to criticism for continuing to put financial stability before defence until almost the eve of the war."[17] The fact is that the first lord was correct; not borrowing money in 1934, or, indeed, even just withholding promised tax cuts that were no longer affordable turned out to be the very definition of penny wise and pound foolish.

Chamberlain's fear of the public response was by far the most central feature of his diagnosis of the political situation at home. From his earliest participation in defense deliberations, Chamberlain articulated the position that the public would not sanction the kind of spending on the army that the Defence Requirements Committee (DRC) report envisioned. In his own memorandum of June 1934, he wrote that spending on the army "appear[s] hardly likely to command immediate public support."[18] In later meetings of the ministerial committee that was considering the DRC report, Chamberlain resisted the military logic of, for example, stationing airplanes in Malta and Gibraltar because the public wanted to see airplanes stationed on the

British Isles.[19] When Baldwin, for one, suggested that the public could be educated as to the true defense needs of the nation that they would then support, Chamberlain dismissed Baldwin as treating the matter of public support in a "lighthearted spirit."[20]

Nor did the passage of time serve to allay Chamberlain's perception of the problem of public support. When the third DRC report came up for discussion in early 1936, Chamberlain reminded his colleagues of his fear that spending on the "Field Force were not likely to get such public support as the proposal for the renovation of the Navy or the expansion of the RAF [Royal Air Force]."[21] In December 1936, when Chamberlain was clashing with Duff Cooper over the equipment of the Territorial Army, Chamberlain wrote to the other ministers, "we should not lose sight of the fact that the political temper of the people in this country is strongly opposed to Continental adventures." And that while he acknowledged that "opinions will, no doubt, differ as to whether or not this almost instinctive aversion from large scale military preparations corresponds with a sound perception of the principles upon which our foreign policy should be founded. . . . at least it is a factor which can never be ignored by those responsible for framing our policies."[22]

Whether Chamberlain's diagnosis of the fragility of public support was accurate or not is, of course, open to debate. Duff Cooper, who sat with Chamberlain in Baldwin's cabinet as war secretary, was not nearly as convinced as the chancellor that public opposition was strong. During the meetings of the Defence Policy Requirements (DPR) Committee in 1936 that discussed the third DRC report, the war secretary "questioned whether the House of Commons would take exception to the renovation of the Field Force. He had himself found no difficulty in the House in his reference to that force."[23] At the same meeting Baldwin, too, expressed less certainty over the degree of difficulty that the government might face in making recommendations on the army than his chancellor did. The prime minister said that "on the political side it would be necessary to carry conviction with the House of Commons and the country, and that might not be easy with some of the recommendations made, although anything which was considered essential would have to be carried through." That certainty that what needed to be done both could and would be done was consistent with what he also had said a year and a half earlier when the subject had arisen. At that time, too, although Chamberlain did not believe that the public could be carried, Baldwin had argued that, once apprised of the true situation, "public opinion might be willing to agree to anything which would prevent foreign air forces from getting any closer than they were to-day," and that included equipping what was then called the Expeditionary Force for use on the European Continent.[24]

If Winston Churchill is to be believed, Chamberlain was simply wrong in the degree to which he expected significant opposition to spending plans for defense. In the speech that he gave on the occasion of the air estimates debate of March 1934, Churchill exhorted Baldwin to lead, saying to and of him, "He has only to make up his mind what has to be done in this matter [armament] and Parliament will vote all the supplies and sanctions which are necessary, if need be within 48 hours."[25]

Noncontemporary observers are likewise less sure than Chamberlain was about the depth of public support. Brian Bond has observed, for example, that "since the Press was largely Tory it could easily have been prompted to campaign for rearmament. It is noticeable that politicians invoked 'public opinion' in support of whatever policy they wished to pursue. Colonel Hankey's assistant, Colonel Pownall thought that ministers . . . such as Neville Chamberlain . . . exaggerated the fear that public opinion would 'rise up in anger at the idea of the Territorials being sent to 'another Passchendaele.'"[26]

Although a final resolution to the question of whether the people would have truly risen up against the government will always remain a great "what if," it is important to recall that the national governments of the 1930s had majorities so large they have yet to be replicated. Weaker governments, with smaller majorities, have accomplished far more, and the idea that the national government would have been turned out to be replaced by George Lansbury was, with no disrespect to the Labour leader, not likely no matter what policy the national government advocated.

Military-Strategic Diagnosis

A leader informed by structural logic and seeking to create an effective balance of power would also have made a strategic diagnosis about the impact of aerial warfare as it related to an overall conception of the requirements of defense. Specifically, he or she would have appreciated that the British concept of border defense needed to be expanded in such a way that it would allow for an understanding that borders mark the perimeter of vulnerability, not just—or even only—the physical boundaries of the state.

To some extent, Chamberlain's appreciation of the nature of the air threat was both in tune and out of it with the other important leaders of the time. Chamberlain, like Baldwin, Churchill, and nearly everyone else, believed that the great threat to the United Kingdom lay in the ability of Germany to wage a war against it from the air. Even army men like General Montgomery-Massingberd and Colonel Hankey, as well as the war ministers Hailsham and Duff Cooper, shared the opinion that the gravest threat to the British Isles lay in German air strength. Where the chancellor differed significantly from the military chiefs, their civilian overlords, and from Baldwin was in the prescription he chose in light of that diagnosis.

Rather than focus on the details of an aerial threat, Chamberlain instead focused on other aspects of the military-strategic diagnosis. Of particular interest to Chamberlain was the timing of the threat. In terms of timing, there was a wide discrepancy between what the experts suggested and what Chamberlain believed. From the very first, the military experts argued that Britain would have to face the reality of a rearmed Germany within three to five years of 1933. In the annual review of October 1933, which, along with Baldwin's speech of November 1932, should be considered the curtain raising of the rearmament process, the chiefs had warned, "in say three to five years' time, when the anticipated military renewal in Germany may have been realized, we shall be in a worse position than to-day."[27] That position was affirmed a few months later in the first DRC report, which also envisioned the German threat being nearly fully realized in five years time, a point that was affirmed yet again in the responses of the chiefs to the ministerial committee questionnaire.[28]

The professionals at the foreign office, including both Sir Robert Vansittart and the various ambassadors to Berlin, shared the timing expectations of the military chiefs. Vansittart had provided a written warning of the alarming pace of German rearmament during the deliberations of the ministerial committee in 1934 and again at a meeting of the Defence Policy Requirements Committee in 1936.[29] At that later occasion, Vansittart had warned that "he did not consider that peace in Europe could be guaranteed for the next 5 or even 3 years. Indeed he was sure that this would not be the case."[30]

A similar position had been taken by Anthony Eden at the DPR meetings in January 1936. Eden, then foreign secretary, had issued the memorandum in support of his claim that "it was not clear that we could afford to wait for 5 years" because Germany may be ready to challenge Britain before then.[31]

From the outset, Chamberlain denied that the timing assessments of either the military or the foreign service experts were accurate. On at least four separate occasions during the discussions of the ministerial committee in 1934 Chamberlain challenged the timing assumption. The first, and by far the oddest, was his comment that "he was quite agreeable to accepting the suggested 5 year period, provided it was understood that it did not necessarily mean that we were tying ourselves down to complete the programme in 5 years."[32] As mentioned earlier, this comment seems to imply both an acceptance and a rejection of the idea of the five-year threat. Thankfully, Chamberlain would clear up the confusion a few meetings later when he said that as near as he understood, the idea of remedying deficiencies within five years was based on the idea that "in five years' time we might want to send an Expeditionary Force to the Low Countries within one month. At the present moment there was not enough evidence to convince him that this pace was necessary."[33] Chamberlain's challenge to the idea of the threat being realized in five years was expressed yet again at the meeting of the ministerial committee on June 25, where he said, "Germany would not be in a position to wage war in the west within five years."[34] Finally, at the meeting of the ministerial committee on June 26, in which Hailsham and Chamberlain had their lengthy exchange, the chancellor acknowledged that he did not believe that the threat would be real in five years.[35]

Taken together, there is a great divergence between what a leader informed by the neorealist structural logic of balancing would have understood the problem to be and what Chamberlain himself understood the problem to be. That tension between theoretical expectations and observed outcomes is brought into even starker relief when it comes to the prescriptions that Chamberlain offered.

PRESCRIPTION

The terms of the null hypothesis are that a leader informed by structural logic and pursuing the aim of effectively balancing Germany would have made two different types of prescriptions. Their political prescription would have been for an explicit commitment to, and guarantee of, the integrity of the Low Countries and northern France so that Germany would be under no illusions about the extent of British interest in those areas. From a military perspective, the leader would have prescribed that Britain raise a modern mechanized army, with independently operated armor units that could be rapidly deployed to the Continent either before the outbreak of war or immediately upon it.

Political Prescription

The issue of Chamberlain's commitment to France and the Low Countries was addressed in the previous section, which argued that

Chamberlain's actions were not motivated by the logic of either buck-passing or distancing. Chamberlain accepted in principle that British security was contingent on the integrity of northern France and the Low Countries. He was not willing, however, to make that guarantee full and explicit and was curiously quiet during the discussion over Sir John Simon's proposed declaration to the House of Commons on the matter. Chamberlain was conflicted because, on the one hand, he accepted that France and Belgium were vital to British security, and on the other hand, as he became convinced that they may not be able to hold out against the Nazis until British help arrived, he looked for other ways to fight the Nazis that were not dependent on allied help. That tension is exposed in Chamberlain's military prescriptions.

Military Prescription

Chamberlain's military prescription was fairly simple. Chamberlain believed that Britain should focus nearly all of what he believed to be her meager resources toward the building up of an air force. It was Chamberlain's hope, expressed on numerous occasions, that the very existence of a large air force would deter Germany from launching an attack against the United Kingdom. In the event that Germany failed to be deterred by the large British air force, that same force would then be the executor of British vengeance. This was the essence of Chamberlain's suggestion from the very beginning of the discussions of the ministerial committee. It is also the logic that lay behind the questions that the committee directed to the service chiefs on May 3, 1934. Those questions probed the chiefs on why British air power could not do unto Germany what the chiefs had argued could be done by Germany unto Britain.

Chamberlain remained committed to this vision of a deterrent force in the air for the remainder of his involvement in British public life until war actually broke out. Where Chamberlain is rightly faulted is that he held this conviction about the power of the air force in defiance of all expert opinion on the topic. At every opportunity when expert opinion was solicited, it argued against the vision of air power as Chamberlain held it. In their response to the 1934 questionnaire, the chiefs had argued that air power could not do what Chamberlain wanted it to. Indeed, even the separate memorandum by the chief of the air staff, Ellington, had reached the conclusion that "it is . . . not too much to say that the occupation and successful defence of the Low Countries against German invasion would be the most effective means of mitigating the severity of German air attack on London."[36]

Despite being warned by both the chief of the air service (CAS) and the air secretary that the air force could not keep the Germans out of Belgium, Holland, and northern France, as was the essential precondition of British security, Chamberlain insisted on increasing the budget for the air service by 94 percent while slashing the money for the army and navy by 50 percent and 64 percent, respectively. Those cuts hit the army hardest, for it was the branch of service that had been the most impacted by the operation of the ten-year rule. Despite being explicitly warned by Lord Hailsham that the chancellor's budget figures would prevent the army from holding France and the Low Countries, Chamberlain went ahead with his plan.

Chamberlain's stance of 1934 was repeated again in 1936. As with the first DRC report, Chamberlain was disturbed to see once again a unanimous insistence by the chiefs and the foreign office for a field force capable of intervention on the Continent. As before, he tried to convince his colleagues, this time along with Lord Weir, that focusing attention on the air force was the best thing to do both from the perspective of politics and from the perspective of deterrence. And, as before, the chief of the imperial general staff (CIGS) retorted that what the chancellor wanted could not be done. Britain simply did not have the industrial capacity or the manpower to overtake German aircraft production. And because all agreed that parity, in some form, was the *sine qua non* of the chancellor's plan, "to challenge Germany to a type of warfare in which we must be in an inferior position would appear to be sheer folly."[37]

The fundamental problem with Chamberlain's prescriptive ability was that he continued to insist on its validity when all the evidence pointed in the other direction, when the experts told him that it could not be done, and most grievously, even when it became clear that it was not even complying to its own internal logic.

This last point is particularly relevant in relation to the parity argument. There is simply no way, even by the immature understandings of deterrence in the 1930s that Britain could have expected to deter Germany without attaining at least qualitative parity with Germany. That much was understood at the time, yet, from 1934 on, Britain found itself on the weaker end of the comparative measure. In 1934, Lord Londonderry had pointed out to Chamberlain that even his unexpected generosity toward the air service "did not provide parity" in the air with Germany.[38] The relative weakness of Britain in the air was brought to the chancellor's attention again in 1936 by Lord Swinton who had replaced Londonderry when Baldwin assumed the premiership. Swinton told Chamberlain at a meeting of the DPR that "at the present time they

[Germany] had a greater number of Service aircraft than we possessed at home, taking into account training aircraft, reserves, aircraft recently sent overseas to meet the temporary emergency, and such proportion of the Fleet Air Arm as might reasonably be assumed as available for co-operation in defence. The German output was larger than ours, and their capacity for future output was larger still."[39]

It is this last part of Swinton's message that is the most crucial. Deterrence relied on parity and parity was beyond reach.

There are several fundamental flaws with Chamberlain's prescriptions. Among the most significant is that Chamberlain showed only the vaguest understanding that inspiring fear of punishment is only one aspect of effective deterrence. A second aspect of deterrence lies in the ability to deny an adversary battlefield success.[40] The force created so as to inspire sufficient awe in the eyes of a potential enemy to keep them from attacking must also, if that awe fails to restrain them, be useful to actively deny the enemy those goals that they seek. That is where Chamberlain is weakest. Even with regard to the air—Chamberlain's preferred arm—the weapons that he envisioned were neither sufficient nor appropriate for fighting a war. Londonderry had pointed out as much when he commented that Chamberlain's armament policy seemed more designed for public consumption than utility because it was devoid of all provisions for the creation of an aerial reserve.[41]

Obviously, the fatal flaw in Chamberlain's prescriptions is that he failed to understand that, as Hailsham explained, "a strong Air Force operating from this country would not constitute a strong deterrent."[42] The appeal of the idea of reliance on air power alone to either deter Germany or, failing that, to deny her access to vital areas, was clear. If it were possible, it would indeed allow Britain to not send men to Europe to fight and die, perhaps in as horrible a way as they had just twenty or so years before. The appeal of the idea was acknowledged even by such land devotees as Field Marshal Montgomery-Massingberd in his January 1936 memorandum.[43] However, the attractiveness of an idea cannot supersede consideration of its feasibility. Chamberlain was warned several times between 1934 and 1937 that the British air forces simply could not do what he was suggesting if they could not operate from Belgium, Holland, and northern France. Chamberlain was also warned that the Low Countries and France could not hold out alone and that a British land contribution was necessary both to bolster their will to resist Germany but more, because, as the chiefs had written, "quite apart from any question of implementing our guarantees under the various Pacts and Covenants which we have signed, the security of this county demands that we should be prepared to fight for the integrity of Belgium and Holland."[44] In other words, the defense of the Low Countries was not a favor to them but a vital British interest that others could not be relied upon to secure. Speaking before the Defence Policy Requirements Committee in 1936, the normally reserved Colonel Hankey had put it well. Hankey said, "Perhaps the nature of armaments might change some day, but that was a matter for the future. If our forces were to provide a deterrent, therefore, our armaments must be broadly on the same lines as other countries."[45] For the moment, then, reliance on air power was untested, and in the isolated cases in which it had been tried, as in Abyssinia, it had not succeeded. Britain needed an army, and the chancellor refused to grant one.

MOBILIZATION

Chamberlain possessed neither the silver tongue of his predecessor nor the sharp wit of his successor. Chamberlain inspired neither affection nor adoration. Chamberlain's public speaking was completely unremarkable. Neville Chamberlain's skill lay, in almost exact contrast to Baldwin's, in garnering support in closed forums such as the cabinet and its committees. Chamberlain possessed the tactical skill of finding a way to speak last or nearly last at committee meetings and thus influence the official conclusions in a manner disproportionate the degree of consensus that they actually reflected. Thus, for example, when the ministerial committee was discussing the prospect of an expeditionary force on May 10, Chamberlain spoke near the end saying that "he thought . . . that the Committee were not entirely convinced in regard to this [the need for an expeditionary force]."[46] A careful reading of the minutes of the meeting shows nothing like the consensus that this comment implies. At a later meeting of the same committee, the chancellor said, "It seemed to him that the Committee had been somewhat startled at first by the Army proposals, but that after full consideration their hesitation had been overcome, although they did not consider that the Army demands should be met in so short a period as five years."[47] As an encapsulation of the intellectual process that Chamberlain himself had passed, however, it is more or less accurate, but whether it reflects anybody else's opinion is more open to question.

In some ways, it is more accurate to say that rather than that Chamberlain was good at mobilizing support, his position as chancellor of the exchequer serving under weak prime ministers made that task less relevant. As during the discussions of the ministerial committee on the first DRC report, Chamberlain was often charged with, or simply took upon himself, the job of setting spending priorities. Those plans would then be presented for what turned out to be an up or down vote on his proposals. Chamberlain was willing to lead—or bully—reluctant colleagues, and although most of them dithered over what needed to be done, he worked diligently to get his vision translated into government policy. In the few instances in which his superiors, especially Baldwin, expressed an attitude contrary to that which Chamberlain himself held, such as Baldwin's willingness to consider the equipment of the Territorial Army in 1936, Chamberlain would manipulate the committee process such that a concrete decision would be either put off indefinitely or, at least, put off until such a time as Chamberlain would no longer have to answer, even nominally, to anybody.

One of Chamberlain's most glaring shortcomings as it relates to the issue of mobilization is the near dread with which he regarded the prospect of having to gain the support of the people for policies that he expected to be unpopular. Chamberlain had, it seems, a rather failing faith in what the people would allow, and as he wrote in his 1936 memorandum, consideration of public feeling is "a factor which can never be ignored by those responsible for framing our policies."[48] Baldwin would have admitted no less, but where Baldwin would have interpreted the statement to mean that more needed be done to advise the people of the truth and thereby gain their support, Chamberlain interpreted it as a call to satisfy the whims of the people at the expense of long term security. Chamberlain's call for air rearmament at the expense of the furbishing of a land army was an outgrowth of his belief that the people could not be led to that outcome.

In the end, Chamberlain did not so much mobilize support even within the cabinet but rather reshaped the cabinet so that support would be his. Where Chamberlain was confronted by collegial adversity, as in the case of Duff Cooper and Anthony Eden, he would either move them to a position less likely to irritate him, or create circumstances in which the offending minister had little choice but to resign.

HISTORICAL CONCLUSIONS

The tragic irony of British defense policies in the 1930s is that the leader who more or less accurately understood both the realities of the situation and the means necessary to correct it proved too timid to force his view on ministerial colleagues whom he viewed as his equals not his underlings. The leader who did, in the end, have the force of character to get his way was the one who had serious flaws in his understanding of what the true nature of the threat Britain faced was and an even weaker grasp on what needed to be done about it.

Chamberlain, of course, did not admit that he was weak in either the capability of diagnosing the reality of Britain's strategic situation or that his prescriptions for its amelioration may have caused more harm than good. The evaluation of Baldwin concluded that although he performed reasonably well in two of the three tasks of leadership, his failure to mobilize cabinet support fatally undermined what could have been an armament process that may have gone farther toward creating a real deterrent or, more likely, a force that would have acquitted itself admirably on the day of battle.

Chamberlain, by contrast, performed none of the three tasks of leadership well. At best, his diagnosis was only partially accurate. Although he did understand that the advent of the age of air had changed Britain's strategic situation, he did not understand that it also required a new perception of where Britain's borders lay.

In terms of prescriptions, Chamberlain charged headlong in the wrong direction and did so in stark opposition to the advice of all who had any degree of professional expertise in the field. Chamberlain did not deny for a minute that he was himself rejecting and urging his ministerial colleagues to reject along with him "the advice of their military advisers."[49] Chamberlain was certain that he knew what was best and has become the embodiment of the principle that one ought to be careful what they wish for, lest they get it. Chamberlain got his focus on the air arm. The army was left in the shambles it had been in when the chiefs of staff had first called attention to its sorry state in October 1933. And although the army fought bravely in the spring of 1940, it also fought in vain because of the decisions taken by Neville Chamberlain throughout the preceding half decade that stripped it of any chance of being able to hold its own against a German nation that took the continued supremacy of land warfare more seriously.

Finally, although Chamberlain got his way, it was less through the successful process of mobilization and more the twin effects of ministerial abdication on the part of his colleagues and a willingness to reshape the cabinet to suit his tastes and remove irksome obstructions so that he could get his way. Chamberlain did not, of course, mobilize the people, because he was too afraid to lead them. Chamberlain allowed his fear of the consequences of sharing the grim strategic truth with the nation that he ostensibly led drive him toward decisions that, while giving succor to public fears, also left Britain weakened in the face of what would be a far more astringent reality.

Much of the early work on the life of Neville Chamberlain, written before access to archival material was allowed, accused the late prime minister as being a "coward" and labeled his policy of appeasement as an act of cowardice. That statement is, in light of the documentary record, not really fair. With reservations, it is accurate to suggest that Chamberlain was not a coward and that he did have the purest of intentions toward British security in his heart. The reservation lies in Chamberlain's allowing the fear of what the public would allow to overrule the sound judgment of what needed to be done. Although that may not be the type of cowardice that Chamberlain's early accusers had in mind, it is a kind that infects leadership in the most grievous of ways because it leads to an abdication of that somber responsibility entrusted to leaders: that they will do what is needed to vouchsafe the security and safety of their nations.

The fitting epithet for the life and leadership of Neville Chamberlain comes from his predecessor, Stanley Baldwin. Years before anyone in England would give thought to the former German corporal whose appetite for domination would soon consume the last great energies of the empire, Baldwin said, "It is a want of imagination and the fear of taking the risk of what could only be a temporary and a local unpopularity [that restrains leaders from doing what is right], but it is that very cowardice that, in the long run, does so much harm to this form of government. A good motive to my mind can hardly be a sufficient excuse for an act of unwisdom."[50]

CHAPTER 7

CONCLUSIONS ON LEADERSHIP AND INTERNATIONAL RELATIONS THEORY

Stanley Baldwin and Neville Chamberlain reflect two possible modes by which leadership matters as the determinative variable in whether an effective balance of power is formed. Baldwin is an example of the leader whose relative inaction led to the nonimplementation of policies to which he basically subscribed. Chamberlain is an example of the leader who is extremely active and determined but who leads poorly. Both types of leaders matter equally. Leaders such as Chamberlain appear to matter more because in their fury of activity they seem to be "doing" more than less active leaders. That is only an illusion, however. Leaders matter both when they take action and when they do not. All that is required for the triumph of evil, to paraphrase Edmund Burke, is that good men do nothing. The same is true for leaders. Although some leaders may be very active, all that is required for an ineffective balance is for a leader to do nothing when something needed to be done. That inaction can have as much impact as any action would.

The failure of the United Kingdom to balance effectively against Germany can be traced in a simple and straightforward manner to Neville Chamberlain. Chamberlain derailed, almost single-handedly, any efforts to get Britain to behave in a manner consistent with what was necessary to create an effective balance. The proper diagnosis about the nature of the German political threat had been articulated by Sir Robert Vansittart, who wrote two strong and pointed memoranda in 1934 in which he had argued that Germany remained unchanged since the days of the Great War and was bent on conquest and revision of its borders now as ever.[1]

The correct appreciation of British strategic vulnerability had been argued by Stanley Baldwin, who sought to convince both his colleagues and the nation that "from an air point of view our frontiers had been moved from Dover to the Rhine."

The appropriate prescriptions for effective balancing policy were not lacking, either. They had been offered by the military chiefs in every document they issued from October 1933 on. The chiefs had even gone so far as to specifically refute Chamberlain's logic of air power as a balancing tool. Chamberlain, however, was able to outmaneuver his superiors and overrule his underlings and translate his own beliefs and preferences about both the nature of the threat and what needed to be done about it into policy. The documentary record shows quite clearly that the explanation for the British armament decisions, which were inadequate for minimizing Britain's own vulnerabilities or for the exploitation of German weaknesses, lies with Chamberlain.

One of the themes of critique running throughout this book is the underspecification of power in structural neorealist theory. Power can take many forms, and the secret to an effective balance lies in a careful analysis by national leaders of their own nation's vulnerabilities, prescribing measures that compensate for those vulnerabilities, and evaluating their rival's vulnerabilities in a similar manner. Chamberlain manifestly failed to do that accurately.

Chamberlain was warned by Montgomery-Massingberd that Germany would not be vulnerable to aerial attack because of its size and the dispersion of its industry, yet he chose nonetheless to take the path of exclusive aerial rearmament.[2] Chamberlain was warned by Londonderry and Ellington in 1934 and by the chief of the imperial general staff (CIGS) in 1936 that Britain's own vulnerability lay in the concentration of industry, military, and political elites in the Greater London area and that no degree of aerial superiority could compensate for that vulnerability. Chamberlain not only overruled the policy choices implied by that observation but also, as shown in his 1936 memorandum on defense coordination, took pride in so doing. Chamberlain believed that his diagnosis and prescription would save Britain. They did not. What they do demonstrate, however, is the degree of control that leaders have in translating their perceptions on how power should be generated for the purposes of balancing a rival into policy outcomes.

Structural neorealist theory has greatly enhanced the social scientific credentials of international relations theory, but it has done so at the cost of taking international relations theory far away from the ability to make accurate and relevant predictions about international behavior. The chapters on Baldwin and Chamberlain have shown how the skills and, more important, limitations of a leader shape the actions of a state and outcomes in international politics far more than systemic structural constraints do. Britain could have spent the 1930s building tanks instead of airplanes and training men for land warfare instead of refusing to arm the nation. To do so would have been possible, but it would have required leaders who recognized the wisdom of the counsel they were receiving and ready to lead the nation in decisions that may have resulted in, as Baldwin said, "only a temporary and a local unpopularity." In the end, Britain did not take those steps because leaders, particularly Chamberlain, were able to redirect policy in a manner consistent with his own frames, perceptions, and preferences. That fact and the divergence that it represents from the expectations of contemporary international relations theory compels a rethinking of the analytic variables considered for inclusion in the discipline. The inclusion of leadership as a variable presents challenges for generalized predictions to be sure, but given that it can explain so much of international affairs, to ignore it or minimize its significance is equally problematic for those who seek to understand the true drivers of behavior in international relations.

CONCLUSION

The publication of Kenneth Waltz's 1979 book *Theory of International Politics* marked an epochal moment for international relations theory. Its publication heralded the promise of a predicatively robust, elegant, and parsimonious theory of international relations, the type that is the aspiration of all social scientific research. The book represented Waltz's attempt to bring the predicative capabilities and theoretical elegance of international relations in line with that achieved in economics. Where economics has long been able to make elegant predications on the basis of a few variables only, international relations theory before Waltz had been encumbered by the habit of its practitioners to draw their inspiration from history and philosophy and with less regard to scientific rigor. Economists, for example, were able to make simple statements that sounded much akin to physical laws: increasing the money supply *will* result in inflation. Lowering interest rates *will* result in increased investment in capital.

Economics, however, its achievements great as they are, is not a natural science. Economic theories often have to be modified to account for human intervention. The purported relationships between interest rates and investment or the money supply and inflation, for example, are predicated on assumptions about extremely limited capital mobility and closed markets that are increasingly not in operation in industrialized nations. This is to say nothing of the often unmet requirement of nearly all economic theory: that its actors be perfectly rational or the profit maximization is their main goal. Despite its reputation as the most scientific of the social sciences, economists often construct elegant theories that fail in their application because of the deviation between the theory's assumptions and reality in practice.

Like economic theory, the promise of structural neorealism as an almost pure material theory that would allow a broad spectrum of predictions about international behavior to be made from two variables only was short-lived. The idea that meaningful theory could be constructed with only knowledge of the number of states in the system and the distribution of the material capabilities between them proved unable to cope when it was applied to observed outcomes. Just as economic theory has required the addition of variables in order to make what were once streamlined and elegant theories comply with reality, so, too, has structural neorealism been modified.

Pure structural materialism has been under attack for more than a decade. Within the structural neorealist school, the reintroduction of ideational variables that structuralism was supposed to have made unnecessary began in 1987 with Stephen Walt's work on the role of threat as a twin component, along with capability, of what makes great powers behave the way they do.

Other theorists were dubious of Waltz's emphasis on the immutability of the impact of systemic structure on outcomes from the outset. Liberal theorists such as Robert Keohane, Stephen Krasner, John Ikenberry, and Daniel Deudney have all long argued that neorealism undervalues the role that international institutions can play in mitigating the most deleterious aspects of international anarchy.[3] And, as mentioned earlier, theorists of the democratic peace also have challenged the primacy of the system level as *the* explanatory variable for international outcomes. They have argued that the character of the regime can explain at least some of the outcomes in international politics.

The apogee of revolution against Waltz has come with the rise of social constructivism. Alexander Wendt's *Social Theory of International Politics*, a book with a title likely as not intentionally in echo of Waltz's own, in order to present a nearly inverted model of international relations theory to materialist structural neorealism. Where Waltz's book was material with a rump ideational element, Wendt's book is the complete reverse, a theory of nearly pure ideation, with only a rump material element.[4]

The creeping back in of nonmaterial variables in international relations theory though, has not gone so far as countenancing a determinative role for leaders, despite an intuitive appreciation that leaders matter. The reasons why leadership remains excluded are manifold, but most are variations of the argument that "although individual leaders matter . . . their influence does not lend itself to the kind of generalizations that political scientists seek."[5] The same cannot be said of ideas. Particular ideas can be predicted to impact reality in particular ways. That at least is the logic behind Wendt's claims as well as those of the theorists of the democratic peace. The widespread diffusion of states regarding one another as friends instead of rivals, Wendt feels comfortable predicting, *will* result in an international system marked by a pacific relations instead of armed conflict. The introduction of ideas has not meant the abandonment of the social scientific enterprise. The variables that are determinative may have changed from material-structural to ideational but ideas-based constructivism still aspires to produce a falsifiable theory.

Building a falsifiable theory that includes a measurement of leadership performance is theoretically possible but unlikely. In Chapter 2, the suggestions of Byman and Pollack on how to operationalize leadership as a variable were considered but ultimately rejected as being not conducive to *a priori* prediction because they relied on subjective data about the leader that could only be known *ex post*, such as their sanity.

The difficulty of fitting leadership into a rigorous scientific rubric should not, however, lead to a refusal to consider it through some other method. Leaders are the occupants of the black box that sits at the heart of the policymaking process. They frame and diagnose a problem, they prescribe corrective measures to meet it, and then they mobilize support to get their prescriptions implemented. Leaders matter, both when they do what other theories predict they will and equally when they do not. Social, systemic, and institutional variables can all impact on what a leader perceives and how they might frame a given problem, but in the end, it is the leader with all their skills and their limitations that shift the levers that result in policy outcomes.

This project used one of international relations most enduring puzzles, that of why Britain did not effectively balance against rising German might to demonstrate the role of leadership as a determinative factor in international politics. By all accounts, Britain should have developed robust capabilities to match Germany's aspirations. Whether as a measure of pure material capability, or even when modified by Stephen Walt's notion that states balance against capability paired with malevolent intention, Germany is the archetype of the state that should be balanced against.

REJECTING NEOREALIST EXPLANATIONS FOR BRITISH BEHAVIOR

Kenneth Waltz's theory does not attempt to explain why any given state in any given situation would or would not act in a particular way. That type of prediction demands a theory of foreign policy that Waltz, with full candor, does not offer. What Waltz argues is that the system will condition states to act a certain way and that, if they fail to do so, they will suffer some sort of consequence. As far as it goes, that is what happened to Britain between the wars. However, not all scholars are as unconcerned as Waltz is about not being able to explain particular outcomes. Two structural neorealist explanations have been offered that purport to explain why Britain in the 1930s did not balance adequately against Germany: buck-passing and distancing.

Once buck-passing and distancing were identified as the leading neorealist explanations for British behavior, the logic that lay behind their claims was explored and evidence that logic was looked for in the historical record. Specifically, the leadership of Stanley Baldwin and Neville Chamberlain as it relates to their involvement in the armament decisions of the 1930s was dissected to seek any motivation for their behavior that would indicate a cognizance of the structural imperatives said to be at work according to those theories.

The first structural theory, buck-passing, had argued that states in a multipolar international system in which perceptions of the dominance of defensive weapons systems prevail may choose to externalize the costs of defense to a second state that is also under threat in an attempt to ride free on the exertions that that state would make for its own defense. If that were so, then we would expect to see evidence of that logic operating in Britain.

The idea of the 1930s being an era of defense dominance is highly problematic. In the first case, in Britain certainly, the fear and obsession was over war in the air. War in the air was believed to have no possible active defense. Interceptor aircraft could punch holes in an attacking force, but they could not stop it entirely. As Stanley Baldwin famously summarized, "the bomber will always get through."

Even beyond air power, however, the idea of the 1930s being an era of defense dominance in land warfare is much a matter of who you ask. Both the Germans and the British recognized that the widespread diffusion of mechanized forces heralded the possibility of restoring the mobility of the offensive that had been lacking for most of the First World War. In predicting the opening stages of a war with Germany, the war office had written in 1935, "Either side may gain a great initial advantage by mobile operations conducted principally by mechanised forces and aircraft. . . . The value of mechanisation as an aid to the offensive is generally realised."[6] Chamberlain himself used the logic that the next war would move rapidly, a condition that indicates offensive dominance, for his claim made during the meetings of the Defence Policy Requirements (DPR) Committee in 1936 that Britain should focus on air power as its land forces would arrive too late to make a difference.[7]

The perception of defense dominance is crucial for the incentives for buck-passing to exist because it implies that the cost of not joining a war immediately will not be as high as they would be if early stages are believed to be decisive. Let us accept, however, despite the argument made earlier, that the 1930s were an era of defense dominance. Even so, the claim that Britain was looking to ride free on the French defensive effort is not substantiated by the documentary record. Certainly Baldwin accepted the idea that British security would rise or fall with France and not separate from her. Baldwin, in fact, expanded his concept of British borders for defense so widely that they included France and the Low Countries as well. Christensen and Snyder infer buck-passing from the lack of a land-based commitment to France. That is an erroneous conclusion. The lack of land-based capability was a fact, not because Baldwin was relying on France to secure Britain, but because he relied on Chamberlain.

Even Chamberlain, however, provides little confirmation of buck-passing. Chamberlain genuinely believed that Britain could contribute to her own security and to the security of France by focusing on air power. Therein lay his great mistake. Chamberlain's intention to secure Britain through its own efforts was sincere; it was his prescription on how to accomplish that task that was flawed.

Distancing logic, argued by Randall Schweller, suggests that Britain sought to distance itself from France because France was the country more immediately threatened by Germany. It was Britain's hope that either the conquest of France would sate German appetites or, at least, by directing attention toward France, Britain would buy time for herself. The record, again, shows no indication that that was happening. Even the policy of appeasement for which Chamberlain is so notoriously recalled was at the expense of eastern states, not France. During the meetings of the ministerial committee in 1934, in fact, Chamberlain recognized France as a reasonable cause worth fighting over, as opposed to Czechoslovakia.

Britain did fail to effectively balance, but not for the structural reasons that Christensen, Snyder, and Schweller suggest. It is, rather, because Baldwin and Chamberlain did not perform their tasks as leaders well. It was their responsibility to oversee the generation of the necessary power to either deter Germany or to deny her access to the air fields and support from which costly attacks on Britain could be launched. That they did not do: Baldwin because he defined his role as leader in such a way that prevented him from asserting authority over a bullying chancellor and Chamberlain because he believed in himself and the wisdom of his insights over the advice of experts.

THE GENERATION OF POWER AND EFFECTIVE BALANCES OF POWER

The previous chapters have looked in great detail at the narrow span of moments in British history when the decisions of how to arm the United Kingdom in the face of a rising Germany were made. These were formative moments. Certain decisions that could have been taken, and indeed were advised to be taken by British military experts, would have produced the kind of material capability and defense posture that may have succeeded in deterring Germany from the western adventure it undertook in the spring of 1940 or at least in blunting its probability of success. That advice was not heeded as British leaders, particularly Chamberlain, produced their own diagnosis of the situation, a diagnosis that was different than that of the military elites. Chamberlain's diagnosis led to a prescription for correction different than what the military favored and ultimately to an emphasis on the production of weapons, which failed to meet the most basic requirement of an effective balance of power.

An effective balance of power, whether it is an intentionally desired outcome or an accidental one, is the result of the matching of the capabilities of state A with the vulnerabilities of state B. That process of identifying the vulnerabilities of a second state and making policy decisions that take advantage of those vulnerabilities is taken by leaders whose relative skill at the task can vary greatly. Leaders can desire to balance sincerely and still fail to do so effectively. Leaders can be smart and rational and still fail to appreciate the exact calibration of their vulnerabilities and capabilities in relation to a rival.

Both Stanley Baldwin and Neville Chamberlain were desirous that Britain should balance against Germany. That was their intention; it was not the outcome. Kenneth Waltz has argued that because, very often, intentions do not match outcomes in international politics, some variable must intervene between the intentions of the leaders and the actual outcomes. Waltz believes that behaviors induced by the structure of the international system explain why intentions and outcomes often do not match up in international politics. Yet, in this case, neither his structural explanation nor those of theorists who attempt to produce subsidiary theories within the structural framework adequately explain this particular outcome.

Waltz is correct that intentions and outcomes do not always match up in international politics. Waltz is also correct that there is a variable that intervenes between intentions and outcomes that explains why that deviation occurs. Where Waltz is mistaken is in his insistence that it is systemic forces that are compelling the deviation. The variable that intervenes between intentions and outcomes in international relations is the skills of the leaders on who sits the responsibility for creating policies that generate the power that is the ultimate arbitrator of international conflict.

The experience of Baldwin and Chamberlain shows how leaders intervene between the intention to balance and the outcome of a failure to balance effectively. Both Baldwin and Chamberlain believed that they were doing what was necessary to create power sufficient to deter Germany and to form a balance. Chamberlain even sought to call attention to the role that he played in "saving" Britain from crisis by overruling the advice of experts. Chamberlain wrote to his colleagues in 1936 to remind them that the experts' "proposals for the treatment of the Air Force were seriously under-estimated and must be substantially increased" and that the correctness of his insistence on building airplanes at the expense of tanks and other land forces "has been proved by what has happened since"[8]

Chamberlain's insistence on air power was misguided. Britain needed a land-based capability for all the reasons that the military chiefs, Robert Vanssitart and Maurice Hankey, had been arguing for years. First of all, it would have represented a token of goodwill to France and Belgium who the Chiefs had pointed out in 1934, esteemed such a contribution. Equally importantly, as Vansittart argued, it would convince the Germans of the seriousness of Britain's intentions to fulfill its guarantee to Belgium and France under the Treaty of Locarno and the Covenant of the League of Nations, although the strongest argument in favor of a land-based army was that British security could not rely on air power alone because even the best air power could not protect Britain if Germany succeeded in establishing air and sea bases on the channel coast. Finally, as Lord Londonderry pointed out, could air power alone could not prevent Germany from establishing such bases.

Colonel Hankey summarized the situation well in his passionately written letter to Baldwin in 1936. "Some day," he wrote, "the future of armaments may change," but that day had not yet come. The only way to either successfully deter Germany from a western adventure to begin with, or hold her back once one began, was to use a mechanized force to thwart the attack.

The traditional supreme aim of British foreign policy has been to deny any continental power from achieving hegemony in Europe. In fulfillment of that role, Britain has been the "balancer," throwing its weight with one side or the other in order to keep the hegemonic aspirations of European powers in check. That role has always demanded that Britain maintain the ability to intervene territorially in Europe. The simple fact is, and was known to be at the time, that if Britain was to prevent Germany from achieving hegemony, she would have to come to Europe with men in arms just as she had in the ages of Marlborough and Wellington.

It is important to note, however, that this is not an endorsement of the view that the military is always correct and should always be listened to. As mentioned earlier, Eliot Cohen has written a convincing account of what makes for effective leaders of democracies in wartime. Cohen has shown that it is not the leaders who follow the advice of their military experts blindly but those who prod, argue, and needle their military men who obtain the best outcomes.

Effective leaders, however, do need to have some understanding of strategy and warfare if their prodding of the military is to yield fruitful results. The example that Cohen gives of Israel's founder, David Ben-Gurion, is most instructive. Ben-Gurion, Cohen writes, cloistered himself for months with military treatises in what he called "the seminar." Ben-Gurion wanted to become conversant in military matters so that he could make *educated* policy decisions when confronted by various options.[9] That, pointedly, is not what Chamberlain was doing. The question of a reliance on air power was less a question of strategy than of capability. Aerial weapons during the 1930s were not technically capable of performing the tasks that Chamberlain's conception of defense required them to be able to do. It was Chamberlain's refusal to listen to that fact that frustrated his advisors who would also, no less than Chamberlain, have liked to be able to spare British soldiers from having to wade once again in the mud of Europe.

Chamberlain's intervention was based on a nearly fatal combination of actual ignorance of military affairs with the ego to think that he understood all things better than anyone else. Baldwin, by contrast, did not challenge the need for Britain to make ready a land based commitment to Europe along the lines of what was recommended to him by the Defence Requirements Committee (DRC). Baldwin's great shortcoming is that he refused to issue an order to the chancellor to finance an effort commensurate with the DRC's recommendations. Baldwin treated Chamberlain as an equal, when in fact he was his superior in both the government and the party. By refusing to issue directives to Chamberlain, he allowed the chancellor to substitute his own spending preferences over those with which Baldwin himself expressed sympathy.

If Baldwin must be found guilty as an accomplice, it is Chamberlain who must bear the brunt of the guilt for Britain's eventual fate. The necessity of a land-based army is not just hindsight wisdom but was known at the time. Although it is true that air power was relatively new, it was not entirely untested. As Field Marshal Montgomery-Massingberd wrote, where a reliance on air power had been tested it had failed to live up to its billing. Air power could not do what it promised to even in conditions, like in Abyssinia or in Spain, for which it was best suited. The uses that Chamberlain conceived of for air power, to include both deterrent impact on Germany and offensive uses if deterrence failed, simply did not account for the technical limitations that Ellington, Londonderry, and Swinton repeatedly apprised him of. British planes could not keep German forces out of France and the Low Countries, could not protect Britain, and could not be used to inflict substantial harm on Germany. All of this Chamberlain was made aware of, yet he insisted on the validity of his own logic over both the evidence and the counsel of professionals.

To the extent that counterfactual reasoning is ever certain, we can be sure that if other statesmen held greater sway outcomes would likely have been very different. Put simply, some senior members of the government understood the imperative of fielding a competent army but they were sidelined by Chamberlain. Lord Hailsham in particular comes to mind as one whom, had he been given a greater position of authority, would have made different decisions. This is to say nothing of Winston Churchill, whom we can only imagine that if he had known the direness that was to befall Great Britain in 1933–39 would have chosen his battles with Baldwin more carefully. If Churchill had not bolted the senior ranks over India in 1931, perhaps he would have been able to return to the chancellorship when the national government was formed. Churchill had ousted Chamberlain from that position before. If that had happened then rather than being a doleful voice in the wilderness, he could have been in 11 Downing Street during the crucial years when decisions needed to be made that would have made Britain more secure in the face of the Nazi threat.

LEADERSHIP IN INTERNATIONAL RELATIONS THEORY: PAST AND FUTURE

Although the key lesson of this book and, indeed, the purpose for which it was written, was to make an argument about the balance of power as a deliberate act of policy created by leaders, for academic theorists, the broader argument about the merit of the inclusion of leadership and other nonmaterial variables in international relations theorizing should be noted as well. Even those variables that will significantly hamper the ability of international relations theory to generate falsifiable predictions should be included in studies of international relations if they can be shown to have had a determinative impact. I agree with Byman and Pollack, who in their consideration of leadership wrote, "We dismiss the contention that parsimony is somehow more important than accuracy when deriving political science theory."[10] They also wrote, however, that "the field of international relations theory is an effort to explain the interaction of states, and, ultimately predict their behavior." Although I agree with the first part of the statement, I have some hesitation over the second. The goal of being able to predict how states will behave is an understandable aim to which to aspire, but the reality is that states, impacted as they may be by systemic or institutional constraints, are governed by people whose relative skills in interpreting what actions those constraints necessitate will vary greatly. Both Baldwin and Chamberlain knew that Britain *should* balance against Germany, but neither of them knew *how* to balance against Germany. And that that made a great deal of difference.

Whatever claims international relations theory makes, whether neorealist, neoliberal, or everything in between, should all be qualified by the recognition that it is leaders who move the machinery of international politics. The goal of theorists should be to develop tools and methods that aid in understanding the impact of those leaders better. Experts on international politics should not pretend that leaders do not matter just because, at present, we do not have great tools for incorporating their role into the type of theory we strive for. The challenge, as Byman and Pollack suggested, remains to find a way to reconcile scientific rigor with difficult to quantify nonmaterial variables.

The conclusions of this project on the determinative role of leaders in shaping outcomes in translating structurally induced constraints into policy outcomes also provide some guidance as to how the guidance proffered to policy makers who wish to be informed by international relations theory should be couched. "This is what theory tells us a rival should do," we can tell those who ask. "What they will do though, depends in large measure, on the skills their own leaders possess in terms of diagnosis, prescription and their ability to mobilize support for their preferred policies."

Finally, the practical takeaway from this project is the insight that effective balance of power formation must be, with the exception of the rare happenstance, the intentional result of a thoughtful pairing of capabilities to vulnerabilities. Simply being strong is not enough to balance a would-be rival. To paraphrase Sun Tzu, a state needs to be strong where the other is weak. Achieving that targeted strength will likely deter a rival state if it recognizes its own vulnerabilities. If it does not, such targeted strength will allow the balancing state to acquit itself well on the field of battle and so prevent a disastrous outcome.

THE BALANCE OF POWER IN THE TWENTY-FIRST CENTURY

Much has obviously changed since the 1930s. The Second World War destroyed the old mutipolar system and a new bipolar structure emerged in its wake. Nuclear weapons that were barely imagined when the war began were detonated in action during the last days of fighting and their proliferation, in absolute numbers of total weapons in the world and in the destructive power of those weapons has grown almost beyond measure. The number of states possessing nuclear weapons is likewise on the rise.

Some scholars have argued that the international system has gotten past war as a means of resolving international disputes and that war is now a disgraced and discarded social institution.[1] Others argue that the suspicion that breeds war in the presence of structural anarchy remains, but that the development of nuclear arsenals capable of causing existential retaliatory damage even in the event of first having absorbed a totally surprising initial blow has made the past poor prologue for the present.[2]

Those of us who witnessed the end of the Cold War are shocked to discover that we have come to miss some of the predictable stability provided by the balance of power between the Americans and the Soviet Union. In the decade of American triumphalism that followed the fall of the Berlin Wall, the question of how to balance power fell completely by the wayside as the newer question of how long America's hegemony might last came to the fore. The conventional wisdom had it that unipolar international systems, which the world experienced in the mid-1990s, were quite unstable, but some prominent scholars argued that they were far more durable than was previously believed.[3]

Regardless, the days of unipolar hegemony are over. The overextension of American military forces during the first decade of this century and the erosion of America's hegemonic role in the world economy have brought the prospect of major power rivalry, if not major power war, roaring back to the present. Russia, although dependent on natural resource commodity exports, has advanced its process of regional reassertion, not least with a quick and successful war in Georgia in the summer of 2008.

China too, has to be taken seriously as a great power. Not only does its enormous population command respect, its bold expansion into the global economy and particularly the vastness of its dollar holdings make it perhaps the second most important player in global finance. Nor have China's military ambitions been neglected. A manned space program and a blue-water navy have both accompanied the independence of Chinese diplomacy of the last several years and fueled that independence as well.

Europe and Japan no longer march in lock step with the United States either. The global economic recession has highlighted some significant differences between the United States and some of its closest residual allies but for Japan especially, the question of east Asian stability among nuclear rivals in China and North Korea is especially vexing.

The proliferation of nuclear weapons, too, has changed the basic calculus. States with small populations and little by way of traditional wealth and power who were irrelevant to international politics in decades past can now command significant attention by dint of their nuclear status. The destructive power of even crude nuclear devices has an equalizer effect in international politics allowing smaller countries to punch above their weight and, more important for this project, raising complicated questions about how to engineer a new and effective balance of power. And that brings the circle fully back to leadership.

The key theme of this book is that the balance of power is a deliberate act of policy and that the effectiveness of balancing behavior in either deterring war or in limiting its geopolitical effects lies in the skills of leaders as diagnosticians of threat, prescribers of remedies, and mobilizers of support to make those often unpopular prescriptions into policy.

The balance of power in the twenty-first century will not be created by accident. Leaders must first diagnose the threats that require balancing against. The proliferation of nuclear weapons is often discussed as a threat and, indeed, preventing Iraq from crossing the nuclear threshold was one of President Bush's core arguments about why the 2003 invasion was necessary. President Obama, and those who will follow him, will need to ask themselves whether *all* nuclear proliferation is a threat, or only nuclear acquisition by certain rogues? If only certain states, which ones? In other words, they must diagnose the nature and the vector of the threat.

These questions matter a great deal as the prescriptions follow therefrom. For example, balancing against a large nuclear power likely requires a significant retaliatory capability in order to promote deterrence, while balancing the power of a smaller nuclear state, like North Korea, may be best achieved by the construction of missile defenses that render the small North Korean arsenal less dangerous but will have little impact on defending attacks from a larger nuclear nation. Alternatively, as Keir Leiber and Daryl Press have argued, perhaps the right prescription will be for a new class of nuclear arms that can effectively preempt small nuclear rogues from using their weapons successfully.[4] From the Chinese perspective, if the relationship with the United States turns more competitive, than their reliance on a few dozen large yield nuclear weapons delivered by slow-to-prepare liquid fueled missiles may need to be rethought if a more effective balance to American might is sought.

Leaders will also have to decide whether conventional war remains likely or even possible and, if it does, which states are the most threatening? These questions, too, will impact the balance of power because if states wish to have the ability to project conventional power as a part of their balancing strategy then prescriptions for enhanced airlift, sealift, communications, and other ancillary technologies—to say nothing of an expansion in the number of troops available for service—may be necessary.

In Western nations other than the United States, it is not hard to see how the return of the balance of power requires the refinement of skills long dormant in their national leaderships. A multipolar world in which the U.S. security guarantee cannot be taken for granted will require European nations to develop new capabilities as a part of their own balancing strategies, and a bit of *schadenfreude* is taken at the thought of European leaders attempting to mobilize support for balancing strategies, which will necessitate arms buildups.

In East Asia the problem is particularly acute as China, Russia, North and South Korea, Japan, the United States, and even nations further afield such as Burma and Australia all find themselves desperately designing new balancing strategies in the untested situation in which multiple states possesses nuclear weapons in a nonbipolar matrix. As with the case examined in this book, there is no model for states to follow in East Asia in terms of how to balance and today's leaders must set themselves to the tasks of diagnosis, prescription, and mobilization if a dangerously unstable situation is to take on the regulated, predictable tensions of a well-balanced international system.

In the final analysis, while much has changed in international politics, much has stayed the same. Today's leaders have much to learn from the past about the roles they are to play, about the combination of humility and confidence that they need to possess, and about the enormity of effort required to produce an effectively balanced and stable international system.

APPENDIX I

BIOGRAPHICAL SKETCH

STANLEY BALDWIN

When Stanley Baldwin was summoned to the cabinet from his vacation at the French resort of Aix-les-Bain on October 1, 1922, he returned to London with the understanding that he was about to quit political life. Baldwin, at the time president of the board of trade, a cabinet post that he had held for a little over a year after five years as the junior minister at the treasury, had had enough of David Lloyd George, a man he referred to as "the Goat." Baldwin deeply resented what he felt to be the loss of the authentic Conservative party of which he was a member, as it ingratiated itself in order to serve in Lloyd George's Liberal-led coalition. When the issue arose during that fall over how the party should present itself in the upcoming elections, as coalitionists or as Conservatives, Baldwin bucked the leadership and demanded to stand as a Conservative. Baldwin summed up the situation in a letter to his mother, saying, "They will follow the G[oat] and I can't, so it means I shall drop out of politics altogether."[1]

Contrary to his expectations, Baldwin's defiance spread like wildfire, and within three weeks of his return to London, the Goat was out and Stanley Baldwin had pushed him there. Bonar Law, the sickly leader of the Conservative Party, assumed the premiership, offering the choice prize of the chancellorship of the exchequer to the man who had restored the fortunes of the Conservative Party. At first Baldwin declined the post, suggesting that Law offer it instead to Reginald McKenna, who had been chancellor in the last Conservative government of Herbert Asquith. When McKenna declined, Law renewed his request that Baldwin accept the post, and this time Baldwin did.

Law, quite ill upon assuming the premiership, did not last long under its strains. Barely a year into his term, he was diagnosed with cancer and was compelled to resign. After a brief period during which King George V deliberated between calling on Baldwin to form the next government or the far more experienced Lord Curzon, the king summoned Baldwin. After less than three years of cabinet experience and barely one as a senior member, Baldwin found himself moving into 10 Downing Street for what would prove to be the first of three terms as prime minister.

Baldwin's first term did not last long. By the beginning of January 1924 he had resigned the premiership, although he remained the leader of the Conservative Party, which was still the largest in the Commons. Baldwin relished this time out of government because it allowed John Ramsay MacDonald to assume the premiership. Mac-Donald was the leader of the Labour Party, a party that, although untested in leadership and almost nonexistent before the Great War, had now overtaken the Liberals as the second largest party in the Commons. The rise of the Labour Party came about, among other things, from the broad expansion of the franchise that came at the end of the war. Baldwin and many others were concerned as to what bent the Labour Party and its voters might take. Given the so recent rise of communism in Russia, the even more recent turn to fascism in Italy, and the tremendous instability of France's Fourth Republic, there was a very real question over whether the Labour Party, following the lead of other European socialists, would try to wrench the United Kingdom toward a radical socialism or whether it would be loyal to the parliamentary rules of the game both in government and in opposition. Baldwin clearly favored the latter outcome and thought that giving Labour a taste of government would go a long way toward maturing the Labour Party, especially since he did not expect Mac-Donald's minority government to last long, which in fact it did not.

Baldwin's second term, which began just ten months after his first ended, was to be his longest uninterrupted stint as prime minister and lasted until 1929. His resignation in June 1929 turned out to be yet another brief interlude away from power. As before, he was succeeded in the premiership by Ramsay MacDonald. The crisis of the world economic collapse brought MacDonald to the brink of resignation. MacDonald went to the king, who urged that a national unity government be formed to deal with the crisis. The king conferred with Herbert Samuel, head of the Liberals, and with Baldwin. The king asked Baldwin whether he would be willing to serve under MacDonald during this time of emergency. Baldwin, despite his bitter recollections of coalition experience under Lloyd George, felt that he could not refuse his sovereign's request. The national government was formed in August 1931 with John Ramsay MacDonald as prime minister and Stanley Baldwin as lord president of the council.

The national government went to the people for a mandate in November 1931. The government won a crushing victory, giving them a majority of 556 seats, of which 473 were Conservative. The opposition was composed of only 85 members in total. Fifty two of those were members of the Labour party who did not support MacDonald and the remainder were members of the Liberal party who were led by Lloyd George. Despite the fact that National Labour only constituted 13 of the government's 556 seats, Baldwin stuck to his promise that MacDonald would be the prime minister. Still, the sheer number of government supporters who came from the Conservative Party meant that Baldwin would have far more power than any previous lord president, or any later one at that. From November 1931 until he assumed the premiership from the physically and mentally failing Ramsay MacDonald in May 1935, Baldwin exercised an influence disproportionate to his formal rank. In many ways, Baldwin was able to exercise a greater influence over events than he might have if he had been prime minister. Baldwin's biographers argue that

> Although only second in command . . . increased power devolved almost automatically on him. When MacDonald was ill, he took the chair in Cabinet and also on the all-important Cabinet Committee on Disarmament, where many decisions about defence and scale of armaments were discussed. . . . MacDonald declined in stature and respect and after the middle of 1934, as he failed physically, Baldwin prepared to fill the gap. Increasingly he took over as Leader of the House of Commons.[2]

Baldwin's biographers comment that with regard to the issue of disarmament and rearmament—around which, perhaps unfairly, much of the debate about Baldwin's legacy hinges—"behind the scenes . . . he was able to do much for rearmament in the air and quite probably more than if he had the myriad responsibilities of Prime Minister."[3]

MacDonald's infirmities became so glaringly obvious as the 1930s wore on that Baldwin, despite having serious reservations about whether he even wanted a third term as prime minister, felt compelled to accept one. Baldwin swapped places with MacDonald in May 1935 and retained the leadership until, having successfully negotiated the painful abdication of King Edward VIII, he, too, chose to leave the stage. As Baldwin commented to the cabinet at their final meeting under his leadership, he had always said that he intended to step down and that he wanted to give Chamberlain at least two years as prime minister before the next general election would be called.[4]

With that, Baldwin's political career came to an end except for a few speeches that he made in the House of Lords, where he was seated after being made the Earl of Bewdley in 1937. Baldwin retired to the family estate at Astley and died there in 1947.

Appendix II

Biographical Sketch

Neville Chamberlain

Neville Chamberlain was the second son of Joseph Chamberlain, a long-serving cabinet minister during the latter part of the nineteenth century whose picture, like that of both of his sons, continues to hang in the National Portrait Gallery in London. Neville's older half brother, Austen, was designated early on as the heir to the political legacy of the family and was sent by Joseph Chamberlain to Cambridge and thence on a grand journey through Europe in order to prepare for the assumption of a prominent role in British public life. Neville, it was decided, would pursue a career in business and manage the family's wealth. Neville did not attend university but, rather, studied engineering and metallurgy at Mason College in Birmingham. After his schooling, Chamberlain set out on the path established for him. Chamberlain's first business undertaking was a risky venture to start a sisal plantation in the Bahamas.

Chamberlain had reported to his father that profits in excess of 30 percent could be expected, and on that basis the elder Chamberlain had authorized the venture. The sisal plantation failed, although the failure of the venture had less to do with Chamberlain's management and more to do with his poor judgment in thinking the Caribbean suitable ground for that particular commodity. Chamberlain returned to the United Kingdom and assumed a position of relative prominence in the banking industry in his home town of Birmingham, where he encountered material success and more than recouped the losses that the Caribbean adventure has created.

With time, however, Chamberlain's interests drew him to politics and by 1915 he became the lord mayor of Birmingham. As mayor he quickly established a reputation for efficiency that attracted national attention; he was called upon in 1915 by the minister of munitions, David Lloyd George, to help regulate the consumption of alcohol during the war. The following years brought Chamberlain more governmental experience when he served as director-general of national service. Chamberlain's tenure in that post was unremarkable save for the fact that it convinced him that he needed to gain parliamentary experience in order to be an effective national statesman. Chamberlain sought election to Parliament in the general election of 1918 and was elected to represent Birmingham in the Commons. Chamberlain's rise from the backbenches was swift, although during these early years of his parliamentary career he was still under the shadow of his more famous elder brother.

When Baldwin assumed the premiership from Bonar Law in 1924, after a time, he transferred the control of the exchequer to Chamberlain. When Baldwin constituted his second ministry in 1924 after ten months out of power, Chamberlain was moved to the health ministry to make way for Winston Churchill, who had returned to the Conservative Party (after his prolonged stint as a Liberal and supporter of Lloyd George) to serve as chancellor. During this ministry, both Chamberlain brothers sat in cabinet, and although Neville worked quite hard, it was Austen, the foreign secretary, who shone, winning the Nobel Peace Prize in 1925 for his role in bringing about the Treaty of Locarno.

Six year later, when Baldwin led the Conservatives into the national government, Austen had agreed to pass on the cabinet post to which he was entitled in order to make room for younger men. Neville became the chancellor of the exchequer and heir apparent to the leadership of the Conservative Party. Chamberlain held on to both positions with tenacity and was rewarded with nearly unparalleled influence as a consequence of the first and eventual supreme leadership as a consequence of the second.

Notes

Introduction

1. Robert O. Keohane and Joseph S. Nye, *Power and Interdependence* (New York: Longman, 2001), chap. 1.
2. Francis Fukuyama, *The End of History and the Last Man* (New York: Free Press, 2006).
3. Robert A. Doughty, "The Maginot Line," *MHQ: The Quarterly Journal of Military History* 9, no. 2 (1997): 48–59, especially 51.
4. Brian Bond, *British Military Policy between the Two World Wars* (Oxford: Clarendon Press, 1980), 201–2.
5. On the insistence of Sir Thomas Inskip, minister for the coordination of defence, to build fighters while the air ministry wanted bombers, see Charles Webster and Noble Frankland, *The Strategic Air Offensive Against Germany: 1939–1945, Vol. 1* (London: Her Majesty's Stationary Office, 1961), 75–77, or Tami D. Biddle, *Rhetoric and Reality in Air Warfare* (Princeton, NJ: Princeton University Press, 2002), 121.
6. J. P. Harris, "British Armour and Rearmament in the 1930s," *The Journal of Strategic Studies* 11, no. 2 (June 1988): 220.
7. Ibid., 236.
8. Ibid., 228.
9. Bond, *British Military*, 180.
10. Ibid., 187.
11. Quoted in Bond, *British Military*, 190.
12. B. H. Liddel Hart, *History of the Second World War* (New York: G. B. Putnam's & Sons, 1971), 117.
13. For more on Percy Hobart, see Trevor J. Constable, *Hidden Heroes* (London: Arthur Baker's Ltd., 1971).
14. Arend Lijphart, "Comparative Politics and the Comparative Method," *The American Political Science Review* 65, no. 3 (September 1971): 683.
15. Ibid., 691.
16. Alexander George, "Case Studies and Theory Development: The Method of Structured, Focused Comparison," in *Diplomacy: New Approaches in History, Theory and Policy*, Paul Gordon Lauren, ed. (New York: Free Press, 1979), 58.
17. James D. Fearon, "Counterfactuals and Hypothesis Testing Political Science," *World Politics* 43 (1991): 169.

18. Fearon, "Counterfactuals," 170.
19. Robert Jervis, *System Effects: Complexity in Political and Social Life* (Princeton, NJ: Princeton University Press, 1987).
20. George, "Case Studies," 44.
21. Baldwin had wanted to bring Churchill into the cabinet but he was thwarted in that endeavor by his Tory colleagues. Baldwin, however, looked on the bright side, and wrote to a friend about Churchill saying, "If there is going to be a war—and no can say there is not—we must keep him fresh to be our War Prime Minister." Quoted in Kenneth Young, *Stanley Baldwin* (London: Weidenfeld and Nicolson, 1976), 112.

CHAPTER 1

1. Kenneth N. Waltz, *Theory of International Politics* (Reading, MA: Addison-Wesley, 1979).
2. Kenneth N. Waltz, "Anarchic Orders and Balances of Power," in *Neorealism and Its Critics*, Robert O. Keohane, ed. (New York: Columbia University Press, 1986), 120–21.
3. Steven R. David, "Explaining Third World Alignment," *World Politics* 43, no. 2 (January 1991): 234.
4. Kenneth N. Waltz, "Anarchic Orders and Balances of Power," 125.
5. See Joseph S. Nye, Jr. "Soft *Power*: The Means to Success in World Politics," *Foreign Affairs* 83, no. 3 (May–June 2004): 136–37. See also *The Paradox of American Power: Why the World's Only Superpower Can't Go It Alone* (Oxford: Oxford University Press, 2002).
6. See, for example, Robert Jervis, *The Meaning of the Nuclear Revolution: Statecraft and the Prospect of Armageddon* (Ithaca, NY: Cornell University Press, 1989) and John Lewis Gaddis, *The Long Peace: Inquiries into the History of the Cold War* (New York: Oxford University Press, 1987).
7. Russia was not a signatory.
8. Pact of Paris, August 27, 1928, Article I.
9. Treaty of Mutual Guarantee between Germany, Belgium, France, Great Britain, and Italy; October 16, 1925, Article 2.
10. E. H. Carr, *The Twenty Years' Crisis 1919–1939: An Introduction to the Study of International Relations* (London: Papermac, 1939/1991), Chapter 4.
11. Ibid., 44–47.
12. *Ibid.*, 52–53.
13. Hans J. Morgenthau, *Scientific Man versus Power Politics* (Chicago: Chicago University Press, 1946), chap. 3.
14. Ibid., chap. 7.
15. Ibid., 191–96.
16. Hans J. Morgenthau, *Politics among Nations: The Struggle for Power and Peace* (New York: Knopf, 1985), 3.
17. Ibid., 3–4.

18. Ibid., 33, 35.
19. Ibid., 39–40.
20. Kenneth N. Waltz, "Political Structures," in *Neorealism and Its Critics*, Robert O. Keohane, ed. (New York: Columbia University Press, 1986), 81.
21. With the exception of the institutions of the European Union (EU), there are no true "supranational" organizations in world politics. And, although it has yet to be tested, the states of the EU remain sovereign and could at any time opt out of the organization entirely should their interests no longer be served by participating in it. Private citizens of a state have no such option vis-à-vis the institutions of the state that have authority over them.
22. Waltz, "Anarchic Orders," 101.
23. Ibid., 103.
24. Ibid., 110.
25. On the difficulty of making predicatively relevant theory in international relations, see Hans J. Morgenthau, *Truth and Power* (New York: Praeger, 1970), 253–58.
26. Waltz, "Anarchic Orders," 121.
27. Ibid., 125.
28. Ibid., 125.
29. Thomas Christensen and Jack Snyder, "Chain Gangs and Passed Bucks: Predicting Alliance Patterns in Multipolarity," *International Organization*. 44, no. 2 (Spring 1990): 137–38.
30. Christensen and Snyder, "Chain Gangs," 138.
31. One expansion of structural neorealism that will not be addressed because it falls outside of the scope of interest of this project but that readers are strongly encouraged to familiarize themselves with is Robert Gilpin's *War and Change in World Politics* (Cambridge: Cambridge University Press, 1981). This book should be viewed as a necessary companion piece to Waltz's because it explains systemic change within a structuralist paradigm.
32. Waltz, "Anarchic Orders," 116.
33. See, for example, Henry Kissinger, *A World Restored: Metternich, Castlereagh and the Problems of Peace, 1812–1822* (Boston: Houghton Mifflin, 1957/1973).
34. Bandwagoning is a behavior in which a state will ally with a stronger power rather than balance against it. Bandwagoning is more fully discussed later in this chapter.
35. Stephen M. Walt, "Alliance Formation and the Balance of World Power," *International Security* 9, no. 4 (Spring 1985): 8.
36. Ibid., 8.
37. There is an entire universe of extremely complex literature on this subject of calculating the "power" of states, generally known as "net assessment." For an illustration of some of the difficulties involved, see William W. Kaufmann, *Assessing the Base Force: How Much Is Too Much?* (Washington, DC: The Brookings Institution, 1992); Stephen Biddle, *Military*

Power: Explaining Victory and Defeat in Modern Battle (Princeton, NJ: Princeton University Press, 2004).

38. This question ties into the ancient one framed by Thucydides that has come to be referred to as the "security dilemma" in which the actions taken in defense by one state are not perceived that way by an adversary who then counters them, purely defensively. This action is perceived by the first state as being hostile and so it takes further measures to counter them and so on and so forth. For a good overview on the security dilemma, see John H. Herz, *International Politics in the Modern Age* (New York: Columbia University Press, 1959), 231–35. The question became increasingly important during the Cold War in terms of nuclear weapons doctrine with "defensive" weapons, like ballistic missile shields being "bad" and "offensive" weapons, like the virtually undetectable submarine-launched ballistic missiles being "good." To sum up the general argument, however, few weapons are either clearly offensive or defensive. For most weapon systems, the question is how they are employed that makes the difference. Other than Herz, the canonical statement on the security dilemma comes from Robert Jervis, "Cooperation under the Security Dilemma," *World Politics* 30 (January, 1978): 167–214.

39. Walt, "Alliance Formation," 12–13.

40. In fact, as Alexander Wendt has recently pointed out, even Waltz has significant ideational elements that lie at the root of his theory, although he is not explicit about them, a point for which Wendt takes him sternly to task. See Alexander Wendt, *Social Theory of International Relations* (Cambridge: Cambridge University Press, 2000), 103–9.

41. Not everyone agrees with the idea that bandwagoning is an alternative to balancing or that the term applies to all "opposite-of-balancing" situations. Steven David argues that in some cases, particularly in the developing world, it is really just a variant of balancing in which the threatened state makes an "accommodation, made to conserve strength for the battle against the prime threat" as a part of "a general policy of resistance." David, "Explaining Third World Alignment," 236.

42. Walt, "Alliance Formation," 16–18.

43. Adolf Hitler, *Mein Kampf*, Ralph Manheim, trans. (Boston: Houghton Mifflin Company, 1943/1971), 3.

44. Very few scholars take issue with the suggestion that Hitler both intended and sought war. Perhaps the most notable detractor from that thesis is A. J. P. Taylor. Taylor's book, *The Origins of the Second World War* (London: Penguin Books, 1961, 1991), makes the argument that Hitler never intended to go to war, certainly not with France and England at least. Taylor makes the case that more than Hitler having defined foreign policy aims, he took advantage of opportunities as they presented themselves. Thus, for example, Taylor argues that the union with Austria as well as the issue of the Sudeten Germans were foisted upon him and were not rather occurring under his direction. To that end, Taylor suggests

that Hitler had no reason to suspect that war would erupt over Poland any more than it had over similar issues and using similar methods as he had with Austria and Czechoslovakia. Even if one accepts that argument that Taylor makes, all he really proves is that the specific events that occurred were not directed by Hitler. He does not, critically, prove that Hitler would not have done something about them sooner or later anyway. The fact remains, as mentioned above, that Hitler makes very plain his ambitions in *Mein Kampf* and that both the union with Austria and the repatriation of all ethnic Germans to the Reich was a necessary step. The great strength of Taylor's argument is not in the detail but, rather, in the theme, which may be simplistically summarized as "What do you expect?" This means that after nearly a full decade of giving Hitler what he wanted, why should Hitler have expected that the issue over which war ultimately was declared would be so treated? It was, after all, no different than any of the others.

45. Waltz, *Theory of International Politics*, 165.
46. Jervis has written about the how the dynamics of the security dilemma are impacted by the dominance of either offensive weapon systems or defensive weapon systems at any given time. See note 37.
47. Christensen and Snyder, "Chain Gangs," 145.
48. Tami D. Biddle, *Rhetoric and Reality in Air Warfare* (Princeton, NJ: Princeton University Press, 2002), 102–10.
49. The only reference that suggests a form of buck-passing to Russia on record is a comment made by Stanley Baldwin to a deputation of Conservative MPs, in which he suggests, "If there is any fighting in Europe to be done, I should like to see the Bolshies and the Nazis doing it." Philip Williamson and Edward Baldwin, eds., *Baldwin Papers: A Conservative Statesman* (Cambridge: Cambridge University Press, 2004), 379.

   Neither the comment nor the implications that could be drawn from it were referred to again in any official forum or in any other private correspondence.
50. Randall L. Schweller, *Deadly Imbalances: Tripolarity and Hitler's Strategy of World Conquest* (New York: Columbia University Press, 1998), 73.
51. Ibid., 71
52. Ibid.
53. Neville Chamberlain noted in a letter to his sister Hilda that although the treaty had annoyed the French, the British would be able to show the French that "the Treaty is good not only for us but for them." Robert C. Self, *The Neville Chamberlain Diary Letters, Vol. 4* (London Ashgate, 2004), 141. By reducing Britain's naval anxieties, the treaty would allow Britain to marshal more of its resources into other arms that would be part and parcel of the British contribution to the limited liability scheme, which will be discussed later.
54. Randall L. Schweller, "Tripolarity and the Second World War," *International Studies Quarterly* 37, no. 1 (March 1993): 87.

55. Presidential Declaration 44 Declaration 2405. May 11, 1940.
56. A. J. P. Taylor, *English History: 1914–1945* (New York: Oxford University Press, 1965), 416.
57. Ibid., 446.
58. Which, if true, would be yet another hard case for Kenneth Waltz, whose *Theory of International Politics* is, as Christensen and Snyder point out, far more interested in demonstrating the inherent stability of bipolar systems than he is in the nuance of either system. (See Christensen and Snyder, "Chain Gangs," 142.)
59. Schweller, "Tripolarity," 88.
60. Schweller, *Deadly Imbalances*, 7.
61. That is, whether they are revisionist or status quo.
62. Randall L. Schweller, *Unanswered Threats: Political Constraints on the Balance of Power* (Princeton, NJ: Princeton University Press, 2006).
63. Randall Schweller, *Unanswered Threats*.

CHAPTER 2

1. The literature in the American Politics subfield has perhaps dealt with the issue most extensively in writings on the role that particular presidents play. The canonical text on this is Richard E. Neustadt, *Presidential Power and the Modern Presidents: The Politics of Leadership from Roosevelt to Reagan* (New York: Free Press, 1990). Another contribution to the genre is Stephen Skowronek, *The Politics Presidents Make: Leadership from John Adams to Bill Clinton* (Cambridge, MA: Harvard University Press, 1997). Some work on the topic has been less directly focused on the presidency and encompasses leadership within the American political culture more broadly. See Adam D. Sheingate, "Political Entrepreneurship, Institutional Change, and American Political Development," *Studies in American Political Development* 17 (Fall 2003): 185–203.
2. For the most part, the international relations literature is silent on the topic, leading students to infer the role that leaders may play more from what is either assumed or not said than what is. Within the discipline, the most illustrative case of the irrelevance of leadership comes from the explicitly structural work of Kenneth Waltz. One of Waltz's most intriguing and controversial contributions comes from his piece *The Spread of Nuclear Weapons: More May Be Better* (London: International Institute for Strategic Studies, 1981). Waltz argues that because nuclear weapons have a stabilizing effect, their spread to conflict zones should be encouraged rather than discouraged. This argument, logical on its face, flies against the common wisdom in policy circles. In Waltz, whether the state is guided by Saddam Hussein or Mother Theresa makes no difference; the stabilizing effect of the weapons is the same. Most people would not agree with that conclusion. Indeed, Scott Sagan has forcefully denounced Waltz's argument in Scott D. Sagan and Kenneth N. Waltz, *The Spread*

of Nuclear Weapons: A Debate (New York: W. W. Norton, 1995). Sagan points out that the efficacy of nuclear weapons as a stabilizing element is contingent on their rational employment by the actor possessing them and that that rationality should not be assumed to apply equally in all cases. The essence of Sagan's argument, although he does not frame it this way explicitly, is that leadership matters and that some leaders can be trusted, while others cannot. A nuclearized Saddamite Iraq was a concern, a nuclearized Israel less so. I thank Steven David for bringing this particular insight on the irrelevance of leadership to my attention. An exception to the silence on leadership is Margaret G. Hermann and Joe D. Hagan, "International Decision Making: Leadership Matters," *Foreign Policy*, Spring 1998, 124–37.

3. Daniel L. Byman and Kenneth M. Pollack, "Let Us Now Praise Great Men: Bringing the Statesmen Back In," *International Security* 25, no. 4 (Spring 2001): 108.

4. Robert C. Tucker, *Politics as Leadership: Revised Edition* (Columbia: University of Missouri Press, 1981/1995), 27.

5. For more examples of cases in which leaders are the *prima facie* cause of foreign policy outcomes, see Byman and Pollack, "Let Us Now," 114–133.

6. Byman and Pollack, "Let Us Now," 109.

7. Remarks by President John F. Kennedy on the occasion of the granting of an honorary citizenship to Winston Churchill, April 9, 1963.

8. Byman and Pollack, "Let Us Now," 108.

9. Ibid., 137.

10. Ibid., 113.

11. Ibid., 140.

12. Eliot A. Cohen, *Supreme Command: Soldiers, Statesmen and Leadership in Wartime* (New York: Free Press, 2002).

13. Jerrold M. Post and Robert S. Robbins, *When Illness Strikes the Leader: The Dilemma of the Captive King* (New Haven, CT: Yale University Press, 1993).

14. For examples of the "psychology of the leader" literature, see Raymond Birt, "Personality and Foreign Policy," *Political Psychology* 14, no. 4 (December 1993): 607–25; Jason M. Satterfield, "Cognitive Affective States Predict Military and Political Aggression and Risk-Taking: A Content Analysis of Churchill, Hitler, Roosevelt, and Stalin," *Journal of Conflict Resolution* 42, no. 6 (December 1998): 667–90; Daniel Rancour-Laferriere, *The Mind of Stalin: A Psychoanalytic Study* (Ann Arbor: Ardis, 1988); and Frederick C. Redlich, *Hitler: Diagnosis of a Destructive Prophet* (New York: Oxford University Press, 1998).

15. Richard J. Samuels, *Machiavelli's Children: Leaders and their Legacies in Italy and Japan* (Ithaca, NY: Cornell University Press, 2003).

16. Ibid., 1–2.

17. Ibid., 6.

18. Kenneth N. Waltz, "Anarchic Orders and Balances of Power," in *Neorealism and Its Critics*, Robert O. Keohane, ed. (New York: Columbia University Press, 1986), 117.

19. Deborah A. Stone, "Causal Stories and the Formation of Policy Agendas," *Political Science Quarterly* 104, no. 2 (Summer 1989): 282.

20. Ibid. 283.

21. Ibid., 282.

22. Robert D. Benford and David A. Snow, "Framing Processes and Social Movements: An Overview and Assessment," *Annual Review of Sociology* 26 (2000): 614.

23. Stone, "Causal Stories," 293.

24. There are several variants of the "theory of the democratic peace." For overviews, see Bruce Russet, *Grasping the Democratic Peace: Principles for a Post–Cold War World* (Princeton, NJ: Princeton University Press, 1993). See also the reader *Debating the Democratic Peace*, edited by Michael E. Brown, Sean M. Lynn-Jones, and Steven E. Miller (Cambridge, MA: MIT Press, 1996).

25. Alexander Wendt, *Social Theory of International Politics* (Cambridge: Cambridge University Press, 1999), 246–312.

26. Tucker, *Politics as Leadership*, 18–19.

27. Robert C. Tucker, "Personality and Political Leadership," *Political Science Quarterly* 92, no. 3 (Autumn 1977): 385–86.

CHAPTER 3

1. For a brief biographical sketch of Stanley Baldwin, see Appendix 1.

2. Not everyone agrees that policy choices leave theoretical fingerprints that explain the choice behind. Barry Posen has recently argued that there need be no forensic proof of the kind that I am suggesting for neorealism's predictions to be vindicated. Posen has written that, "States and statesmen are not necessarily expected to couch their actions in balancing language— the theory does not require statesmen to understand the theory for the theory to explain their actions." Barry Posen, "European Union Security and Defense Policy," *Security Studies* 15, no. 2 (2006): 165.

3. *Parliamentary Debates*, 5th ser., vol. 286 (1932), col. 2078.

4. DC(M)(32) 117, Vansittart Minute, 2 June 1934, Cab 16/111. "DC(M) (32)" in these citations refers to the Ministerial Committee on Disarmament, which was formed in response to the global disarmament talks initiated in 1932. Papers and memoranda submitted to the committee were assigned numbers (as here, 117). Not all documents have formal titles. When they do not, as here, I have described the content of the paper.

5. Keith Middlemas and John Barnes, *Baldwin: A Biography* (London: Weidenfield and Nicolson, 1969), 732.

6. *Parliamentary Debates*, 5th ser., vol. 270 (1932), cols. 630–31.

7. Ibid., col. 631.

8. Ibid., col. 632.
9. Ibid., col. 632.
10. Ibid., col. 634.
11. Ibid., col. 634.
12. Ibid., col. 637.
13. Ibid., col. 638.
14. Middlesmas and Barnes, *Baldwin*, 730.
15. COS310 Annual Review, 12 October, 1933, Cab 53/20. "COS" refers to the papers of the Chiefs of Staff committee.
16. Ibid.
17. Ibid.
18. Ibid.
19. Ibid.
20. Ibid.
21. The three were Field Marshal Sir Archibald A. Montgomery-Massingberd (Army), Admiral Sir Ernle Chatfield (Navy), and General Sir Edward Ellington (RAF).
22. Defence Requirements Committee (DRC), First Report, Cab 16/109.
23. DC(M)(32), Paper 109, Cab 16/111.
24. DC(M)32 46th Cons., 17 May 1934, Cab 16/110.
25. Ibid.
26. Ibid.
27. See Memorandum by the Secretary of State for Foreign Affairs, 6 June 1934. DC(M)(32), Paper 118, Cab 16/111.
28. DC(M)(32), 48th Cons., 11 June 1934, Cab 16/110.
29. Baldwin framed the idea even more boldly at a gathering of the Conservative Party in October 1935 when he suggested that the new situation in the air had made Britain as it must have been long ago, before the waters of the channel flooded the area between Britain and France.
30. DC(M)(32), 50th Cons., 25 June 1934, Cab 16/110.
31. Ibid.
32. Ibid.
33. CP205(34), Amended & Revised Defence Requirements Committee Report, 31 July 1934, Cab 24/250. "CP" refers to paper submitted to the cabinet. In this case, it is the 205th paper submitted to the cabinet in 1934.
34. See Lord Londonderry's comments during the meeting of the ministerial committee held on June 26, 1934. DC(M)32, 51st Cons., Cab 16/110.
35. *Parliamentary Debates*, 5th ser., vol. 292 (1934), col. 2339
36. Ibid.
37. *Parl. Deb.* 5th ser., vol. 270, col. 633.
38. *Parl. Deb.* 5th ser., vol. 286, col. 2076–77.
39. Ibid., col. 2078.
40. *Parl. Deb.* 5th ser., vol. 292, col. 2337.
41. Michael Howard, *The Continental Commitment* (London: Temple Smith, 1972), 113.

42. Middlemas and Barnes, *Baldwin*, 757. Similarly, Thomas Jones, a close friend and confidant of Baldwin's, writes the following to a friend of his in America on March 1, 1934: "At any rate, rightly or wrongly, all sorts of people who met Hitler are convinced that he is a factor for peace." See Thomas Jones, *A Diary with Letters: 1931–1950* (London: Oxford University Press, 1954), 125.

43. DC(M)32 51st Cons. 16 June 1934, Cab 16/110.

44. Cmd. 4827, Statement Relating to Defence, 11 March, 1935.

45. Ibid.

46. Ibid.

47. Ibid.

48. *Parliamentary Debates*, 5th ser., vol. 299 (1935), cols. 47–48.

49. *Parliamentary Debates*, 5th ser., vol. 317 (1936), col. 1144

50. G. M. Young, *Stanley Baldwin* (London: Weidenfeld & Nicolson, 1976), 200.

51. C. T. Stannage, "The East Fulham By-Election, 25 October 1933," *The Historical Journal* 14, no. 1 (1971): 183.

52. Stannage, "East Fulham," 186.

53. *Times* (London), April 9, 1935.

54. Ibid.

55. *Times* (London), June 10, 1935.

56. Ibid.

57. *Times* (London), October 4, 1935.

58. Ibid.

59. *Times* (London), November 1, 1935.

60. *Parl. Deb.* 5th ser., vol. 317, col.1144

61. DRC (37) Third Report, Cab 16/123.

62. DRC 3rd Report, Cab 16/123.

63. Ibid. It is interesting to note the change in the title of the proposed force. In the 1934 report it was called the "Expeditionary Force," the same title that had graced the troops sent to fight in Europe in 1914. This new report calls the same body a "Field Force," perhaps in the hope that a new name might weaken resistance to the task for which it was being created.

64. DPR(DR) 2nd Meeting, 14 January 1936, Cab 16/123.

65. Ibid.

66. Ibid.

67. Ibid.

68. Letter from Hankey to Baldwin, 15 January 1936, Cab 21/422A.

69. Brian Bond, *British Military Policy between the Two World Wars* (London: Oxford University Press, 1980), 224.

70. DPR(DR), 4th Meeting, 16 January 1936, Cab 16/123.

71. Ibid.

72. This conclusion was in fact passed on to the cabinet, which approved it at their meeting on February 25, 1936. See the conclusions from the tenth cabinet meeting of 1936, abbreviated as Cab10(36).

73. DPR(DR), 1st Meeting, 13 January 1936, Cab 16/123.
74. Ibid.
75. DPR(DR), 1st Meeting, 13 January 1936, Cab 16/123.
76. Cab13(36), 2 March 1936, Cab 23/83. This refers to the minutes of a meeting of the cabinet, in this case the 13th meeting of the cabinet in 1936.

CHAPTER 4

1. Letter from Hankey to Baldwin, 15 January 1936, Cab21/422A.
2. Thomas Jones, *A Diary with Letters: 1931–1950* (London: Oxford University Press, 1954), 123–24.
3. See discussion of "Speech to the Peace Society," in Chapter 3.
4. DC(M)(32), 48th Cons., 11 June 1934, Cab 16/110. "DC(M)(32)" in these citations refers to the Ministerial Committee on Disarmament which was formed in response to the global disarmament talks initiated in 1932. "48th Cons" refers to the 48th meeting
5. *Parliamentary Debates*, 5th ser., vol. 292 (1934), col. 2339.
6. *Times* (London), October 4, 1935.
7. DC(M)(32) 46th Cons. 17 May 1934, Cab 16/110.
8. *Times* (London), October 4, 1935.
9. *Parliamentary Debates*, 5th ser., vol. 270 (1932), col. col. 633.
10. *Parliamentary Debates*, 5th ser., vol. 286 (1932), col. 2078.
11. Letter from Hankey to Baldwin, 15 January 1935, Cab 21/422A.
12. DPR(DR) 4th Meeting 16 January 1936,Cab 16/123.
13. Roy Jenkins, *Baldwin* (London: Collins, 1987), 65.
14. Hankey to Baldwin, 15 January 1936, Cab 21/422A.
15. Brian Bond, *British Military Policy between the Two World Wars* (London: Oxford University Press, 1980), 248.
16. *Parl. Deb.*, 5th ser., vol. 286, col. 2074. Churchill's use of the idea of power with responsibility was not a casual reference. It was an attempt to remind Baldwin of his own words from three years before. In a speech given in March 1931, Baldwin indicted press lords Beaverbrook and Rothermere, who opposed his stance on trade, with the biting comment: "What the proprietorship of these papers is aiming at is power, and power without responsibility—the prerogative of the harlot throughout the ages." *Times* (London), March 18, 1931. The phrase, incidentally, was suggested to Baldwin by his cousin, Rudyard Kipling.
17. *Parliamentary Debates*, 5th ser., vol. 317 (1936), col. 1144.
18. See Stephen M. Walt, "Alliance Formation and the Balance of World Power," *International Security* 9, no. 4 (Spring 1985), and the discussion in Chapter 1 of this book.
19. Richard J. Samuels, *Machiavelli's Children: Leaders and Their Legacies in Italy and Japan* (Ithaca, NY: Cornell University Press, 2003), 1–2.

CHAPTER 5

1. For a brief biographical sketch of Neville Chamberlain, see Appendix 2.
2. Keith Neilson, "The Defence Requirements Sub-Committee, British Strategic Foreign Policy, Neville Chamberlain and the Path to Appeasement," *English Historical Review* 118, no. 477 (June 2003): 681.
3. Neville Chamberlain Papers, 18/1/910A, 23 March 1935. This reference refers to the papers of Neville Chamberlain held at the University of Birmingham.
4. COS310 Annual Review, 12 October 1933, Cab 53/20. This reference refers to papers authored by the chiefs of staff subcommittee. In this case, it the 310th paper that the subcommittee generated in 1933.
5. For the CID discussion see CID, 261st Meeting, 9 November 1933, Cab 2/6. For the cabinet approval of the creation of the DRC, see the minutes of the cabinet meeting held on 15 November, Cab 62(33), Cab 23/77. Meetings of the cabinet are recorded as the sequential meeting number of the cabinet followed by the year of the meeting in parenthesis. Here this is the sixty-second meeting of the cabinet held in 1933.
6. CP113(34) "Imperial Defence Policy" Memorandum by the Secretaries of State for War and Air, and the First Lord of the Admiralty 20 April 1934, Cab 16/109. "CP" refers to cabinet papers which are numbered for any given year. This paper is the 113th cabinet paper for 1934.
7. Defence Requirements Committee, First Report, Cab 16/109.
8. DC(M)(32), 41st Cons., 3 May 1934, Cab 16/110. These references refer to the meetings of the Ministerial Committee on Disarmament first convened in 1932. This is a reference to the forty-first meeting, which was held in 1934.
9. Ibid.
10. Ibid.
11. Ibid.
12. DC(M)(32), 42nd Cons., 4 May 1934, Cab 16/110.
13. Neilson, "Defence Requirements," 673.
14. Ibid., 680.
15. DC(M)(32) 109, COS Response to DC(M) Questionnaire, Cab 16/111.
16. DC(M)(32)109, COS Response to DC(M) Questionnaire, Response to Question 2, Cab 16/111
17. DC(M)(32) 117, Vansittart Minute, 2 June 1934, Cab 16/111.
18. DC(M)(32) 109, COS Response to DC(M) Questionnaire, Response to Question 5, Cab 16/111.
19. DC(M)(32) 109, COS Response to DC(M) Questionnaire, Response to Question 6, Cab 16/111.
20. DC(M)(32)109, COS Response to DC(M) Questionnaire, Enclosure 2, "The Strategical Importance of the Low Countries," Cab 16/111.
21. Ibid.
22. Ibid.
23. DC(M)(32), 44th Cons., 10 May 1934, Cab 16/110.

24. Ibid.

25. DC(M)(32) 111(34), Archibald A. Montgomery-Massingberd, French Fortifications, 14 May 1934, Cab 16/111.

26. Ibid.

27. DC(M)(32) 111, A Reply by the Chief of the Air Staff to Question 2, 14 May 1934, Cab 16/111.

28. Ibid.

29. Ibid.

30. Ibid.

31. Michael Howard, *The Continental Commitment* (London: Temple Smith, 1972), 111.

32. DC(M)(32), 44th Cons., 10 May 1934, Cab 16/110.

33. DC(M)(32), 45th Cons., 15 May 1934, Cab 16/110.

34. Ibid.

35. Ibid.

36. Ibid.

37. Ibid.

38. Neilson, "Defence Requirements," 680.

39. DC(M)(32) 120, Note by the Chancellor of the Exchequer on the Report of the Defence Requirements Committee, 20 June 1934, Cab 16/111.

40. Ibid.

41. Ibid.

42. DC(M)(32), 51st Cons., 26 June 1934, Cab 16/110.

43. Ibid.

44. Ibid.

45. Ibid.

46. Ibid.

47. Neilson, "Defence Requirements," 680.

48. DC(M)(32), 50th Cons., 25 June 1934, Cab 16/110.

49. Ibid.

50. Ibid.

51. Quoted in RAC Parker, *Chamberlain and Appeasement: British Policy and the Coming of the Second World War* (New York: St. Martin's Press, 1993), 93.

52. DC(M)(32), 54th Cons., 17 July 1934, Cab 16/110.

53. Cab31(34), 31 July 1934, Cab 23/79.

54. DC(M)(32), 50th Cons., 25 June 1934, Cab 16/110.

55. Defence Requirements Committee—Third Report, 21 November 1935, Cab 16/123.

56. Ibid.

57. Parker, *Chamberlain and Appeasement*, 273–74.

58. DPR(DR), 1st Meeting, 13 January 1936, Cab 16/123. This reference refers to the minutes of meetings held by the Defence Policy Requirements committee, which considered the third DRC report.

59. Ibid.
60. CP13(36), The German Danger, 20 January 1936, Cab 24/259.
61. Ibid.
62. DPR(DR), 1st Meeting 13 January 1936, Cab 16/123.
63. DPR(DR) 4, Memorandum by Lord Weir, 9 January 1936, Cab16/123.
64. Ibid.
65. Ibid.
66. CP205(34), Amended and Revised Defence Requirements Committee Report, 31 July 1934, Cab 24/250.
67. DPR(DR) 6, Note by the CIGS on the Memorandum by Lord Weir, Cab 16/123.
68. See the discussion of the memorandum of the CAS as a part of the 1934 DRC meetings earlier in this chapter.
69. DPR(DR) 6, Note by the CIGS on the Memorandum by Lord Weir, Cab 16/123.
70. DPR(DR), 2nd Meeting, 14 January 1936, Cab 16/123.
71. Ibid.
72. Neilson has noted that during the consideration of the first DRC report Hankey did complain privately: "Hankey . . . was annoyed by the fact that consideration of the DRC's report had been turned over to Chamberlain" because that meant that the task of determining how British defense needs would be met was now in the hands of people who have no "experience in Imperial Defence." Neilson, "Defence Requirements," 674.
73. DPR(DR), 2nd Meeting, 14 January 1936, Cab 16/123.
74. DPR(DR) 6, Note by the CIGS on the Memorandum by Lord Weir, Cab 16/123.
75. Ibid. This plea was followed the next day by the letter from Hankey to Baldwin, covered extensively in Chapter 3. There is no evidence that Chamberlain saw the letter, and so it is excluded from consideration herein.
76. Cab10(36) 25, February1936, Cab 23/83.
77. DPR(DR)6, Note by the CIGS on the Memorandum by Lord Weir, Cab 16/123.
78. CP38(36), Memorandum by the Chancellor of the Exchequer on Defence Co-Ordination, 11 February 1936, Cab 24/260.
79. Ibid.
80. DC(M)(32), 51st Cons., 26 June 1934, Cab 16/110.
81. CP38(36), Memorandum by the Chancellor of the Exchequer on Defence Co-Ordination, 11 February 1936, Cab 24/260.
82. DPR(DR) 6, Note by the Chief of the Imperial General Staff on the Memorandum by Lord Weir, Cab 16/123.
83. COS 537, "The Role of the British Army," Memorandum by the Secretary of State for War, 14 December 1936, Cab 53/29.
84. COS 537, Memorandum by the Chancellor of the Exchequer, 11 December 1936, Cab53/29.
85. Ibid.

86. Ibid.
87. CP2(37), "The Role of the British Army and its Equipment," Memorandum by the Secretary of State for War, 5 January 1937, Cab 24/267.
88. Ibid.
89. Cab5(37), 3 February 1937, Cab 23/87.
90. Vansittart was perhaps the most prolific antiappeaser of them all. Examples of his stance on Germany can be found in the memoranda that he wrote for the ministerial committee discussing the first DRC Report (CP104[34], "The Future of Germany," Cab 16/111, The Vansittart Minute of 2 June 1934, Cab 16/111, or his comments at the meeting of the Defence Policy Requirements Committee, 11 June 1936, Cab 16/136).
91. Howard, *The Continental Commitment*, 115.

CHAPTER 6

1. DPR(DR) 4, Memorandum by Lord Weir, 9 January 1936, Cab 16/123. This reference refers to documents submitted to the DPR. Where the document has a formal title it has been used. Where there is no formal title I have summarized the content of the document.
2. Memorandum on the Future Organisation of the British Army September 1935, WO32/4612. This reference refers to a memorandum from the war office files.
3. DPR(DR), 1st Meeting, 13 January 1936. See also DPR(DR), 4th Meeting, 14 January 1936, Cab 16/123.
4. DC(M)(32) 120, Note by the Chancellor of the Exchequer on the Report of the Defence Requirements Committee, 20 June 1934, Cab 16/111. This reference is from documents submitted to the ministerial committee on disarmament.
5. DPR(DR), 2nd Meeting, 14 January 1936, Cab 16/123.
6. Ibid.
7. DC(M)(32), 46th Cons., 17 May 1934, Cab 16/110.
8. Barry Posen, *The Sources of Military Doctrine* (Ithaca, NY: Cornell University Press, 1984), 158.
9. Robert C. Self, *The Neville Chamberlain Diary Letters: Vol. 4* (London: Ashgate, 2005), 141.
10. Thomas Jones, *A Diary with Letters: 1931–1950* (London: Oxford University Press, 1954), 125.
11. Quoted in RAC Parker, *Chamberlain and Appeasement: British Policy and the Coming of the Second World War* (New York: St. Martin's Press, 1993), 162.
12. Ibid.
13. DC(M)(32), 51st Cons., 26 June 1934, Cab 16/110.
14. DC(M)(32), 50th Cons., 25 June 1934, Cab 16/110.
15. Michael Howard, *The Continental Commitment* (London: Temple Smith, 1972), 99.

16. DC(M)(32), 50th Cons., 25 June 1934, Cab 16/110.
17. Brian Bond, *British Military Policy Between the Two World Wars* (Oxford: Clarendon Press, 1980), 249.
18. DC(M)(32) 120, Note by the Chancellor of the Exchequer on the Report of the Defence Requirements Committee, 20 June 1934, Cab 16/111.
19. DC(M)(32), 45th Cons., 15 May 1934, Cab 16/110.
20. DC(M)(32), 50th Cons., 25 June 1934, Cab 16/110.
21. DPR(DR), 2nd Meeting, 14 January 1936, Cab 16/123.
22. COS537, Memorandum by the Chancellor of the Exchequer, 11 December 1936, Cab53/29. "COS" refers to papers of the chiefs of staffs subcommittee.
23. DPR(DR), 2nd Meeting, 14 January 1936, Cab 16/123.
24. DC(M)(32), 46th Cons., 17 May 1934, Cab 16/110.
25. 286 H.C. Deb. 5th ser., col. 2074.
26. Bond, *British Military Policy*, 217–18.
27. COS310, Annual Review, 12 October 1933, Cab 53/20.
28. DC(M)(32) 109, May 1934, Cab 16/111.
29. CP104(34), Vansittart Essay, 9 April 1934; CP116(34) 23, April 1934, Cab 16/111.
30. DPRC, 22nd Meeting, 11 June 1936, Cab 16/136. This reference comes from the minutes of the Defence Policy and Requirements Committee, which was different than the DPR.
31. DPR(DR), 1st Meeting 13 January 1936, Cab 16/123; CP13(36), "The German Danger," 17 January 1936, Cab 24/259. This reference is both to the minutes of a meeting of the DPR and to a document submitted to the cabinet as cabinet paper 13 in 1936.
32. DC(M)(32), 41st Cons., Cab 16/110.
33. DC(M)(32), 44th Cons., 10 May 1934, Cab 16/110.
34. DC(M)(32), 50th Cons., 25 June 1934, Cab 16/110.
35. DC(M)(32), 51st Cons., 26 June 1934, Cab 16/110.
36. DC(M)(32) 111, A Reply by the Chief of the Air Staff, 10 May 1934, Cab 16/111.
37. DPR(DR) 6, Note by the CIGS on the Memorandum of Lord Weir, Cab 16/123.
38. DC(M)(32), 51st Cons., 26 June 1934, Cab 16/110.
39. DPR(DR), 4th Meeting, 16 January 1936, Cab 16/123.
40. Robert Jevis, *The Meaning of the Nuclear Revolution: Statecraft and the Prospect of Armageddon* (Ithaca, NY: Cornell University Press, 1990), Chapter 2.
41. DC(M)(32), 51st Cons., 26 June 1934, Cab 16/110.
42. Ibid.
43. DPR(DR) 6, Note by the CIGS on the Memorandum by Lord Weir, Cab 16/123.
44. DC(M)(32) 109, COS Response to DC(M) Questionnaire, Cab-16/111.

45. DPR(DR), 2nd Meeting, 14 January 1936, Cab 16/123.
46. DC(M)(32), 44th Cons., 10 May 1934, Cab 16/110.
47. DC(M)(32), 50th Cons., 25 June 1934, Cab 16/110.
48. COS537, Memorandum by the Chancellor of the Exchequer, 11 December 1936, Cab53/29.
49. Cab20(37), 5 May 1937, Cab 23/88.
50. "Democracy and the Empire" speech to the Junior League 3 May 1924 in Stanley Baldwin, *On England and Other Addresses* (London: Phillip Allan and Co., 1926), 221.

CHAPTER 7

1. Vansittart Memorandum on the Future of Germany, 9 April 1934, Cab 16/111.
2. DPR(DR) 6, Note by the CIGS on the Memorandum by Lord Weir, Cab 16/123. This note refers to the papers submitted for consideration by the Defence Policy Requirements committee. In this case, paper 6. Where there is a formal title, I have used it, otherwise I have described the contents of the paper.
3. See, for example, Robert O. Keohane, *After Hegemony: Cooperation and Discord in the World Political Economy* (Princeton, NJ: Princeton University Press, 1984); Stephen D. Krasner, "Structural Causes and Regime Consequences: Regimes as Intervening Variables," in *International Regimes*, Stephen D. Kranser, ed. (Ithaca, NY: Cornell University Press, 1983); and G. John Ikenberry and Daniel Deudney, "The Nature and Sources of Liberal International Order," *Review of International Studies* 25, no. 2 (April 1999): 179–96.
4. The idea that Waltz's theory is purely material has been debunked by Randall Schweller and by Alexander Wendt. Both have argued that Waltz's theory has implicit assumptions about the status quo biases of states, which are an ideational factor not a material fact. That ideational assumption that states are interested in the maintenance of their relative position in the international system underlies much of Waltz's theory. See Randall Schweller, "Neorealism's Status-Quo Bias: What Security Dilemma?" *Security Studies* 5, no. 3 (1996): 90–121. Not all structuralists share that assumption. John Mearsheimer has argued that states seek security through expansion and the pursuit of hegemony, not through the maintenance of their relative position. The dynamic of the international system as governed by Mearsheimer's "offensive" realist assumption yields a vastly different system than Waltz's "defensive" realism. See John J. Mearsheimer, *The Tragedy of Great Power Politics* (New York: W. W. Norton, 2000).
5. Daniel L. Byman and Kenneth M. Pollack, "Let Us Now Praise Great Men: Bringing the Statesmen Back In," *International Security* 25, no. 4 (Spring 2001): 108.

6. Memorandum on the Future Organization of the British Army September ber 1935, WO32/4612.
7. DPR(DR), 2nd Meeting, 14 January 1936, Cab 16/123.
8. CP38(36) Memorandum by the Chancellor of the Exchequer on Defence Co-Ordination, 11 February 1936, Cab 24/260. This note refers to a cabinet paper (CP)—that is, papers submitted to the full cabinet for its consideration. In this case, it is the 38th paper in the year 1936 to be submitted.
9. Eliot A. Cohen, *Supreme Command: Soldiers, Statesmen and Leadership in Wartime* (New York: Free Press, 2002), 142–54.
10. Byman and Pollack, "Let Us Now," 113.

EPILOGUE

1. Robert Mueller, *Retreat from Doomsday: The Obsolescence of Major War* (New York: Basic Books, 1990).
2. Robert Jervis, *The Meaning of the Nuclear Revolution: Statecraft and the Prospect of Armageddon* (Ithaca, NY: Cornell University Press, 1989).
3. William C. Wohlforth, "The Stability of a Unipolar World," *International Security* 24, no.1 (1999): 5–41.
4. Keir A. Lieber and Daryl G Press, "The Nukes We Need: Preserving the American Deterrent," *Foreign Affairs* 88, no. 6 (November/December 2009).

APPENDIX 1

1. Quoted in Roy Jenkins, *Baldwin* (London: Collins, 1987), 50.
2. Keith Middlemas and John Barnes, *Baldwin: A Biography* (London: Weidenfield and Nicolson, 1969), 719.
3. Ibid., 802.
4. Cab 22(37), Cab 23/88. See this reference for the minutes of the 22nd cabinet meeting held in 1937 where Baldwin explained his logic.

A NOTE ON PRIMARY SOURCES

The primary source material in this book comes from the collections of the National Archives of the United Kingdom and the Hansard Record of Parliamentary Proceedings. The text of Stanley Baldwin's speeches given outside Westminster are taken from the *Times of London* newspaper, which transcribed the full text of his speeches during his years both as Lord President and as Prime Minister.

The documents from the National Archives are all from the Cabinet series as follows:

Series 16—Records of the Cabinet sub-Committees on Defence, including the Ministerial Committee on Disarmament (1932) and the Defence Policy Requirements Committee
Series 2—Records of the Committee on Imperial Defence
Series 23—Records of the meetings of the Cabinet
Series 24—Papers circulated to the Cabinet
Series 53—Records of the Chiefs of Staff Committee

BIBLIOGRAPHY

Baldwin, A. W. *My Father: The True Story*. London: George Allen & Unwin Ltd., 1956.

Baldwin, Stanley. *On England and Other Addresses*. London: Philip Allan and Co. Ltd., 1926.

Benford, Robert D., and David A. Snow. "Framing Processes and Social Movements: An Overview and Assessment." *Annual Review of Sociology* (2000): 611–39.

Biddle, Tami D. *Rhetoric and Reality in Air Warfare*. Princeton, NJ: Princeton University Press, 2002.

Birt, Raymond. "Personality and Foreign Policy." *Political Psychology* 14, no. 4 (December 1993): 607–25.

Bond, Brian. *British Military Policy between the Two World Wars.* Oxford: Clarendon Press, 1980.

Byman, Daniel L., and Kenneth M. Pollack. "Let Us Now Praise Great Men: Bringing the Statesmen Back In." *International Security* 25, no. 4 (Spring 2001): 107–46.

Carr, E. H. *The Twenty Years' Crisis 1919–1939: An Introduction to the Study of International Relations.* London: Papermac, 1939/1991.

Churchill, Winston S. *Memoirs of the Second World War: An Abridgement of the Six Volumes of the Second World War.* New York: Houghton Mifflin, 1959.

Cohen, Eliot A. *Supreme Command: Soldiers, Statesmen and Leadership in Wartime.* New York: Free Press, 2002.

Colvin, Ian. *The Chamberlain Cabinet.* London: Victor Gollancz, 1971.

Constable, Trevor J. *Hidden Heroes.* London: Arthur Baker's Ltd., 1971.

David, Steven R. "Explaining Third World Alignment." *World Politics* 43, no. 2 (January 1991): 233–56.

Dunbabin, J. P. D. "British Rearmament in the 1930s: A Chronology and Review." *The Historical Journal* 18, no. 3 (September 1975): 587–609.

Fearon, James D. "Counterfactuals and Hypothesis Testing Political Science." *World Politics* 43 (January 1991): 169–95.

Feiling, Keith. *The Life of Neville Chamberlain.* London: Macmillan & Co., 1946.

Gaddis, John Lewis. *The Long Peace: Inquiries into the History of the Cold War.* New York: Oxford University Press, 1987.

George, Alexander. "Case Studies and Theory Development: The Method of Structured, Focused Comparison." In *Diplomacy: New Approaches in History, Theory and Policy, edited by* Paul Gordon Lauren. New York: Free Press, 1979.

Gibbs, N. H. *Grand Strategy: Volume I-Rearmament Policy.* London: Her Majesty's Stationary Office, 1976.

Gilpin, Robert. *War and Change in World Politics.* Cambridge: Cambridge University Press, 1981.

Harris, J. P. "British Armour and Rearmament in the 1930s." *Journal of Strategic Studies* 11, no. 2 (June 1988): 220–44.

Herrmann, David G. *The Arming of Europe and the Coming of the First World War.* Princeton, NJ: Princeton University Press, 1996.

Herrmann, Richard K., and Jonathan W. Keller. "Beliefs, Values and Strategic Choice: U.S. Leaders' Decisions to Engage, Contain, and Use Force in an Era of Globalization." *The Journal of Politics* 66, no. 2 (May 2004): 557–80.

Herz, John H. *International Politics in the Atomic Age.* New York: Columbia University Press, 1959.

Hitler, Adolf. *Mein Kampf,* translated by Ralph Manheim. Boston: Houghton Mifflin Company, 1943/1971.

Howard, Michael. *The Continental Commitment: The Dilemma of British Defence Policy in the Era of the Two World Wars.* London: Temple Smith, 1972.

Ikenberry, G. John, and Daniel Deudney, "The Nature and Sources of Liberal International Order." *Review of International Studies* 25, no. 2 (April 1999): 179–96.

Jacoby, William G. "Issue Framing and Public Opinion on Government Spending." *American Journal of Political Science* 44, no. 4 (October 2000): 750–67.

Jenkins, Roy. *Baldwin*. London: Collins, 1987.

Jervis, Robert. "Cooperation under the Security Dilemma." *World Politics* 30 (January 1978): 167–214.

———. *System Effects: Complexity in Political and Social Life*. Princeton, NJ: Princeton University Press, 1987.

———. *The Meaning of the Nuclear Revolution: Statecraft and the Prospect of Armageddon*. Ithaca, NY: Cornell University Press, 1989.

Jones, Thomas. *A Diary with Letters: 1931–1950*. London: Oxford University Press, 1954.

Keohane, Robert O. *After Hegemony: Cooperation and Discord in the World Political Economy*. Princeton, NJ: Princeton University Press, 1984.

Kissinger, Henry. *A World Restored: Metternich, Castlereagh and the Problems of Peace, 1812–1822*. Boston: Houghton Mifflin, 1957/1973.

Krasner, Stephen D. "Structural Causes and Regime Consequences: Regimes as Intervening Variables." In *International Regimes*, edited by Stephen D. Kranser. Ithaca, NY: Cornell University Press, 1983.

Liddel Hart, B. H. *History of the Second World War*. New York: G. B. Putnam's & Sons, 1971.

Lijphart, Arend. "Comparative Politics and the Comparative Method." *The American Political Science Review* 65, no. 3 (September 1971): 682–93.

Maurer, John. "Arms Control and the Anglo-German Naval Race before World War I: Lessons for Today?" *Political Science Quarterly* 112, no. 2 (Summer 1997): 185–206.

Mearsheimer, John J. *The Tragedy of Great Power Politics*. New York: W. W. Norton, 2000.

Middlemas, Keith, and John Barnes. *Baldwin: A Biography*. London: Weidenfeld and Nicolson, 1969.

Morgenthau, Hans J. *Scientific Man versus Power Politics*. Chicago: Chicago University Press, 1946.

———. *Politics among Nations: The Struggle for Power and Peace*. New York: Knopf, 1985.

———. *Truth and Power*. New York: Praeger, 1970.

Mowat, C. L. "Baldwin Restored?" *The Journal of Modern History* 27, no. 2 (June 1955): 169–74.

Murray, Williamson, and Allan R. Millett. "Armored Warfare: The British, French and German Experiences." In *Military Innovation in the Interwar Period*, edited by Williamson Murray and Allan R. Millett. Cambridge: Cambridge University Press, 1996.

Neilson, Keith. "The Defence Requirements Sub-Committee, British Strategic Foreign Policy, Neville Chamberlain and the Path to Appeasement." *English Historical Review* 118, no. 477 (June 2003): 651–84.

Neustadt, Richard E. *Presidential Power and the Modern Presidents: The Politics of Leadership from Roosevelt to Reagan.* New York: Free Press, 1990.

Nye, Joseph S., Jr. "Soft Power: The Means to Success in World Politics." *Foreign Affairs* 83, no. 3 (May–June 2004): 136–37.

———. *The Paradox of American Power: Why the World's Only Superpower Can't Go It Alone.* Oxford: Oxford University Press, 2002.

Parliamentary Debates. Commons, 5th ser., vol. 270 (1932)

Parliamentary Debates. Commons, 5th ser., vol. 286 (1932)

Parliamentary Debates. Commons, 5th ser., vol. 292 (1934)

Parliamentary Debates. Commons, 5th ser., vol. 299 (1935)

Parliamentary Debates. Commons, 5th ser., vol. 317 (1936)

Parker, R. A. C. *Chamberlain and Appeasement: British Policy and the Coming of the Second World War.* New York: St. Martin's Press, 1993.

Post, Jerrold M., and Robert S. Robbins. *When Illness Strikes the Leader: The Dilemma of the Captive King.* New Haven, CT: Yale University Press, 1993.

Rancour-Laferriere, Daniel. *The Mind of Stalin: A Psychoanalytic Study.* Ann Arbor, MI: Ardis, 1988.

Redlich, Frederick C. *Hitler: Diagnosis of a Destructive Prophet.* New York: Oxford University Press, 1998.

Russet, Bruce. *Grasping the Democratic Peace: Principles for a Post–Cold War World.* Princeton, NJ: Princeton University Press, 1993.

Samuels, Richard J. *Machiavelli's Children: Leaders and their Legacies in Italy and Japan.* Ithaca, NY: Cornell University Press, 2003.

Satterfield, Jason M. "Cognitive Affective States Predict Military and Political Aggression and Risk-Taking: A Content Analysis of Churchill, Hitler, Roosevelt, and Stalin." *Journal of Conflict Resolution* 42, no. 6 (December 1998): 667–90.

Schweller, Randall. *Deadly Imbalances: Tripolarity and Hitler's Strategy of World Conquest.* New York: Columbia University Press, 1998.

———. "Tripolarity and the Second World War." *International Studies Quarterly* 37, no. 1 (March 1993): 73–103.

———. "Neorealism's Status-Quo Bias: What Security Dilemma?" *Security Studies* 5, no. 3 (1996): 90–121.

———. *Unanswered Threats: Political Constraints on the Balance of Power.* Princeton, NJ: Princeton University Press, 2006.

Sheingate, Adam D. "Political Entrepreneurship, Institutional Change, and American Political Development." *Studies in American Political Development* 17 (Fall 2003): 185–203.

Skowronek, Stephen. *The Politics Presidents Make: Leadership from John Adams to Bill Clinton.* Cambridge, MA: Harvard University Press, 1997.

Snyder, Jack. "Civil-Military Relations and the Cult of the Offensive." *International Security* 9, no. 1 (Summer 1984): 108–46.

———. *The Ideology of the Offensive: Military Decision Making and the Disaster of 1914.* Ithaca, NY: Cornell University Press, 1984.

Snyder, Jack, and Thomas Christensen. "Chain Gangs and Passed Bucks: Predicting Alliance Patterns in Multipolarity." *International Organization* 44, no. 2 (Spring 1990): 137–68.

Stannage, C. T. "The East Fulham By-Election, 25 October 1933." *The Historical Journal* 14, no. 1 (March 1971): 165–200.

———. *Baldwin Thwarts the Opposition.* London: Croom Helm, 1980.

Stinchcombe, Arthur L. *Constructing Social Theories.* New York: Harcourt, Brace and World, 1968.

Stone, Deborah A. "Causal Stories and the Formation of Policy Agendas." *Political Science Quarterly* 104, no. 2 (Summer 1989): 281–300.

Taylor, A. J. P. *The Origins of the Second World War.* London: Penguin Books, 1991.

———. *English History 1914–1945.* New York: Oxford University Press, 1965.

Thayer, Bradley A. "Bringing in Darwin: Evolutionary Theory, Realism, and International Politics," *International Security* 25, no. 2 (2000): 124–51.

Tucker, Robert C. *Politics as Leadership: Revised Edition.* Columbia: University of Missouri Press, 1995.

———. "Personality and Political Leadership." *Political Science Quarterly* 92, no. 3 (Autumn 1977): 385–86.

Van Evera, Steven. *The Causes of War: Power and the Roots of Conflict.* Ithaca, NY: Cornell University Press, 1999.

Walt, Stephen M. "Alliance Formation and the Balance of World Power." *International Security* 9, no. 4 (Spring 1985): 3–43.

Waltz, Kenneth N. "Reductionist and Systemic Theories." In *Neorealism and Its Critics, edited by* Robert O. Keohane. New York: Columbia University Press, 1986.

———. "Political Structures." In *Neorealism and Its Critics, edited by* Robert O. Keohane. New York: Columbia University Press, 1986.

———. "Anarchic Orders and Balances of Power." In *Neorealism and Its Critics,* edited by Robert O. Keohane. New York: Columbia University Press, 1986.

———. *The Spread of Nuclear Weapons: More May Be Better.* London: International Institute for Strategic Studies, 1981.

Waltz, Kenneth N., and Scott D. Sagan. *The Spread of Nuclear Weapons: A Debate.* New York: W. W. Norton, 1995

———. *Theory of International Politics.* Reading, MA: Addison-Wesley, 1979.

Webster, Charles, and Noble Frankland. *The Strategic Air Offensive against Germany: 1939–1945, Vol. 1.* London: Her Majesty's Stationers Office, 1961.

Wendt, Alexander. *Social Theory of International Politics.* London: Cambridge University Press, 1999.

Williamson, Philip. *Stanley Baldwin: Conservative Leadership and National Values*. Cambridge: Cambridge University Press, 1999.

Young, G. M. *Stanley Baldwin*. London: Rupert Hart-Davis, 1952.

Young, Kenneth. *Stanley Baldwin*. London: Weidenfeld & Nicolson, 1976.

Zakaria, Fareed. *From Wealth to Power: The Unusual Origins of America's World Role*. Princeton, NJ: Princeton University Press, 1998.

Index